Dr Jo Stanley FRHistS is a creative historian specialising in gender and maritime history, including women pirates and pioneers. She is Honorary Research Fellow at the University of Hull's Maritime Historical Studies Centre and runs the blog: http://genderedseas.blogspot.com. Her book *From Cabin 'Boys' to Captains: 250 Years of Women at Sea* was one of the winners of the Mountbatten Maritime Literary Prize in 2016.

This book is dedicated to JP, who enabled it so generously, and to the memory of Vera Stanley, who helped me so much with its founding stages. I offer it with esteem to all women in the naval world who gave without counting the cost.

A History of the Royal Navy Series

A History of the Royal Navy: The Age of Sail
Andrew Baines (ISBN: 978 1 78076 992 9)

A History of the Royal Navy: Air Power and British Naval Aviation
Ben Jones and Tim Benbow (ISBN: 978 1 78076 993 6)

A History of the Royal Navy: The American Revolutionary War
Martin Robson (ISBN: 978 1 78076 994 3)

A History of the Royal Navy : Empire and Imperialism
Daniel Owen Spence (ISBN: 978 1 78076 543 3)

A History of the Royal Navy: The Napoleonic Wars
Martin Robson (ISBN: 978 1 78076 544 0)

A History of the Royal Navy: The Nuclear Age
Philip D. Grove (ISBN: 978 1 78076 995 0)

A History of the Royal Navy: The Royal Marines
Britt Zerbe (ISBN: 978 1 78076 765 9)

A History of the Royal Navy: The Seven Years War
Martin Robson (ISBN: 978 1 78076 545 7)

A History of the Royal Navy: The Submarine
Duncan Redford (ISBN: 978 1 78076 546 4)

A History of the Royal Navy: The Victorian Age
Andrew Baines (ISBN: 978 1 78076 749 9)

A History of the Royal Navy: Women and the Royal Navy
Jo Stanley (ISBN: 978 1 78076 756 7)

A History of the Royal Navy: World War I
Mike Farquharson-Roberts (ISBN: 978 1 78076 838 0)

A History of the Royal Navy: World War II
Duncan Redford (ISBN: 978 1 78076 546 4)

The Royal Navy: A History Since 1900
Duncan Redford and Philip D. Grove (ISBN: 978 1 78076 782 6)

A HISTORY OF THE
ROYAL NAVY

Women and the Royal Navy

Jo Stanley

I.B. TAURIS
LONDON · NEW YORK

in association with

THE NATIONAL MUSEUM ROYAL NAVY

'Modern armed forces must represent the societies they defend if they wish to remain relevant in the modern world. Jo Stanley's expertly contextualised book explains how the modern Royal Navy successfully integrated women into seagoing service, a key example of transformation that has benefitted the navy, the nation and all those involved.'
Andrew Lambert, Laughton Professor of Naval History, Kings College, London

'My grandmother Dame Katharine Furse [the Women's Royal Naval Service's first director] convinced me that a woman could achieve whatever she set her mind to. Jo Stanley's wonderful book will inspire women worldwide.'
Hon. Elizabeth Furse, United States Congresswoman (retired)

'The author gives an authoritative and dynamic account of the vital role women in naval uniform have played in the shaping of today's maritime forces – it is recognition long overdue. She asks the questions, skilfully provides the answers and tells it as it is. For anyone with an interest in things naval and women in particular this is an inspirational book which deserves a place in everyone's library. An excellent sequel to her previous book *From Cabin 'Boys' to Captains*.'
Commodore Muriel Hocking RD* Royal Naval Reserve, the first and only woman in command of the RNR and the navy's first ever female commodore

'A meticulously researched tribute to women's immense contribution to naval service, mirroring their sisters' with the air force and army.'
Mary Mackie, author of *Wards in the Sky: The RAF's Remarkable Nursing Service*

'Jo Stanley's work is distinguished by the trouble she takes to uncover and explain the "how" and the "why" of women's full integration into the Royal Navy, rather than merely reporting the "what". Both as a military reference and a social commentary, the end result is important and compelling.'

Commodore Carolyn Stait, CBE, Naval Base Commander Clyde (Faslane), 2004–7

'Naval Nurses of the QARNNS are respected members of the longest serving women's service within the Royal Navy. This book shows the evolution of the Service from the days of the lob-lolly boys who assisted the ship's surgeon, to the highly trained defence nurse specialists available to serve aboard ship or ashore, home or abroad.'

Nora Lewis, author of *Nursing in the Navy*, and former QARNNS Sister

'The Royal Navy loomed large in my family history. To my delight this book makes clear the enormous but hidden role played by women in the Senior Service life. It is based on sound research and engagingly written and deserves to find a wide audience.'

Dr Susan Rose, lecturer, maritime author, and granddaughter of Admiral of the Fleet Sir John Jellicoe

Praise for *From Cabin 'Boys' to Captains: 250 Years of Women at Sea*:

'This book is a compendium of years of research which she presents in a clear concise style ... [it] should be mandatory reading for maritime history courses.'

The Mariner's Mirror

Published in 2018 by
I.B.Tauris & Co. Ltd
London • New York
www.ibtauris.com

Copyright © 2018 Jo Stanley

The right of Jo Stanley to be identified as the author of this work has been asserted by the author in accordance with the Copyright, Designs and Patents Act 1988.

All rights reserved. Except for brief quotations in a review, this book, or any part thereof, may not be reproduced, stored in or introduced into a retrieval system, or transmitted, in any form or by any means, electronic, mechanical, photocopying, recording or otherwise, without the prior written permission of the publisher.

Every attempt has been made to gain permission for the use of the images in this book. Any omissions will be rectified in future editions.

References to websites were correct at the time of writing.

ISBN: 978 1 78076 756 7
eISBN: 978 1 78672 313 0
ePDF: 978 1 78673 313 9

A full CIP record for this book is available from the British Library
A full CIP record is available from the Library of Congress
Library of Congress Catalog Card Number: available

Typeset by Mach 3 Solutions Ltd, Bussage, Gloucestershire

Printed and bound in Great Britain by T.J. International, Padstow, Cornwall

Contents

List of Figures	ix
List of Tables	xiv
List of Colour Plates	xv
Foreword by HRH The Princess Royal	xvii
Series Foreword	xviii
Acknowledgements	xx
Introduction	1
1. 'Assisting Behind the Scenes' – and More: 875–1884	19
2. The War Needs Veiled Warriors – in Navy Blue: 1884–1919	37
3. Wrens in World War I	53
4. Nursing in the Peacetime Navy: 1919–38	77
5. Naval Women Win World War II	85
6. Women Care for Wartime Patients: 1939–45	113
7. Struggling Seawards: The WRNS 1946–90	129
8. Women become Doctors and Men become Nurses: 1946–90	159
9. All in the Defence Medical Services Team: 1991 to Today	171
10. On towards Diversity and Inclusion: 1991 to Today	179

Appendices

1.	Women and Naval Services: A Select Timeline	203
2.	Finding Out More about Naval Services Women: Selected Reading	212
3.	Filmography	223
4.	Women in Perspective: Other Organisations	228
5.	Heads of WRNS and QARNNS	231

Notes — 237

Index — 257

List of Figures

00.1.	HRH The Princess Royal and Commander Rosie Wilson OBE (chair of the WRNS Benevolent Trust) joke as HRH is presented with a silver Women's Royal Naval Service brooch in celebration of her thirty-five years as patron of the WRNS Benevolent Trust (hereafter BT), 2010. Picture courtesy of WRNS BT.	xix
0.1.	HMS *Brilliant*'s first women matelots get ready to sail, Devonport 1990. Picture courtesy of the WRNS BT.	1
0.2.	'RN: "Really Nice"'. Women as a shore-based pleasure. Postcard, origin unknown, *c.* 1920. Eve Tar Archive.	5
0.3.	Maritime traders were temporarily welcomed visitors: 'From the old world to the new. The bumboat women come on board at Queenstown', by William Lionel Wyllie, 1893.	5
0.4.	At best women were welcomed as valued visitors who humanised the ship. 'A Ball on Board a Battleship', by Arthur Hopkins, *The Graphic*, 31 July 1894, pp. 70–1.	9
0.5.	Heart-warming camaraderie was most Wrens' chief pleasure in naval life. Wrens Armourers from HMS *Martello*, Weymouth, 1943. Picture courtesy of WRNS BT.	9
0.6.	Women's wartime service could confer prestige upon parents, some of whom had been initially uneasy that their daughters would become Amazons. 'Senior Service takes precedence. MY daughter's in the W.R.N.S.', Joseph Lee, *Evening News*, 28 August 1942. By courtesy of the British Cartoon Archive (JL2264) and Associated Newspapers/ Solo Syndication.	15
0.7.	'Lady Admirals' are on the agenda (AIB means Admiralty Interview Board).Cartoon by Smiles, December 2004. Picture courtesy of *Navy News*.	16
1.1.	Britannia: that shifting emblem of gendered Britain. *Punch*, 1859.	20
1.2.	Batches of camp followers and their children shared the vicissitudes of warriors on the move in a later period. Thomas Rowlandson, *Soldiers on a March: 'To pack up her tatters and follow the Drum'*, 1811. Wikimedia commons.	22

1.3.	A male cabin boy, which indicates cross-dressed women did not have to look extremely masculine. Thomas Rowlandson engraving, 1799. Wikimedia commons.	25
1.4.	Ann Perriam, veteran of the Battle of the Nile, 1860. Picture courtesy of Exmouth Library, Devon Archives and Local Studies Service, EXM001153.	27
1.5.	Sailors' partners make merry: *Sailors in Port/ Matelots au Port*, mezzotint, Thomas Stothard and William Ward, 1794. Picture courtesy of UK Government Art Collection, GAC 9882.	28
2.1.	Sister Louisa Hogg (centre, seated), when Head Sister at Haslar Hospital. *The Navy and Army Illustrated*, 19 February 1879.	39
2.2.	In the Boer War, ladies' roles in defence included fundraising for sailors' and soldiers' wellbeing: 'Sisters of Mercy', *Punch*, November 1899.	42
2.3.	QARNNS sister, well-disciplined patients, sick berth staff and no MO: Chatham Royal Naval Hospital, *c.* 1912. Postcard, Eve Tar Archive.	44
2.4.	Red Cross nurses were often shown as the most upsetting victims of German atrocities in World War I. Coloured chalk drawing by Louis Raemaekers, 1918. Picture courtesy of Wellcome Library ICV No 8538, Creative Commons Attribution only licence CC BY 4.0.	46
2.5.	Nurse at Mount Stuart Royal Naval Auxiliary Hospital, Bute, waiting in the operating theatre, which was the Marchioness's former Horoscope Room. Picture courtesy of Wellcome Library, London, V0030789ETR.	47
2.6.	QARNNS sisters in lifejackets enjoying their veils being blown in the wind. Capes and veils could be an occupational hazard, especially for lightweight women in strong gusts, caught up almost like kites. Picture courtesy of National Museum of the Royal Navy (hereafter NMRN).	49
3.1.	Katharine Furse in tricorn hat, the first director of the WRNS. Picture courtesy of University of Bristol Library, Special Collections, SC004695.	54
3.2.	Cooks were some of the first women to be taken up by the WRNS. All Wrens were seen as daughters of the Senior Service. Picture courtesy of George Malcolmson, P2012.40.12.	58
3.3.	Even before the war women enjoyed dressing up in sailor kit at photographic studios (left). In the war, some Wrens actually wore a version as uniform (right) and looked like counterparts of their brothers and sweethearts. Images from Eve Tar Archive and George Malcolmson Archive.	60
3.4.	Wren ratings lining up by the sea, summer 1918. Picture courtesy of University of Bristol Library, Special Collections SC 004692.	67
3.5.	Arguably the most fortunate WRNS personnel: those in Malta, late 1918. Ida Jermyn is in the centre. Picture courtesy of NMRN.	70
3.6.	WRNS posing on surrendered German U-boat, *U-123*, probably at Cowes, 22 November 1918. Picture courtesy of WRNS BT.	71

List of Figures

3.7.	Wrens marching in peace celebrations, Portsmouth, 1918. Picture courtesy of WRNS BT.	73
3.8.	Stewards (General) demobilising in 1919. Would they become housemaids or emigrants? Picture courtesy of NMRN 1989_447_2.	74
4.1.	Olga Franklin: from VAD to QARNNS. Photograph by Hay Wrightson, © National Portrait Gallery, NPG x74231.	77
4.2.	MP Nancy Astor dancing with a Royal Navy sailor on Plymouth Hoe. Picture courtesy of Plymouth City Council, PLYMG AR.1985.345.6.	80
5.1.	When the navy opened its doors to women Wrens were 'almost sailors' but did not quite share sailors' vicissitudes, such as carrying heavy kit bags and sleeping in hammocks that bowed their backs. 'Bent to it. Oh yes, just like the men, in hammocks …', Joseph Lee, *Evening News*, 24 November 1942. By courtesy of the British Cartoon Archive (JL2250) and Associated Newspapers/Solo Syndication.	86
5.2.	Widowed Vera Laughton Mathews, Director WRNS throughout the war, with her children in 1946. Eve Tar Archive.	86
5.3.	Ruins of the bombed Wrennery in Queen's Road, Great Yarmouth, 18 March 1943. Photo courtesy of Norfolk Libraries.	95
5.4.	'Wrens climb from the quarter boom, "Thirty seconds from deck to deck", Scotland 1943', by Lee Miller [5077–181]. © Lee Miller Archives, England 2016. All rights reserved. www.leemiller.co.uk.	96
5.5.	Protecting females from marauders: Wrens at the Aviary camp on the road to Cairo. Courtesy of the WRNS BT.	99
5.6.	Second Officer Kalyani Sen visits Rosyth, with Chief Officer Margaret L. Cooper, Deputy Director of the Women's Royal Indian Naval Service (WRINS) in June 1945. The WRINS began in February 1944. Photo courtesy of Imperial War Museum (hereafter IWM), IWM A29070.	100
5.7.	Pioneering WRNS air mechanics at the WRNS-only technical training establishment Mill Meece, Staffordshire, September 1943. Picture courtesy of Peggie Carmichael.	101
5.8.	WRNS boarding officer in unwise but regulation summer gear, climbing unknown ship to deliver confidential information, 1943. Picture courtesy of IWM, IWM A29071	103
5.9.	Wartime service meant Wrens could now be boys' role models: Frank Reynolds' cartoon from 17 January 1945. Picture courtesy of *Punch* Ltd.	108
5.10.	Women's valour was not recognised by medals but by practical support. Chief Wren Nye, Naval Family Welfare Service, arranges for children to be cared for until the poorly sailor's wife can resume her family duties. Picture courtesy of IWM, IWM D 26077.	109
6.1.	Out in Alexandria at the naval hospital in February 1945. The women are (left to right): Surgeon Lieutenant Ailsa Whitehouse, Medical Officer in Charge WRNS; Miss K. N. Cooper, Acting Principal Matron, QARNNS; Miss Phyllis Shipton, Acting Senior Sister, QARNNS; and Reserve Miss M. G. E. Maher-Loughnan, Acting Senior Sister, QARNNS. They are being inspected by Admiral Sir John Cunningham, C-in-C Mediterranean. Picture courtesy of IWM, IWM 205159130	114

6.2.	Varied but united in health care: HMS *Cabbala* Signal School sick bay personnel in 1943. Left to right on back row: the Wren steward who cleaned the ward; two Red Cross VADs; the RNVR medical officer; a St Johns VAD, Norma Wilson; and the WRNS writer who did the sick berth's clerical work. Front row: a St Johns VAD and the QARNNS sister. Picture courtesy of Norma Wilson (Hanson).	114
6.3.	A VAD wields the willow with convalescent psychiatric patients at RNAH Cholmondeley Castle, Cheshire. Photograph courtesy of IWM, IWM A11524.	121
6.4.	Nursing POWs at sea: Sister S. M. Augustus attends Captain (DO) H. G. Camp, Royal Artillery, aboard the hospital ship *Oxfordshire* in Hong Kong harbour following the reoccupation of the Crown Colony in 1945. Picture courtesy of IWM, IWM ABS 846.	121
6.5.	Ceylon, 1946. VAD Enid Crouch and Yeoman signaller Ernie Crouch enjoy the guard of honour at their wedding. Enid's colleagues, all naval nursing VADs, use splints instead of swords. Ernie's signalling pals brandish signal flags. Picture courtesy of Norma Hanson.	125
7.1.	The joke was both in the ample evidence of naval service and in the wife's presumption that she had really been *in* the Royal Navy, not just part of naval services. Cartoon for the *Ditty Box*, July 1946 by Ionicus (Joshua Armitage), courtesy of Judith P. Woodman.	130
7.2.	Limited opportunities for women. Wren stewards (general) enjoying stand-easy at the Duchess of Kent Barracks, 1959. Picture courtesy of WRNS BT.	134
7.3.	Women combatants without arms were increasingly an anomaly. 'I thought it about time they had something with which to present arms.' Cartoon for the *Ditty Box*, November 1945, by Ionicus (Joshua Armitage), courtesy of Judith P. Woodman.	136
7.4.	Formality in freewheeling times: a WRNS marchpast at HMS *Excellent*, the salute being taken by HRH The Princess Royal, 1970s. Picture courtesy of NMRN, 1981-349-3.	139
7.5.	Mary Talbot (far right), Nancy Robertson in the middle, and colleagues. Picture courtesy of the WRNS BT.	141
7.6.	A 'Happiness is Wren-shaped' sticker, which was in circulation in the 1970s. Picture courtesy of Lawrie Phillips from his forthcoming fifth edition of *The Royal Navy Day by Day*.	144
7.7.	Wrens lucky enough to be posted to Gibraltar work at the tape relay centre, a form of telephone communication via punched paper tape, which preceded fax and email, 1977. Picture courtesy of WRNS BT.	146
7.8.	Wren Joan Roberts enjoys photographers' rights to roam on ships, briefly and just in daytime. She is seated on a capstan on HMS *Lion*, a light cruiser at Rosyth in 1973. Picture courtesy of Joan Roberts.	149
7.9.	Commandant Anthea Larken in blue, not yet gold, braid, 1988. Picture courtesy of the Association of Wrens.	151
7.10.	Caroline Coates, at the time of working on the West report. Picture courtesy of Caroline Fuller-Webster.	153

List of Figures

8.1.	QARNNS sisters and matron Barbara Nockolds on hospital ship *Maine* during the Korean War. Courtesy of Ruth Stone (seated on lowest seat).	160
8.2.	Ann Whatford and some of the last WRNS SBAs play at Haslar, c. 1960. Picture courtesy of Ann Dickerson.	161
8.3.	QARNNS Sister Liz Law at the time of the Falklands Conflict. Picture by courtesy of Liz Ormerod.	164
8.4.	Surgeon Lieutenant Collette Green begins her naval training in Portsmouth, July 1963. IWM, IWM A34746.	167
8.5	QARNNS increasingly served abroad: team on exercise load patient into a Land Rover in Norway, 1980s. Picture courtesy of NMRN.	170
9.1.	Medical team including QARNNS in a tented unit on an exercise in the 2000s. Picture courtesy of NMRN.	175
10.1.	Seagoing women creating a new naval tradition. Smiles' *The Girlhood of Jenny* (February 1991) is a take-off of Millais' 1870 *Boyhood of Raleigh*. Cartoon courtesy of *Navy News*.	181
10.2.	The first Chief Naval Officer for Women, Julia Simpson, stands by the board honouring all the directors who preceded her, 1994. Picture courtesy of WRNS BT.	184
10.3.	Anxiety about women bearing arms changed: Vicki Taylor RN and her gun in Afghanistan, 2009. Picture courtesy of WRNS BT.	187
10.4.	Blue Wrens remain passionately loyal via the Association of Wrens. The Yeovil branch of the association visits Somerset's Fleet Air Arm Museum, 2007. Picture courtesy of WRNS BT.	192
10.5.	Pilot Natalie Grainger in a Merlin, 2016. MOD Crown Copyright picture, 2016, VL160053008.	199
10.6.	Exhilarating camaraderie: World War II Wrens classically enjoying 'the time of their lives' in naval service, Plymouth, October 1945. Picture courtesy of WRNS BT and Sheila Hamilton (left).	202

List of Tables

3.1.	Top five roles for WRNS ratings in 1917–19	68
4.1.	QARNNS locations in 1930	82
5.1.	Numbers of WRNS members by year and area in World War II	94
6.1.	Numbers of women and men giving health care in World War II, by year	116
7.1.	The WRNS as part of RN services, 1944–90	132
8.1.	Women Medical and Dental Officers, 1945–89	167
9.1.	Trained Regulars in Royal Navy Medical Branches, 2000–16	175
10.1.	Where are they now: RN women and men in 2016	198
A.1.	Total Women and Men in Royal Naval Services, 1660–2016	233
A.2.	What Did Naval Women Do? 2004 and 2014	235

List of Colour Plates

1. Hannah Snell, cross-dressed marine, c. 1750. Painting attributed to Daniel Williamson, courtesy of National Trust RNM 1988/51.
2. Women nursing the wounded during the Battle of Trafalgar, 1805. Detail from Daniel Maclise, *The Death of Nelson*, 1859–64.
3. Women were part of waterfront life and traded goods, including sex, with seagoers. *Portsmouth Point*, etching by Thomas Rowlandson, 1811. Picture courtesy of NMRN.
4. Sex industry workers and alcohol were rowed out to moored ships. The women sometimes worked and partied aboard for several days: *Exporting Cattle not Insurable*, by William Elmes, printed by Thomas Tegg, 1813.
5. Women and men alike joined in the admiration of the nation's greatest naval hero, Nelson: *England's Pride and Glory*, by Thomas Davidson, 1894. Picture courtesy of Royal Museums Greenwich, NMM BHC181.
6. A sailor takes his girlfriend to pay homage to his hero. Postcard, undated but c. 1900. Eve Tar Archive.
7. World War I WRNS recruiting poster by Joyce Dennys, 1917. Picture courtesy of NMRN.
8. Decorative Wrens at the waterside: *WRNS Officer and Ratings: Boat-cleaning at the Coastal Motor Boat Base, Haslar Creek, Portsmouth*, by A. D. M'Cormick, 1919. Picture courtesy of IWM, IWM ART 2619.
9. On ships men and boys did 'women's work'. Postcard, undated, Eve Tar Archive.
10. Girls in novels and reality learned about the sea as Sea Rangers and Girls' Nautical Training Corps members sometimes as a prelude to joining the WRNS or reserves. Detail from P. B. Hickling's cover of *Sea Rangers at Sloo*, Blackie & Sons, 1948.
11. World War II recruiting poster, undated. Picture courtesy of NMRN.
12. Recruiting poster of the 1960s inviting Wrens to serve 'with', not 'in', the Royal Navy. Picture courtesy of NMRN.
13. Leading Wren Margaret Young, the WRNS' only female blacksmith in World War II. She is working here as a moulder's mate. Picture tinted from NMRM image.
14. Leading Wrens on a survival course at HMS *Dryad*, 1960s. Picture courtesy of NMRN.

15. WRNS stewards give finishing touches to the dining tables at RNAS Culdrose, Helston, Cornwall, 1985. Picture courtesy of WRNS BT.
16. Cleaning materials being given to a Wren, probably by a Wren steward, 1970s. Picture courtesy of NMRN.
17. Naval women undergo Tarzan assault course at Royal Marines Commando Training Centre, Lympstone, Devon, 1996. Picture courtesy of WRNS BT.
18. One of the many Wren dental surgery assistants playing a key role in the delivery of dental services, 1970s. Dental surgeons were rarely females at this point. Picture courtesy of NMRN.
19. Naval women on the firefighting course which all personnel have to undergo, 2001. MOD Crown Copyright photograph, 2001, 04101572.
20. Marine engineering artificer apprentice Liz Meggit using a pillar drill at HMS *Sultan*, in 1993. Picture courtesy of Liz Howard.
21. Leading Steward Teisha Freckleton on HMS *Somerset* takes part in a refuelling at sea operation with a Royal Fleet Auxiliary ship *Fort Victoria*, 2001. Crown Copyright photograph 2001. FZ110159036.
22. The Royal Navy's leading women. Commodore (then Captain) Inga Kennedy (left) and Captain (then Commander) Ellie Ablett, 2013, Portsmouth. MOD Crown Copyright photograph, 2013, FX130323011.
23. Former navy LGBT activist Mandy McBain (left) and Sherry Conway, a serving RAF squadron leader critical care nurse, enjoy a mainly female guard of honour after their wedding in April 2016. Photo courtesy of photographer Kim Collins.
24. Combined Services co-operation on HMS *Illustrious*'s sickbay in a Role 2 Afloat training exercise, 2012. MOD Crown Copyright photograph 2010, IL120392073.
25. Women and the Royal Navy exhibition, National Museum of the Royal Navy, Portsmouth, 2017. Picture courtesy of NMRN.
26. Sailor relaxing by her ship: unnamed naval woman from HMS *Sheffield*. Picture courtesy of WRNS BT.
27. Royal Fleet Auxiliary CDT(X) Laura Frudd taking a reading with a sextant on the bridge wing of RFA *Fort Victoria*, 2010. MOD Crown Copyright photograph 2010, NE100433157_2.

Foreword
by HRH The Princess Royal

BUCKINGHAM PALACE

As Chief Commandant for Women in the Royal Navy, I watch with fascination and admiration as women rise up the ladder of promotion towards the rank of Admiral. The women in my family have always been closely involved with the Royal Navy both as wives and daughters of the Women's Royal Naval Service and the Queen Alexandra's Royal Naval Nursing Service. We know "life in a blue suit" and we have worn the uniform.

To read these pages is to understand how much women, including the women of naval families, have contributed to the Naval Service and to our Nation. The words and pictures show the steps that have been made in taking a full and complete role in today's diverse and inclusive Royal Navy, which is as busy as it has ever been. Life at sea holds many challenges, not least separation, and women continue to rise to this particular challenge in an inspiring way.

Anne

Fig. 00.1. HRH The Princess Royal and Commander Rosie Wilson OBE (chair of the WRNS Benevolent Trust) joke as HRH is presented with a silver Women's Royal Naval Service brooch in celebration of her thirty-five years as patron of the WRNS BT, 2010.

Series Foreword

The Royal Navy has for centuries played a vital if sometimes misunderstood or even at times unsung part in Britain's history. Often it has been the principal, sometimes the only means of defending British interests around the world. In peacetime the Royal Navy carries out a multitude of tasks as part of government policy – showing the flag, or naval diplomacy as it is now often called. In wartime, as the senior service of Britain's armed forces, the navy has taken the war to the enemy, by battle, by economic blockade or by attacking hostile territory from the sea. Adversaries have changed over the centuries. Old rivals have become today's alliance partners; the types of ship, the weapons within them and the technology – the 'how' of naval combat – have also changed. But fundamentally what the navy does has not changed. It exists to serve Britain's government and its people, to protect them and their interests wherever they might be threatened in the world.

This series, through the numerous individual books within it, throws new light on almost every aspect of Britain's Royal Navy: its ships, its people, the technology, the wars and peacetime operations too, from the birth of the modern navy following the restoration of Charles II to the throne in the late seventeenth century to the war on terror in the early twenty-first century.

The series consists of three chronologically themed books covering the sailing navy from the 1660s until 1815, the navy in the nineteenth century from the end of the Napoleonic Wars, and the Navy since 1900. These are complemented by a number of slightly shorter books which examine the navy's part in particular wars, such as the Seven

Years War, the American Revolution, the Napoleonic Wars, World War I, World War II and the Cold War, or particular aspects of the service: the navy and empire, the women in Royal Navy services, the Royal Marines, naval aviation and the submarine service. The books are standalone works in their own right, but when taken as a series present the most comprehensive and readable history of the Royal Navy.

Duncan Redford
Series Editor

The role in Britain's history of the Royal Navy is all too easily and too often overlooked; this series will go a long way to redressing the balance. Anyone with an interest in British history in general or the Royal Navy in particular will find this series an invaluable and enjoyable resource.

Tim Benbow
Defence Studies Department,
King's College London at the
Defence Academy of the UK

Acknowledgements

Creating wide-ranging history books require hard work. Glamorous it ain't. Key people who have helped me make *Women and the Royal Navy* are Celia Saywell, the public relations officer of the Association of Wrens, who has been invaluable to me from the moment she said, 'Let me help you make writing this book as enjoyable and easy as possible.' That is such a gift to a writer. M. J. Fish, expert statistician and blogger on WRNS history, has been indispensable in helping me with the statistical side.

Writing books like this requires incorporating the help of the many before me who have done primary research. I stand appreciatively on the shoulders of giants such as Kathleen Harland and Claire Taylor, the QARNNS experts. The WRNS key contemporary experts are Kath Sherit, Hannah Roberts and Vicky Ingles. In the past Ursula Stuart Mason, M. H. Fletcher, Lesley Thomas, Chris Howard Bailey, and Second Officer J. Hardy created path-breaking chronicles of the institution, too. These augment the many personal memoirs, not least by the two wartime directors who wrote as impressively as they led. My late friend Suzanne J. Stark did pioneering work on women in the early navy.

I have had the honour of meeting many admirably dynamic and focused women involved in naval services. For their generosity in speaking to me – in person, by letter, email and phone – to help me understand the big picture from their individual stories and views, I thank the following and assure them that although *all* their words may not be here, their riches certainly inform the book and will fertilise many future articles and talks too:

Penny Abbott, Ellie Ablett, Jane Allen, Rosemary Booth (née Codman), Betty Calderara (née Maguire), Peggie Carmichael (née Morris), Liz Chislett-Milne, Ann Dickerson (née Whatford), Emma Fox (née Parkhurst), Caroline Fuller-Webster (née Coates), Pauline Gifford, Val Gleave, Grace Gough, 'Angela Green', Norma Hanson (née Wilson), Dawn Higginson, Stephanie Higham, Liz Howard, Penny Hockley (née Lee), Joy James (née Freeman), 'Philippa James', Anne Jones, Marion Kettlewell, Val Knight (née White), Ann Lacey, Polly Laird, Anthea Larken (née Saville), Alison Lawrence, Thelma Leach, Elaine Hanby, Nora Lewis (née Miller), Mary Milton (née Burdett), Jean Morton, Carol Murray-Jones (née Fell), Karen Nimmo-Scott (née Linstead), Lucy Ottley, Liz Ormerod (née Law), Shelagh Packwood, Joan Payne (née Hobhouse), Annette Penfold, Georgie Peters, Stephanie Piggot, Carole Ralph (née Quinn), Dorothy Runnicles, Karen Sawyer (née Crosbie), Julia Simpson, Carolyn Stait, Ruth Stone, Mel Thompson, Phyllis Tull (née Le Seelleur), Joy White (née Bennington), Margaret Whitehouse, Linda Williams (née Oldridge), Rosie Wilson, Penny Wright.

Many more preferred that their names did not appear and I appreciate them equally. Others were standing by to help but we ran out of time; I hope they will join in by sending stories to the Association of Wrens publications and my blog on the gendered sea.

Many people who are not women in naval service now but know the field gave me information, pictures and ideas. Those who can be named include:

Bill Alexander, Len Barnett, Richard Cobbold, Mike Coombes, Sue Diamond and the Bear, Godfrey Dykes, Jean Edwards, Nicola Fear, Elizabeth Furse, Peter Hore, Rick Jolly, Charles Johnston, Daphne Joynes, Frank Judd, Andrew Lambert, Jan Larcombe, Brian Lavery, Sue Light, David McLean, Della Rebours, Mike Farquharson-Roberts, Susan Rose, Ann Savours Shirley, Robin Spittle, Chris Terrill and Kevin Winter.

The various organisations that have enabled this study include the Association of Wrens; the WRNS Benevolent Trust, especially Sarah Ayton; the National Museum of the Royal Navy, particularly Kate Braun, Stephen Courtney, David Eaton, Alison Firth, Giles Gould, Nick Hewitt, Vicky Ingles, George Malcolmson and Alice Walsh; and the QARNNS Archive. At the National Maritime Museum some of the many helpful people include Laura Humphrey, Sara Wajid and Tracey Weller, as well as the library staff. The National Archive and British Library have been invaluable: digitisation has made such a difference, as it has to the Royal College of Nursing's Archive and the British Red Cross Archive too. For their help with finding naval VADs I thank Emily Oldfield at the BRC archive, and Sue Hawkins who was responsible for the digitisation. The SCONUL access scheme has enabled many scholars to access university libraries: mine include Bradford, Huddersfield, Hull, Leeds, Liverpool, Liverpool John Moores, the London School of Economics and Manchester. While going through Katharine Furse's archives at the University of Bristol I was aided by Hannah Lowery, Jamie Carstairs and Michael Richardson. Naval help has included those at the MoD press office and the statisticians who responded to my Freedom of Information queries; Jennie Wraight and George Gelder at the Naval Historical Branch; and Jane Wickenden at the Institute of Naval Medicine Library. The Royal Marines Museum and the RM Historical Society helped all they could, as did Sue Huggett of the RM Band Service. In the world of MOs and DOs, Ben Davis at the British Medical Association and Rachel Bairsto of the British Dental Association have generously given much remote assistance.

The series editor Duncan Redford is appreciated for his insightful and erudite editing. So too is Jo Godfrey at I.B.Tauris for her integrity, deftness and alacrity. Two old friends have been my stalwart 'Fast Response Unit' in preparing a text that is now a third the original length, much less snippy, and in much better English: Janet Perham and Teresa Stenson.

I have been more subtly sustained by the worldwide communities of historians of women, of gender and of maritime and naval pasts, as well as of oral historians. Tellingly, these seldom overlap. Those in the water-focused world include my colleagues at the University of

Hull Maritime Historical Studies Centre; the Kings Maritime History Seminar participants; port studies scholar; gender and military masculinities studies researchers; and many worldwide in the International Commission for Maritime History. Nourishment for authors comes from many sources. I am grateful to early mentors Sarah Palmer, Skip Fischer and Anna Davin, as well as my inspirations Greg Dening, Marcus Rediker, Isaac Land and Sari Maenpaa. Claudine Hick, Hong Tao Wang, N. B., Anthony Hall, Keith Helmsley and Gerry Tompkins gave essential practical help. Creating books costs money, rather than making it, so I am grateful to the Society for Nautical Research's Anderson Award for some travel expenses and to all the people who have accommodated or fed me far from home.

Acquiring pictures that are unusual yet somehow typical, *and* high resolution *and* affordable is a feat for any author. This is especially hard when copyright laws are so stringent and smartphone camera shots are too low-resolution for publication. I deeply thank my friends for sponsoring some of the institutional pictures. Hazel Seidel's gift is in memory of her father, Russell Seidel, a lecturer at Dartmouth. Neil Hanson gave in memory of Don Hanson, a naval radiographer. The Lee Miller photo was sponsored by Jean Margetts, an admirer of Miller's work, in memory of the murdered MP Jo Cox. Musicians Annie Dearman and Steve Harrison funded the photo of the WRNS boarding officer. Their gift is in memory of their Thames sailing barge shipmate, musical collaborator and wedding witness Barry Callaghan, who died suddenly in 2007. Hester Dunlop sponsored two health-related pictures. A. S. generously helped out with three wartime photos that my heart groaned for. In memory of Jean Shaw Rimmer Grayson, former nurse Shirley Irving donated the costs of a nurse photo. The A. D. M'Cormick painting is reproduced thanks to the help of Jan Buttifont in memory of her aunt Edith Sowerbutts. Edith is my heroine, a pioneer woman seafarer who also helped World War I ex-Wrens emigrate as part of her early work at the Society for the Overseas Resettlement of British Women.

I am grateful to the many other people who helped with images. Some are credited in the captions of each individual picture but I additionally thank Neera Puttapipat at the IWM; the Fleet Air Arm museum staff including Barbara Gilbert; the Government Archives Collections Office; Steve Saywell; *Navy News*; Judith Armitage; Wellcome Collection; staff and Elspeth Millar at the University of Kent Special Collections. Astonishingly kind eBay sellers and Bryan Bartholomew, the postman, who never bends a single precious envelope, enabled me to create the Eve Tar Archive. For miraculously enhancing hopeless pictures I am indebted to John Blakeborough and artist Laura Crane.

For the final stages of making this book I appreciate Tia Ali, Magdalene Abraha, Elizabeth Stone (a wonderfully astute editor) and Sophie Campbell.

Inevitably authors temporarily forget many who deserve to be acknowledged. I value them all, whether they appear here or not. I alone am responsible for any errors of fact and understanding. At the request of some RN officers the following disclaimer has been agreed:

> The views and opinions expressed, and the interpretations made, are those of the author and her informants alone. They should not be taken to represent those of Her Majesty's Government, MOD, HM Armed Forces or any government agency.

In a climate where some 'insiders' mistrust questers as, at worst, paparazzi scum and, at best, irredeemable ignoramuses, it has been a joy to be welcomed so hospitably by so many naval people, even at their private gatherings.

Thank you all.

Jo Stanley, South Pennines, August 2017

Introduction

Fig. 0.1. HMS *Brilliant*'s first women matelots get ready to sail, Devonport 1990.

In Devonport on Monday 8 October 1990 a team of 20 sailors in neat blue trousers walked up the gangway to join their ship. Sailors worldwide had done just that for centuries. However, those joining HMS *Brilliant* that day made national news. I, an admirer of women's progress in maritime life, wish I had been there to see this landmark moment. Cameras were rolling. It was a fanfare occasion.

Why? Because these were the very first group of females to sail as an integral part of a warship's complement. Headed by Lieutenant Elizabeth A. Spencer, a married meteorologist and oceanographer, the team of 'Jenny Wrens' included radio operators, stewards and writers. The 16 ratings (meaning lower-rated personnel) and four officers of the Women's Royal Naval Service joined the type-22 frigate at Devonport ... and soon found themselves in a war zone: the Gulf.

This was not just a score of women going to a new UK workplace, a 254-strong community. They were part of a move that resulted in all naval services women being formally integrated into the Royal Navy. This included being armed, seagoing and fulfilling the navy's motto 'If you wish for peace, prepare for war'.

These pioneers represented the bridging of a divide that had earlier seemed impossible. For centuries there has been a long-standing gap between the way society imagined the armed forces and how it saw women. This disparity mirrored archetypal ideas of masculinity and femininity in wider society. Women and war were allegedly an incompatible pairing, like oil and water. So that Monday in 1990 saw the triumphant end of centuries of formally excluding half the people of Britain, of women only being *associate*, not full members. The move was the consequence of there simply not being enough people to staff the fourth most powerful navy in the world (in terms of numbers of ships, submarines, naval aircraft and personnel, as well as firepower, global reach and influence). Women's inclusion on HMS *Brilliant* was the start of today's navy in which D&I (diversity and inclusion) are cornerstones. The navy has moved light years in three decades.

Going away to sea might seem like every girl's dream: enjoying your hair tossing in breezes tangy with salt and spices; visiting the delights of exotic ports; watching porpoises playing in iridescent waters; gazing up, alone, at vast expanses of star-spangled skies over vast oceans; not to mention looking great in your white and gold uniform. Metaphysical elation might seem available by the truckload.

That uncomplicated, romanticised version probably never could be achieved by any adult mortal. Women old and young working on commercial ships managed a more realistic version from about 1820. They were part of the human cargo world: imperial travel, emigration, then tourism. By contrast, in the defence-focused Royal Navy, there had been no female equivalents of Jack Tar until 1990 when the *Brilliant* women set a new pattern and inadvertently helped create a new sort of integrated and family-friendly navy.

Naval women

The long-term story of women in the Royal Navy is largely one of women ashore and their progress towards becoming seafarers. This book is about the tens of thousands of women who could have lived next door to you and me, and maybe did. Some sailed as part of what is now called 'living life in a blue suit'. All were ship-minded and many were related to generations of Jack Tars, committed to enabling that mythical Britannia to rule the world's waves.

These women were, in varying ways, part of the stylish-looking and prestigious 'Senior Service', the oldest of the nation's armed forces. Two key bodies of women within naval services were crucial in harnessing all that women could do; uniforming them, training them, housing them and encouraging them up the limited ladders. First, in 1884, came the Naval Nursing Service, which was renamed Queen Alexandra's Naval Nursing Service (QARNNS) in 1902. QARNNS was initially a small force of female nursing officers, born of the idea that hospitals benefited from the type of superior female care championed by pioneering nursing administrator Florence Nightingale. QARNNS still exists today as a separate force but now includes men too.

The second, much larger, organisation came into being 34 years later when the short-handed navy needed extra personnel in World War I. The Women's Royal Naval Service (WRNS) was established in order to free men to go to sea. It lasted from 1917 to 1919. Then it was restarted, for the same reasons, from 1939. This time when war ended the WRNS moved from being an auxiliary to a permanent service. It continued until 1993, when Wrens were included as a full part of the navy.

Being in the QARNNS or the WRNS meant you were seen as being in naval *services*. By contrast, women doctors, dentists and medical assistants were *in* the navy itself, specifically in the medical service. Such medics were always part of the inner sanctum of the Royal Navy (although sometimes administratively positioned as part of its reserve). Women working as Voluntary Aid Detachment (VAD) staff (under the aegis of the British Red Cross and the Order of St John) were managed by the charities themselves. They assisted in naval hospitals and sick bays, usually just in wartime emergencies.

Apart from these organisations, women and girls were to be found in many navy-related bodies. Increasingly from 1915 civilian workers were employed in admiralty establishments. The very young joined Girl Guide-influenced organisations such as the Girls' Nautical Training Corps and the Sea Rangers. In the late twentieth century, adults volunteered in naval reserves including the Women's Royal Naval Service Reserve, the Royal Naval Auxiliary Service, the Royal Naval Reserve and now the Maritime Volunteer Service. Evening and weekend training and exercises could mean women had a navy-related life from girlhood through to WRNS, to the naval reserves and to the grave. Public-spirited lady activists also took leading roles in naval charities and in campaigning groups such as the Navy League. They made the navy their business.

Women's sense of community was strengthened because they were also proxies; women felt they were part of the navy, albeit supporting from shore, because their relatives and partners were its loyal members. They experienced the navy as an embracing and sociable way of life, not simply as their husband's or father's job. It was also a source of money for the women who traded with naval personnel, including as sex industry workers, landladies and bumboat women (waterborne traders) taking vegetables, alcohol and souvenirs as well as their services to customers on moored ships.

However, naval life was a world where a certain sort of masculinity had dominated. For centuries Jack Tars had rallied to the navy's official march with its chorus:

> Heart of Oak are our ships,
> Jolly Tars are our men,
> We always are ready: Steady, boys, Steady!
> We'll fight and we'll conquer again and again

Men were told going to sea 'would make a man of you', while their sisters were associated with the opposite: pleasantness, recreation, tranquillity, the creation of new life, domestic comforts. Like Emma Hamilton and Fanny Nisbet Nelson – the lover and wife of Admiral Horatio Nelson, respectively – women were regarded as innately

Fig. 0.2. 'RN: "Really Nice"'. Women were appreciated as a shore-based pleasure. Postcard, origin unknown, *c.* 1920.

Fig. 0.3. Maritime traders were temporarily welcomed visitors: 'From the old world to the new. The bumboat women come on board at Queenstown', by William Lionel Wyllie, 1893.

suited to welcoming men home, rather than themselves being leaders of naval battles at sea or the nation's stalwart and nobly selfless heroes.[1]

These female pioneers in *Brilliant*, and their successors, represented a bridging of what had appeared an impossible divide of two species. Female sharp-shooters such as Annie Oakley had been rare in the bronco-busting Wild West. Pioneering women in the male-dominated industries of the 1970s had had to set up supportive networks such as Women in Manual Trades in order to get on. Authoritative female crime-stoppers had been such an innovation that late twentieth century TV dramas were built around characters in shows such as *Charlie's Angels* and *Cagney and Lacey*.

These pages trace women's long progress from being under-recognised, over-sentimentalised non-combatants in whose name war was fought to becoming part of the 3,000-strong highly valued female naval professionals in today's defence team. Their story has parallels to that of Nicole Stott, one of 60 women space travellers since 1963; Cressida Dick, who in 2017 became the first woman Metropolitan Police Commissioner; and solo long-distance yachtswoman Dame Ellen MacArthur. These navy women parallel the air force's women pilots and the army's potential women tank crew members.

Being able to sail away is as pivotal as being able to take to the skies. Not without reason were Royal Air Force women nicknamed 'Penguins', birds with wings who could not fly. Now, of course, the navy not only embraces women but people of all sexual identities, including those who have transitioned.

A different sort of naval history book

Two sorts of naval history book predominate. Prominent are accounts of battles fought at sea against other nations, where justice-seeking male warriors on their sea steads vanquished enemies and maintained a 'wooden wall' around the British Isles. Other works tell of a life at sea, omitting the elephant in the room: that it was taken for granted that males predominated and ruled ships (and usually society too), as the ultimate father figures who could never be gainsaid.

Naval histories are full of names and events that have become famous in the national story of Britannia's efforts to rule the waves, from Sir Francis Drake's moves against the Spanish Armada in Elizabethan times to the battle of Jutland in 1916. Drake, Walter Raleigh and Horatio Nelson are key names in national, not just naval, history.

In these pages you will find another, or alternative, history to that canonical naval story. Songs, films, poems used to speak of sailors' lives in terms of braving terrible storms, using remarkable sea skills, feeling loyalty to their men-o'-war, firing powerful guns across tropical waters, enduring weevil-filled biscuits, enjoying 'a girl in every port'. Ruggedness was celebrated.

The story of women's naval lives is different because fewer were at sea and they took part in large numbers only long after sailing ships had been replaced by vessels that were easier to handle. These were real women, not Britannias with their tridents or idealised muses represented as wooden figureheads. *Their* naval life was furnished with objects of support: wound-dressings, accurate wage slips and mountains of mashed potatoes. Widowly, sisterly and maternal grief at men slain was common; they fought the press gangs that sought to snatch men away to sea, rather than themselves being seized for service.

Servicewomen's work tools included typewriters, not guns. Instead of making model ships in bottles they knitted. On top of their paid labour they did the emotional labour, such as encouraging civility and raising morale, that is expected of women. When men were hostile to them as invaders of the institution, or sexually harassed them, they handled it deftly with a smile and without complaint, so as to maintain group cohesion and women's reputations as good sorts. Above all, they had the additional gendered job of being always professional and acting as staunch colleagues in the face of expectations that females inevitably could not pull their weight and simply did not belong at sea. They repeatedly proved their worth. With impressive generosity, most men were fast to recognise that they had been wrong and that women indeed made excellent colleagues.[2]

The book's theme is about the variety of contributions women have made to naval life in different periods. It shows how the diverse parts of the navy brought about women's inclusion and eventually came to instigate and accept women's presence alongside, in some sectors. I have not just added women into a story that once left no gaps for this relegated group of human beings. Instead the focus is on how largely hyper-masculine naval services handled the women within them. You will find the book is written with questions in mind such as what exactly were women doing in naval life, and why, and how did that relate to what men did? If women were not there, what was behind that? Were they not capable, not suitable, or something else again? How did women feel about the navy, the limitations it placed on what they could do and the unexpected opportunities it gave them?

Women do things differently to men at times: multi-tasking being an obvious example. So how did they maintain their values and usual ways when they did not fit with masculine lifestyles? I take a perspective that recognises that women and men are different but equal, and that much can be achieved through training and setting aside stereotypes – as it eventually has been.

Have all women, always, been somehow naturally and forever unable to lead, decide strategy and successfully adopt unconventional tactics to save their nation? What if an accident of fate had led to all men being expected to home-make, not trained to develop naval expertise? Similarly, no woman is celebrated for deliberately putting her blind eye to her telescope and insisting she could not see the order to cease action, as Nelson famously did at Copenhagen in 1801. If she had, would her (male) senior officers not have refused her authority as feminine dottiness? In essence, the book asks 'what has been the navy's problem with including women? Why would any organisation exclude potentially useful personnel?' And it shows that, from 1989, the navy realised it should welcome them far more fully and opened its doors, with ever-increasing enthusiasm.

At the same time the story is of the thousands of women who, despite the intrinsic difficulties, loved extrinsic aspects of their time in naval services: the camaraderie, the jaunts by boat out to ships and the pleasure of keeping company with naval men. The navy incidentally gave thousands of women 'the time of their lives', confidence, training in a transferable skill, and a way to leave home and travel safely. And finally it gave them integrated and satisfying roles.

Fig. 0.4. At best women were welcomed as valued visitors who humanised the ship. 'A Ball on Board a Battleship', by Arthur Hopkins.

Fig. 0.5. Heart-warming camaraderie was most Wrens' chief pleasure in naval life. Wrens Armourers from HMS *Martello*, Weymouth, 1943.

My story

When they heard I was writing this book people inquired 'Were you a Wren, then?' When I wrote about women pirates they also asked if I was a would-be buccaneer. In fact I am an explorer who uses questions not cutlasses, who likes creating the first maps of barely glimpsed territory. As a cultural historian I am interested in the fact that going to sea can give people, especially women, the opportunity to fulfil themselves in unexpected ways.

My earliest 'meeting' with women in naval life was through the BBC radio programme *The Navy Lark*, which featured crisp and charming Wrens. Listening with my Dad, a World War II radio operator, was a way of understanding the most important organisation in the life of the man who was, at that stage, the most important male in my life.

I puzzled that none of his stories were about women colleagues. Surely that absence of women, and absence of explanation for it, eventually led to my becoming an expert on gender on merchant, not naval ships: the women who were there and the men who preferred to act like women there, the camp crew in floating 'queer heavens'. My interest in the women of the commercial navy consolidated in 1970s Liverpool when I began exploring the life of my Great Aunty May, a stewardess on Elder Dempster Line ships to West Africa. After hearing scores of seagoing women's testimonies, I have produced many articles, books, talks, exhibitions and even plays. The story of these gallivanting pioneers in commercial shipping helped me grasp how ordinary women without money managed the extraordinary feat of seeing the world: they worked their way round it. Dusters, shorthand notebooks, nurses' fob watches, hairdressing scissors and dance shoes were their passports.

Since then I have sought to know how all sorts of women 'intruders' handled life at sea, and how they, in turn, were handled by shipmates. It is a truism that sometimes men saw women aboard as bad luck, as 'Jonahs'. However, why was this superstition so oddly intermittent and suspiciously contingent? Women seemed to be quite accepted when men wanted the services they provided.

In order to understand something of the history of seagoing women I have climbed the mast on the tall ship *Stavros S Niarchos*. I can also understand what it is like to be in a ship under fire because in the Crimea I fired an ancient cannon and found, for days, that your ears really do ring as if you lived in 24/7 in a belfry. Naval nursing became clearer to me when I was shown around Haslar, the pride of naval hospitals, by the former matron-in-chief of naval nursing officers, Claire Taylor. At Britannia Royal Naval College, Dartmouth, in 1977, I met and briefly sailed with women pioneering in command roles, Lieutenants Suzanne Moore and Melanie Robinson. I felt I was witnessing the emergence of a new sort of naval life: they were so accomplished and were treated with respect.

My work for maritime museums, especially as founder of the National Maritime Museum's Women and the Sea Network, has helped me learn enormous amounts about women's overlooked contributions to the maritime past, which documentary research and oral interviews strengthened.

Surprisingly ...

Yet surprises always abound as you research and write up a book – in listening to experts and veterans, as well as scouring archives. I found out how little the naval push to send women to sea was impelled by a belief in equal rights; it was principally the outcome of demographics: navy statisticians identified the need for bright personnel in 1989. Women were available. Simple.

I became curious about seeming contradictions. Why, having served in the *military*, did many recall their time as a good time with other girls, disassociated from defence work, which can involve slaughter? Until 1977 naval women were civilians, and officially of the navy. So why, like so many army women too, did they 'explicitly consider ... themselves to be in "in" – or at least equivalent to – the Army' and Navy, despite male officials refuting the preposterous idea that they were fully members and equal? It seems that a subtle message created the continued confusion. At the National Maritime Museum in 1991 I happened to meet WRNS historian and former WRNS officer Ursula Stuart Mason, just after naval women were integrated. Almost shaking with outrage, she insisted that putting hormonal young people together in tin box far from home would only lead to sexual trouble. In my regrettable ignorance, I could not understand how any woman would be opposed to women's seagoing, and on such grounds.

Eating pizza on Portsmouth seafront with one of the wives who had protested at the dockyard gates that mixed-sex crews would lead their husbands towards adultery on board ship, I absolutely empathised with her concern of 25 years earlier. Equally, sitting down with earnest male sailors who had genuinely feared their cherished institution would suffer from erosion and even pollution, I understood the reasons why they wanted to shield it from women.

I had expected naval women to have joined up primarily out of patriotism. In fact, many were like the stewardesses, social directors and hotel-side managers from passenger ships I had also interviewed. Naval women, too, often just fancied life away from home and were fascinated by the sea.

The invariably dynamic Wrens, QARNNS and VADs I have met were empowered by being part of a proudly women-only organisation that had early been shaped by suffragettes and suffragists. So how could any of them have embraced the idea that women and men had different places and that women's natural place was not at sea or in combat situations? Why could not they see that they were a kind of feminist?

Finding out

One of my key resources was naval records. Historians recognise that official records are frequently reticent or even entirely absent. Formal minutes may mask more than they reveal, especially in organisations where high security is normal and where minorities have developed the habit of being self-protective. Organisations weed out a staggering percentage of their archives before putting them in the public domain. This book is based partly on such unsatisfactory troves. That has to mean it is a partial narrative.

Sparse remaining documented history is helpfully, but again patchily, expanded by what naval women have told me, or told the world on the record. As historian Penny Summerfield explained in her discussion about how wartime women remember and how writers work with that, remembering is a complex construction. Retrieving a memory is not like pulling a frozen pea from a packet, intact as when it was put there. Many influences cause rememberers to rewrite many times, not least to avoid offending or to not seem out of step. Naval women's public stories have been upbeat, loyal and polite. This means there are important omissions, usually about men's failure to be fair and respectful, and about bad living conditions, miscarriages of justice and petty restrictions. For example, Bletchley Park Wrens working on breaking the Enigma code often felt excruciatingly bored; heroic status was only later thrust upon them. So there are at least two sorts of absences: missing documents and tactful silences.[3]

Naval women's history will benefit from many people in the future telling the story in other ways – and more fully. Modern thinking is that there is no such thing as a right and true account, only versions and subjective interpretations. So please read on with your antennae atwitch, knowing that there is much between the lines. Greg Dening, my favourite cultural historian, wrote that an ethnographic history is 'an attempt to represent the past as it was actually experienced in such a way that we understand both its ordered and disordered natures.' The orderliness that a narrative suggests and the order it imposes is seldom real; life, even in the orderly navy, is a bumpy and awry business full of contradictions and anomalies. My angle is far from the only one, although it is valuable because it draws on the wider world of women as sailors, explorers and adventurers who sought fulfilment on the ocean wave.

It is not a story of heroines. I am not making naval pioneers into swashbuckling Amazonian adventurers like Buffy the Vampire Slayer or Wonder Woman. Nor am I seeing them simplistically as happy pals in dorms, as in Angela Brazil boarding school novels. The story is of an institution that shifted, and the women who were for and against that shift. It is complex and I hope you will enjoy wondering at it.[4]

Naval life for women

In my discovering process, I came to understand naval life somewhat. So I hope that readers who do not know much about its history will accept my offer of some points that I wish I had known when I set out. They will help you contextualise the diverse women in these pages.

The Royal Navy was enormous and comprised many sub-sections. It was not just water-focused. The RNRM (as the Royal Navy and Royal Marines is now commonly called) also had its own infantry force (the Royal Marines, from 1755) and air force (the Fleet Air Arm Branch, from 1924). Women had varying and sometimes expert knowledge of these many parts and increasingly worked with them, with remarkable corporate loyalty. Although QARNNS, Wrens, VADs and medics were in separate organisations, they saw themselves as branches of the main, as 'family'. Rivalry was usually amicable and politely low-key.

This book could almost have been called 'Such camaraderie!' or 'The time of my life', because naval servicewomen remember enjoying it so much. Their recollected pleasure is similar to young people living collectively away from home and being able to access new experiences – such as those who found jobs on cruise ships, or young women in some college hostels. They appreciate, especially in retrospect, a life where infectious serotonin highs created a happy atmosphere, whatever the actual circumstances. Some women were in both the commercial and defensive navies at different times, such was their ardour for the sea, travel and substitute 'families away from home'.

Any island nation seeking dominion focused on its navies as its primary seaborne fighting force. This means its members understood their significance to the nation's strength and future. Most naval women felt honoured to be part of the 'Senior Service', at least for a time. For many that pride continues. In addition, marrying into it and having children who joined it, helped consolidate a striking sense of patriotism and public service. It is no accident that some also had links with the police and fire service. These were women with an exceptional sense of duty to others. They were happy to take on any responsibility, as required, and ignore personal difficulties in a culture where it was not done to complain or challenge. Only later did they become questioning, or even pacifists.

Fig. 0.6. Women's wartime service could confer prestige upon parents, some of whom had been initially uneasy that their daughters would become Amazons. 'Senior Service takes precedence. MY daughter's in the W.R.N.S.', Joseph Lee, *Evening News*, 28 August 1942.

Navies are part of a nation's defensive system, like armies and air forces. Seeing themselves as protective of 'weaker' people, members necessarily had trouble accepting that the 'weaker sex' might be part of that protective force, rather than protectees. Women seemed anomalous in knightly roles and the risk of their being wounded or killed was distressing to the many chivalrous males. This attitude was slow to change. Transition was eased as women's roles in wider society, after the 1970s, expanded and they moved from marginalised status.

In the past, worldwide, women were seen as 'naturally' unsuitable as armed fighters, including in the Royal Navy. Combat was regarded as a solely male province – until an alteration to the Geneva Convention in 1977, and a UK change in 2016. In most countries changes only really began in the 1970s. They are still ongoing. Members of the Royal Navy are confident there will soon be women admirals. Serving personnel now generally believe that allowing women in combat roles is fair enough; is necessary because of personnel shortages; and is an equal rights victory consistent with our changed times.

These armed forces are controlled by decisions made for political, and sometimes financial, reasons. So the inclusion of women full-time in almost all roles – flying, going to sea, joining infantry battalions – has been a political and economic decision. Reasons for opening up the navy

Fig. 0.7. 'Lady Admirals' are on the agenda (AIB means Admiralty Interview Board). Cartoon by Smiles, December 2004.

include shortages of personnel, women being seen as ideal for many fiddly or boring indoor tasks, and also that – until 1949 – they could be paid less. Reasons against were that women would not be suitable because society was thought unready to accept women bearing arms, not babies, in their arms; they might not be good enough and so could potentially reduce overall operational effectiveness; and they would leave early because they married – they were not in it for lifetime careers. At times in the past sea life was seen as unsavoury and therefore unfit for ladies, so a kind patriarch would of course ensure a lady was not besmirched through mixing with common tars. Finance-based fears included that lack of physical strength would mean two women had to be employed in place of one man, and that having separate female forces would cost extra money for set-apart accommodation, especially toilets, and administration.

Finally, decision makers worried about sexual intercourse at sea. 'Sex. There, I have said it', wrote Commander T. R. Harris. 'My job is to require them [people on board] to confine their interest to a time not just off duty, but off ship. Anyone who thinks that you can prevent something like that happening ... may have forgotten their own youth!'

In the past, concerns about illicit shenanigans were partly based on the old gallant ideas that the fair sex should be protected, especially if young and innocent. (Behind this lay concern that experienced Lotharios could be forcefully desirous.) Concern was also practical: romancing and rivalry would distract people from their duties, upset shipboard discipline and disrupt group cohesion. Pregnancies in mid-crisis, when all hands were needed, would be a disaster. For many reasons 'mixed manning', as it is still called, was opposed until the 1990s. It is now entirely accepted, and women are reaching the higher echelons.[5]

Shipboard life mirrors the larger organisation, so a ship is indeed a microcosm and a place of hierarchies. Everyone on board is focused on agreed goals, such as 'We have got to rescue these poor refugees on that tiny unseaworthy boat', even though various subcultures may disagree about rules, for instance allowing everyone only two cans of beer per day. It may be worth reminding ourselves that a ship at sea truly is a prison. It is a vehicle, so getting to places matters. So does the sea itself, which determines daily living conditions. Also it is a community where people live in quarters that are usually too close, and so become adept at the art of getting on together. They are dependent on each other for survival, which creates strong bonds.

These ships are the expensive offshore real estate that are as crucial as the air force's planes and more important than the army's tanks, because they are also residential accommodation. Ships are the outward face of navies. And they are institutions. An institution's job is to keep itself going. Women's inclusion, especially in ships, enabled the navy to carry on at times when men were unavailable. It was hard for the institution to change its exclusionary ways, which were based on deeply held personal beliefs – as in wider society – that women could only play secondary and home-based roles.

Since naval women became seagoing in 1990 they have faced arguably greater challenges than women in any of the other UK armed forces. It is not just that the sea can kill, maim and cause distress. Coping with unwarranted blocks to their acceptance as equals requires more stamina when young people are away from home in a relatively small floating residential workplace with its own tight culture. For anyone, including women in commercial seafaring, it is onerous to be so long and so far away from home life and to live in what they call a goldfish bowl, where peer pressure to conform is demanding and where prolonged barbed banter can be wearing.

Finally, it is important to understand the importance of two words the navy uses today: operational effectiveness. The Royal Navy diversity manifesto affirms that 'embracing Diversity and Inclusion ... maximises the Operational Effectiveness of the Naval Service'. Reading that helped me grasp a key truth about why the navy has progressed so far in embracing those it previously excluded: it wants to succeed. It prides itself on resolving issues and finding solutions. So it has well-staffed ships which conduct successful operations. Including enough competent people (some of whom happen to be women) is a way being operationally effective – which is what all armed forces need to be.[6]

Women's successes and struggles in negotiating their way in this changed navy, including their immense tact and respect for institutional tradition and entrenched habits, deserve a book in their own right. For all these reasons, women and their mutating, often deeply enjoyed, place in naval life deserve attention, as the following chapters show.

Chapter 1

'Assisting Behind the Scenes'— and More: 875–1884

Come all you maids both near and far / And listen to my ditty,
'Twas near Gravesend there lived a maid, / She was both neat and pretty....
In her jacket blue and trousers white, / Just like a sailor neat and tight,
The sea, it was the heart's delight, / Of the female rambling sailor.

(Traditional)

Britannia, that armoured goddess with her upstanding trident, ruled the waves of the nation she personified. So said the rousing patriotic song of 1740. What of the more complex story of real women, power, arms and waves? If women sailed in the very first recorded 'English Navy' in 875, they would have been aboard in minuscule numbers and only occasionally. The main opportunity would have been to go as a well-camouflaged boy. Or else they would have been there as what were later called 'accompanying wives' or 'camp followers'. 'Navy' at this point meant a small fleet powered by sail and oarsmen, on specialist warships, not just co-opted cargo vessels for carrying goods.

The navy grew, changed and formally consolidated between 875 and 1660; the state maintained permanently employed sailors and dedicated ships. Seemingly the navy still offered infinitesimal opportunities to women, except for the few accompanying their husbands. (Women are not recorded, but chroniclers do tend to disregard anomalies.) Women in Hastings, Dover, Sandwich, Romney and Hythe

Fig. 1.1. Britannia: that shifting emblem of gendered Britain. *Punch*, 1859.

BRITANNIA—THE UNPROTECTED FEMALE!!

– the so-called Cinque Ports – were more likely to be involved than those in the north. This navy was an organisation of people who sailed in the national interest but for personal gain too.[1]

Crusades against Islam in the eleventh and early thirteenth centuries were only patchily chronicled. Experts on the medieval past differ widely on interpretations, including the extent to which women sailed, were armed and fought to kill. Historian Thomas Ashbridge estimates that women, children and other non-combatants constituted at least a third of those in the First Crusade in 1095 and that they numbered 20,000–40,000. Latin Christian noblewomen who were sisters, widows and wives of travelling knights, plus lowly women who did support work and even killed Muslim prisoners, went to Palestine on ships subcontracted for use in these weaponised Christian 'pilgrimages'.

Oddly, the voyage provided an intellectual and political opportunity for Queen Eleanor of Aquitaine (1122–1204), which was to have a key effect on maritime life for centuries. Learning from her time in Jerusalem, on the way back in 1160 she ordered a record of the Oléron maritime court judgments. It became the first internationally recognised protocol for mariners, evolving into the Black Book of the

Admiralty: its 'bible'. Most crusades women took the opportunity to be, in effect, self-employed domestic servants doing freelance laundering, nursing, cooking and sex work for a captive market on ships. It was an extension of what wives and mothers traditionally did within their families. Older women 'washed the clothes and heads ... [of the soldiers]. Women were as good as monkeys at getting rid of the fleas.'[2]

There were two key sorts of non-elite women on these ships, and their roles are significant to understanding the history of women in the later navy. Some were there because their warrior spouse was there. Others were helpful traders or what was later called sutlers/ *vivandières*. Marginally they sold services to men in war situations.

The two roles overlapped; for example, a wife might launder for her husband's friend or go on to marry him if her spouse died. He became her children's step-father and her earnings from doing tasks for other men funded him if he lost his income – say if he had a non-compensated injury. Both categories of women came to be called 'camp followers' in around 1800 and the term was used in laws. It meant someone not officially connected with a military unit (including a warship), or someone espousing a group's aims even if she did not quite belong. Initially not labelled in that way, 'dependent' women were commonly part of armed bodies of men travelling for war, for at least six centuries.

Their template helps us understand how the navy came to have a vision of women as naturally being loyal adjuncts and associate members. 'Accompanying wives' were seen as having varying levels of usefulness and irksomeness. They were not full participants who could be commanded, as directly employed men could. However, their value was that they met human needs, raised morale, and humanised voyages and battlefields. They supplemented for what the military was sometimes too preoccupied by war to do. Even better, they did not have to be waged or pensioned. As a category, even a stereotype, such batches of (effectively) self-employed stewards, became *a sort* of loyal member of the larger team, sharing its values and vicissitudes. They were an enduring indication that this is what women could be expected to do in conflicts: faithfully assist warriors in their efforts, but to the side.[3]

Fig. 1.2. Batches of camp followers and their children shared the vicissitudes of warriors on the move in a later period. Thomas Rowlandson, *Soldiers on a March: 'To pack up her tatters and follow the Drum'*, 1811.

However, we must first return to the story of the navy that was emerging and would later utilise such women. In the thirteenth century something a little more like today's Royal Navy was beginning to take shape. Landowning men commanded ships that were hired from the merchant fleet. These elite males briefly sailed for national ends and sometimes for their own fortunes. They went to sea when required, not as a career. A few ladies and their women servants may have been aboard such 'warships' at times, not least to sweeten the harshness of sea life for the noblemen in command. Possibly female exporters and shipowners may have voyaged on business too.[4]

Women's principal role in naval life in this early period was at home. As wives and mothers they enabled those men to be away for years. They did so by acting as their proxies, including as heads of households. Women went briefly aboard when ships were moored, before or after the great voyages like Drake's circumnavigation, the wars against Spain from 1585 and the Dutch wars from 1652. Overwhelmingly they were the 'hidden navy', the behind-the-scenes personnel who served what was becoming a nation establishing itself all over the world, thanks to sea power.

However, as with camp followers, there was an overlap. Some women sailed for months or years. Two categories of women sailed in warships: pretend men, and wives. The most daring women who dressed and acted as sailors are now seen as heroic and 'liberated'. Yet was it as simple as that: spinster ladettes and floating housewives, traversing oceans on military sea steeds?[5]

Girls looking like sailor boys

Bold, diligent, physically capable and rare as unicorns. That is how the few women disguised as boys at sea and in armies are portrayed – usually admiringly. Of the three camouflaged naval women listed in the 1690s, Anne Chamberlayne (1667–91) was described most vividly. In keeping with the convention that women doing men's work were somehow akin to legendary Amazons and not interested in heterosexual relationships, 23-year-old Anne was (later) depicted as:

> long declining wedlock, and aspiring above her sex and age, fought under her brother, with arms and manly attire, in a fireship against the French, for six hours [at Beachy Head] on the 30th June 1690; a maiden heroine! Had life been granted, she might have borne a race of naval warriors.[6]

Why did Anne and her successors go to sea as boys? Several ballads claimed they were following their sweethearts. Actually, from the scant factual reports it seems that mainly they were from broken families and rather adrift. Some needed an escape route. They would be paid higher wages than if in domestic service ashore. Others grabbed a waiting opportunity for a breakaway experience, rather like a modern teenager's gap year. It is possible that a few were intersex people (then called hermaphrodites) and seeking an accepting context. Being in the armed forces was a means to an extrinsic end: survival and even adventure and 'liberty'. It was possible for women to pass as boys because their officers did not look too closely; clothes were loose and ships dark enough below decks to conceal anomalous body shapes. Disguised women used horns as a funnel, a bit like today's bright plastic 'she-wees', when standing to urinate. And perhaps collectively dependent shipmates, who had learned to be tolerant of all, more readily accepted the unusual, including 'boys' who never grew beards.

After Anne Chamberlayne, disguised women kept on joining ships to do lower-deck jobs. It was relatively easy to become a ship's boy. These were the stewards and odd-jobbers doing work usually called 'women's', including preparing vegetables and cleaning hen coops. They worked in both commercial and naval ships, in roughly equal numbers. In the period 1690–1899, 20 were in the Royal Navy and 29 in merchant ships. At least three are known to have sailed in naval vessels between 1720 and 1750, a further nine between 1750 and 1791 and six in the nineteenth century.

They are usually only known through a few column inches in newspaper reports about their revelation. Images of Anne Mills (born c. 1720), who allegedly sailed cross-dressed in the frigate HMS *Maidstone* in 1740 brandishing her French enemy's severed head, were typical of the common lurid fanciful illustrations of their alleged extreme bloodthirstiness.

Some lived on in a male identity. Cross-dressing landswomen successfully courted and married other women. Others lived more precariously in poverty. Samuel Bundy/Sarah Paul was the most famous sailor of this type. In 1760 she returned to seagoing to avoid her duped wife's wrath, after pawning the wife's clothes to help them survive. After serving on a man-o'-war, the *Prince Frederick*, Samuel came to the Southwark magistrate's attention for the theft, but not for fraudulently masquerading as a man. Her/his wife did not appear to give evidence against her. The case was dismissed. However, the magistrate intervened. He 'ordered her man's apparel to be burned in his presence, and laid the strictest injunction on her never more to appear in that character.' The marriage of this 'very sensible woman' seemed set to continue. It is possible that poverty forced her to sea or to crime again.[7]

No known records exist of any woman rising to command a ship. Women were usually not at sea long enough to rise to petty officer status, let alone to take the midshipman-to-admiral route. Usually they were unmasked in a matter of months. Most were reported, admiringly, as able to do the required 'manly' tasks such as climb aloft and take risks. Females were ejected immediately on being uncovered as imposters, however much their labour was needed. Worcester-born Marine Hannah Snell (1723–92, see colour plate 1) disclosed her own identity then profited by her ruses. On the 14-gun sloop *Swallow* she returned to England in 1750 and told her shipmates in a Westminster alehouse: 'In a word, gentlemen, I am as much a woman as my mother ever was.' Illiterate, her much-hyped story, *The Female Soldier*, was created by publisher Robert Walker. She spent the rest of her life performing a hammy but exhilarating version of 'A Female Marine' for public audiences. Embroidering the way she had 'ventured on the Main / facing death and every danger / Love and Glory to obtain', her

Fig. 1.3. A male cabin boy, which indicates cross-dressed women did not have to look extremely masculine. Thomas Rowlandson engraving, 1799.

stylish singing and drilling augmented her military pension (which women were rarely awarded). She was living proof that women could be effective seafaring soldiers and she may have inspired successors.[8]

'William Brown' was the last naval woman to be revealed. She was also the only known black woman to pass as a sailor. As a 21-year-old Grenadian sailing on the *Queen Charlotte* as a landsman (the least skilled status afloat), she was discovered within a month of being mustered (navalese for being formally registered as being present) in 1815. After that year no more women in disguise were recorded in the navy. This was partly because the huge need for hands dropped as wars decreased, as the 1814 ending of impressment indicates. Also sailors undressed and washed more as hygiene was enforced to improve naval health. This meant shipmates saw each other's bodies. Pre-entry medicals were also becoming more thorough.[9]

Wives as helpers in crises

Mrs Sailing Master, Mrs Boatswain, Mrs Gunner, Mrs Purser, Mrs Cook, Mrs Carpenter, Mrs Sailmaker, Mrs Cooper and Mrs Trumpeter lived on ships by the eighteenth century. On large ships there could be Mrs Surgeon and Mrs Chaplain too. Wives sailed with their men who were part of the hierarchy of proficient, literate male specialist class which had emerged on naval ships. *Standing* officers (the boatswain, gunner and carpenter) were warrant officers who were needed aboard at all times to maintain the vessel. They made homes on the ships, with their spouses and children.[10]

Ann Perriam (1768–1865), the wife of Edward Hopping, lived for five years on board HMS *Crescent* and appears to have been a warrior's assistant when required. She proudly claimed to have taken part in Nelson's victories at L'Orient (June 1795), off Cape St Vincent (November 1797) and the Battle of the Nile (August 1798). A newspaper maintained 'Mrs. Perriam's occupation while in action lay with the gunners and magazine men, among whom she worked, preparing flannel cartridges for the great guns ... [aged 93 she recalled] incidents of the hard-won fight in which she discharged a man's – more than a

Fig. 1.4. Ann Perriam, veteran of the Battle of the Nile, commemorated in 1860.

woman's – part.' Her feat was later celebrated and she was pictured in a Calotype, the first woman in Nelson's fleet to be photographed.[11]

Ann and other wives' daily life at sea can only be deduced from a few documents about dealing with the presence of the more troublesome of these non-employees. Wives-in-residence were formally allowed only a marginal place on naval ships. They were not officially borne on the muster books, meaning they were not provided for as persons in their own right (and so historians cannot know much about them). Food was whatever portion of their husband's food he shared. Depending on his status their space could be his canvas-curtained cubicle with its standard single bed. Informally, their social position partly depended on their husband's standing, the on-board role they negotiated for themselves (which would have been influenced by their stage in pregnancy and number of accompanying children), and whatever the commanding officer allowed in the varying circumstances. On the *Minotaur* in 1805 a washerwoman combined being the wife of a seaman with her laundry work (around 590 potential customers were on board) and with having a baby called 'Horatio Nelson'.[12]

Wives on warships were varyingly seen as somewhere in between invasive hindrances who had to be tolerated and idealised helpmeets who stabilised a shipboard community: civilising a fighting machine, and mothering the boys. 'Bless 'em, they're the sailor's sheet anchor, his joy ashore, his hope at sea ... [T]hey're the treasures that reward

Fig. 1.5. Sailors' partners make merry: *Sailors in Port/Matelots au Port*, mezzotint, Thomas Stothard and William Ward, 1794.

the toils of life and the sweets that enable us to taste its sours without making wry faces,' rejoiced a fictional tar in the 1756 play *Eliza*. Real accounts are tender, too.[13]

How many sweet sheet anchors were there, especially in the classic age of naval battles by the expanded fleet of sailing ships (1689–1815)? The navy had 272 ships by 1700. So at the very least 700 wives would have been routinely aboard naval vessels, slightly fewer than the women at sea today in their own right. A hundred years later there were 950 ships, which were being built at twice the size. So an absolute minimum of 2,850 of wives would have sailed. In practice hundreds, if not thousands, of other spouses and common-law partners sailed too. Some were navy wives, some marines' wives. At least three marines' wives were *officially* allowed (more actually went) in every 200-strong company of marines taking passage out to colonial service. They also accompanied their husbands on active service.[14]

At the most famous British naval engagement, the 1805 battle of Trafalgar, Nelson's *Victory* was staffed by 500 males, of whom 70 were petty officers. In addition there were 146 marines (the principle was one marine for every ship's gun). If the usual ratio of accompanying wives was applied, this could mean a few score naval wives plus two or three marines' wives were aboard. Possibly 75 women were in the 33 ships at Trafalgar, but it is likely that there were fewer as non-essential personnel were removed, whatever their gender.[15]

Official and unofficial naval views of women sailing as accompanying wives varied. On the official side the Admiralty circulated several sets of instructions forbidding women to be taken to sea. It also turned a blind eye because their presence usually meant a ship was happier, which in turn meant the men were less likely to desert. However, the navy did not take responsibility for wives, not even for feeding them. Even if they helped as a kind of steward or medical aide they were not given any sort of wage (although a few later were given pensions if a senior officer spoke up for them).

Several naval officers over the centuries complained about these human distractions. The most queried story is that Admiral Sir John Mennes, the Navy's Comptroller, claimed in 1666 that women were aboard to such an extent that ships were 'pestered with women … as many petticoats as breeches'. If there really were so many 'petticoats', and if they really were a nuisance, then why were not they removed? It suggests women must actually have been convenient.

The most famous story of an officer's distress about women is that Admiral John Jervis in 1796 and 1797 threatened that the seamen's wives who 'infested' ships and did laundry would be shipped home immediately if they continued to waste fresh water by rinsing clothes in it. (Before ships had desalination systems all water had to be hauled on board in barrels, and was therefore a very precious resource.) Historians vary as to whether he was being peevish about the 'alarming evil' or appropriately wary about saving a scarce asset during an operation. Horatio Nelson shrugged that women on ship 'always will do as they please. Orders are not for them – at least I never yet knew one who obeyed.'[16]

Despite the practical difficulties, these part-time sailors-in-skirts went to sea in battles and on replenishing trips, probably in increasing numbers as the navy expanded.

However, by 1810 the number of wives aboard had dwindled. This was likely to have been because of naval practicalities rather than wives' reluctance to venture. By 1880, as sail made way for steam, it is thought that women's ship-dwelling had decreased to zero, except for jaunts or visits in port to the 58,000 naval men.[17]

Seagoing wives cannot be glorified as their husband's deputies. They were passengers and corporate spouses who were sometimes temporarily required to be casual workers, especially laundering and giving health care. They were contingent *associate* members of the shipboard community.

Securing Jack Tar's health and welfare

Nursing on ships

An embryonic naval nursing force began from 1660, when the navy became the Royal Navy – if not earlier. These untrained nursing aides were said to be drunken, inefficient and dishonest. So were males in the same work, probably because alcohol was used as self-medication in an unpleasant and fairly hopeless job. No proper hospitals existed. The Reformation had brought a major decline in nuns as convent-based nurses. Landladies gave ad hoc naval health care in 'a kind of public–private partnership'. The Commission for Sick and Hurt Seamen attempted to regularise this. From 1702 the Fifth Commission began planning naval hospitals, and the care of Jack Tars became centrally organised.[18]

Two sorts of women nursed at sea: naval wives and employed nursing aides on hospital ships. Naval wives, unpaid, helped out in their warship as part of the collective effort in a sea battle. The wives might be regarded as unqualified A&E temps. Only one surgeon to every 80 men was the usual ratio. Lucky ones had help from surgeon's assistants or stewards who were known as loblolly boys because they served gruel (loblolly). Faced with such shortages ships needed extra hands, including auxiliary 'nurses'. Women assisted at operations such as amputations, fed the weak, changed the bedding and looked after the equipment, for example washing the pestle and mortar. Seemingly they were not referred to as loblolly women.

The Death of Nelson (1859–64) (see colour plate 2) is possibly the first colour image of female defence nursing at sea: a woman staunches wounds amid a terrible debacle on HMS *Victory*. Before Daniel Maclise painted this, he interviewed survivors, so this may be a somewhat accurate impression of what other seafaring wives did in the Napoleonic Wars.

Nelly Giles (1770–1860) had been in HMS *Bellerophon* in the 1798 battle of the Nile and has since become the most famous wife-nurse of that world. She and surgeon George Bellamy tended 201 casualties on a ship of 550 men during the two-day battle. When Mr Bellamy asked for help from the warrant officers' wives who were 'all together, panic stricken, in some cabin on the ship ... At first none of them would come'. Then coxswain's wife Mrs Giles stepped forward. Some sources say she was three days away from giving birth.

Terror had immobilised the other wives. Their situation was similar to having an explosives factory, with your husband in it, blowing up – just the other side of your living room or tent wall. On top of that you were blindfold. You were also as trapped as any manacled prisoner. The women on the *Bellerophon* and the other 14 British ships would have been cooped up in darkness and forbidden to venture out. They could do nothing about what was going on or even understand much about the battle's progress from the sounds. At least 28 of the *Bellerophon* 32-pounder guns would have been rolling back and forth noisily on the wooden deck just above their heads. The ship's fabric was being torn by enemy broadsides. Outgoing and incoming shots at least once a minute from the 32 other ships involved would have created an unbearable din. Near at hand were the cries of wounded men, shouted orders, the falling of the mizzen mast and rigging plus enemy musket fire. Fire broke out several times. Male combatants had adrenalin to keep them going. Maybe Mrs Giles and her like on other ships were able to endure the tumult because, if they were involved in nursing, they were active participants, not impotent bystanders.[19]

These ad hoc nurse-wives were counterparts of the 60-odd women on the six hospital ships that existed by 1697. Usually six nurses and four laundresses were aboard each hospital ship, some of which followed the fleet as a kind of floating annexe. Nursing and laundering were very much linked, because of the growing understanding that hygiene promoted health. Laundresses, but not nurses, were hired in the eighteenth century after female nurses were seemingly phased out after the Seven Years War (1753–63). The navy gave preference to naval widows over 50. Such as selection system meant they were deserving but not necessarily appropriate health care workers.[20]

Nursing on land

At varying times the navy allowed women to nurse. This included in the naval hospitals being built at Greenwich in 1694, then Plymouth, Chatham and Haslar. In some periods, the nursing staff on land were all females, probably to free male counterparts for the fleet. Women were employed on an 'as required' basis, which meant there could be no team of usefully committed personnel accumulating skills. They served under a matron at each hospital, meaning there were at least two tiers of women. Both ward matrons and store matrons mainly acted as supervisors of women, not men. In a similar way, male ward masters were later to supervise male sick berth staff. Matrons served for decades and were usually wives or daughters of officers. Their status can be guessed because Martha Hewett and Mary Shoveller, the matrons at Haslar in 1780, were paid an eighth of physician James Lind's pay, but twice that of the nurses.[21]

Male naval sick berth attendants (later called SBAs) were phased in during 1833. The good female nurses were still probably kept on, as male applicants were few. Neither the females nor males had any training. Some had no aptitude. In other words, the new male 'nurses' were not necessarily better than the previous women. Hospitals went on to become places where SBAs were the largest category of workers. The matron position seems to have vanished in the early nineteenth century, although there were still stores matrons in the early twentieth century. They were always called Mrs.[22]

Meanwhile, outside of defence nursing as it is now called, women in the wider world were starting to move into professional nursing and even towards training as apothecaries and doctors. The first women qualified in 1865. Quaker Elizabeth Fry (1780–1845) founded modern civilian nursing in 1830, inspiring Florence Nightingale and thereby paving the way for what was later to become the Naval Nursing Service. It was a slow start. Novelist Charles Dickens' drunken Sairy Gamp figure had from the mid-1840s created a horrifying stereotype of domiciliary nurses as dissolute and incompetent rascals. New professional lady (meaning genteel and sometimes educated, not working-class) nurses had to overcome this hurdle.[23]

The Nightingale Watershed

In the Crimean War (October 1853–February 1856) wives and sutlers, including black Afro-Caribbean Mary Seacole, were among the casualty 'nurses' near the battlefield, just as such 'camp followers' helped on ships. Major hospital facilities were two days' sail away from Balaclava, the front line. The army set up a hospital in Constantinople and the Board of Admiralty established a separate naval hospital on the opposite, European, side of the Bosphorus at Therapia, an ancient and paradisiacal healing refuge once known as Pharmakos.

In this now-suburb of Istanbul the naval hospital's bed capacity grew from 50 to 150 in the 1850s. Finally 17,775 patients were treated there, under the navy's equivalent of Miss Nightingale. Mrs Eliza Mackenzie, the later feted lady superintendent, appears to have been an unpaid volunteer. The five 'rather upper' (meaning socially superior) paid nurses replaced 23 male naval rating 'nurses' who were unsatisfactory and seven 'useless' marines.[24]

Mary Erskine (1810–83) was Mrs Mackenzie's deputy from 1854. This somewhat trained 'Park Village' lady nurse stayed on, and was later in charge, until summer 1856. Miss Erskine's copious letters home reveal three patterns that continued to be true of defence nursing. Most of the nurses were devoted workers who truly cherished their poorly boys in blue. Clever ladies in charge did not always get on with their less-elevated and even obstreperous colleagues who did the donkey work. Also nurses with opinions clashed with surgeons, especially those who had an overbearing or uncaring style. Mary wrote feelingly of the difficulty of finding a replacement lady superintendent who would obey the Medical Officer in Charge, John Davidson, who

> I'm sure dislikes any independent power in his hospital, would rather have everyone strictly under martial law, with no right to an opinion of their own ... [T]his is the almost universal feeling among doctors I believe and the cause of their jealousy... They hate interference in any shape and ladies of course are to a certain extent beyond their control. [Underlining is Mary's][25]

Defence medicine practitioners learned from the Crimean War. As a result, a new professional style of nursing by ladies with a sense of noble purpose emerged. The navy began moving towards change by 1871 as these officer-level nurses became available. Progress was influenced by post-Crimea thoughts about military health care and the army's first steps from 1861 under Jane Shaw Stewart, a Crimea veteran and disciple of Miss Nightingale.

A further war seems to have given the process a nudge. Henrietta Stewart (1838–c. 1901) was one of the National Aid Society nursing sisters in the Anglo-Egyptian War of 1882. Some 24 women served in hospital ships. In the 200-odd bed *Carthage*, moored at Ismailia, Sisters Stewart, Fellowes, King and Solly were part of the new superior sort of trained nurses.[26]

The 1883 Morley Committee of Inquiry into Army Nursing resulted in the birth of the women-only Army Nursing Service, which later became Queen Alexandra's Imperial Nursing Service. Could the navy do other than follow suit? A naval committee was set up in June 1883 to enquire into the organisation and training of SBAs and nurses. After visiting many hospitals the navy's Hoskins Committee reported to the Admiralty: 'We are convinced that trained female nursing staff is of the highest value to the sick and wounded and there is every reason to believe that nothing but good will result from its introduction.' However 30 medical officers' views were canvassed. Half were against female nurses. The other half thought them only acceptable in exceptional circumstances and in small numbers.[27]

Despite resistance, the Naval Nursing Service (NNS) was founded in 1884. It was part of Admiralty-led reforms, including of sick berth staff. Reasons for welcoming nursing sisters were that they raised standards and that women could be paid less than men. Reasons against included that additional men had to be employed because females did no heavy lifting; women could not be sent to sea on warships; and they were not expected to treat venereal cases, although sexually transmitted disease sufferers were in the top five sorts of armed forces problems. Also lady nurses required servants because they 'saw themselves as specialist health providers': an elite with opinions, who merited respect.[28]

After a thousand years the navy had its first female corps. The NNS was to be staffed by ladies trained in civilian hospitals under Fry- and Nightingale-influenced matrons, then inculcated into navy-style nursing in naval hospitals. War veteran Henrietta Stewart was to be the NNS's most controversial founding figure.

Such centrally placed nurses were working in subtle parallel with female benefactors on naval margins ashore. All navies need fit personnel, who ideally are not alcohol-addicted and who lead untroubled home lives. By 1880 many philanthropic ladies, not only commanding officers' wives, were involving themselves in welfare and in health in its widest sense. Agnes Weston (1840–1918) was the key female figure in this. From 1876 she founded temperance-based hostels for sailors, which were later iconic as 'Royal Sailors' Rests' or 'Aggies'.

Just as public-spirited civilian women were taking up new roles such as Poor Law Guardians, naval ladies were also increasingly involved in many charities for sailors, including the Soldiers' and Sailors' Families Association (SSFA, later SSAFA) from 1885. In benevolent organisations they were especially active on ladies' committees, which raised funds through handicraft sales and tea parties.

In other words, females now had had several permitted authoritative roles in shaping situations where naval men were cared for as embodied human beings, not just 'hands'. What could such ladies bring about and how would the navy respond to their efforts?

CHAPTER 2

The War Needs Veiled Warriors – in Navy Blue: 1884–1918

She was an Hospital Nurse you'll remember, a gem in nature's crown,
Tending the sick and the wounded, as well as our own.

('Nurse Cavell', Anon.)

Virtuous officers with military vocations: 1884–1914

Veterans Henrietta Stewart and Belle Story were the two pioneers in the new Naval Nursing Service. In the years between the setting up in October 1884 and World War I, their corps helped create the foundations for today's defence nurses. Adventurous, Scottish and indefatigable, Henrietta Stewart and the reportedly cheerful, amiable and cultured Sister Story were its first twin pillars, at Haslar (Portsmouth) and Stonehouse (Plymouth) naval hospitals respectively.

Belle and Henrietta had returned from the Anglo-Egyptian War of 1882 at a time when the navy's medical director general had already begun questing for 'ladies of character and culture'. Following an earlier army initiative, as early as June 1881 he had noted he wanted to give sailors the good nursing now available in Florence Nightingale-influenced civilian hospitals. The 1883 Morley Committee on army medicine and its counterpart, the Hoskins Committee for the navy, advanced matters. Seemingly the 12 existing 'non-Nightingale' female naval nurses were to be replaced by the new breed: officers who were 'embodiments of Christian virtue', ladies with a calling akin to that of nuns. These members of the all-female, all-officer Naval Nursing Service (NNS) force of 11 worked with male sick berth staff and possibly a few remaining female remnants of the old loblolly-boy style assistants, whom the lady officers supervised. Sisters were civilian, and not under the Naval Discipline Act like the men. Formally, they were rather separated from the Royal Navy proper because they were ladies. However they were far from being as alien as subcontractors or that later phenomenon, bank staff from agencies.[1]

Despots, not darlings?

Belle Story made a 'brilliant start', according to naval nursing historian Kathleen Harland. However, at Haslar the director cautioned Henrietta three times for having a 'harsh unconciliatory manner and a considerable want of tact and judgment'. She had already 'caused trouble' in the hospital ship *Carthage*.

A similar problem had happened with the army's tough first nursing sister, too. It seems likely that all parties had to find an acceptable model for females exerting power in situations where men and fierce service discipline had held sway. Being like the fair but firm matriarch or doyenne of a large household, working with – but under – the patriarch (the navy medical service's director-general) must have seemed the right style. It is telling that people later joked that the Royal Army Medical Corps initials stood for 'Run Away, Matron's Coming'. The terrifying female ruler archetype, later to be overplayed by the bullying Hattie Jacques in *Carry On* films, had emerged.

After only six months Henrietta Stewart was told to resign, which she trenchantly opposed. Kathleen Harland's view is that medical men saw the clash as just a personality problem. It was not, she implies, the now recognised problem that somes males resist females who wield authority with a similar assertiveness and sense of entitlement to that

Fig. 2.1. Sister Louisa Hogg (centre, seated), when Head Sister at Haslar Hospital.

of men. She said the Sister Stewart controversy 'left unshaken' medical men's opinion 'that female nursing Sisters brought professional skill into the wards and exercised a civilising influence'. The stories behind this adjustment will never be known. However, they can be glimpsed through the fragmentary story of Sister Louisa Hogg (1845–1910). A protégée of Florence Nightingale, she rose to be a major figure in the wider sphere of British nursing politics world as well as Haslar's head sister, a successor of Belle Story, in effect the top navy nurse, for nearly two ground-breaking decades.[2]

Establishing the basis of women's naval nursing

Florence Nightingale, that female civilian leader of health care reform, was widely consulted on defence nursing matters. So the navy established the Naval Nursing Service partly under this campaigning statistician's influence, with army nursing parallels in mind. Her trainees were at the forefront. The NNS was not initiated by opinionated ladies wanting patients looked after in the way they thought right. Instead it emerged from a thorough rejig of defence medicine, which sought better nursing support along with an improvement in male aides' standards. Professional but non-navy ladies were to deliver it. The NNS status is illustrated by its being allocated a place in the *Navy List*, the navy's internal who's who. From 1885 women officers were there for the first time, listed as a separate service just after the Royal Naval Medical Service team.

What was an NNS sister? She was in 'the position of gentlewoman ... in naval service'. Young enough to be active (age 25–40) she was also mature, with at least three years' experience of working in civilian hospitals, with male patients. A civilian, she could never be court-martialled or forcibly retained. She had officer status, which was seen as compatible with being a lady, and not a contradiction in terms. A member of the decorous species, she should never see male bodies below the shoulders, except for feet. By virtue of being female she would not have strength enough to deal with paralysis and insanity.

Sisters' uniforms *looked* somewhat naval, as well as typical of female nurses of the time: their serge dresses were grey, like the army nurses, but their capes were navy blue, not army scarlet. Their stockings, boots, under bodices and corsets appear to have been their own affair. Aprons and frilled caps were white. On their right arms they bore a red 'Geneva' cross on a white background, which had from 1863 become the internationally recognised symbol of humanitarian aid. Sisters did not have equivalent ranks to male medical officers (MOs) at that stage. They were formally lower – just. Patients and staff were expected to call sisters 'Madam'. It may now sound chilly but, was consistent with addressing male officers as 'Sir', and later women naval officers as 'Ma'am': a proper recognition of status. In that new phenomenon, nurses' homes, NNS officers had the privilege of individual 'cabins' – they did not share dormitories.[3]

Generally the navy saw these new nursing sisters as a restraining and humanising force which greatly improved standards of care and morale as Jack was made fit for duty again. This was very consistent with the services' view that females made situations more home-like, which was seen as positive when men needed nurturing back to fitness. It was around this point that appreciative patients in general, not only in the forces, began referring to nurses as angels of mercy. Men tended to stop swearing and to take care of their appearance if 'a lady' was present, as in the rest of Victorian society too. By contrast, opponents argued that the presence of such intruders in the military was somehow weakening. Females were a distraction. Worse, they were evidence that men were in mollycoddled situations, which could later weaken operational effectiveness.

The reality appears to be that defence nursing officers were not indulgent but decisive. Louisa Hogg was later active on the executive committee of the Royal British Nurses' Association, akin to the doctors' British Medical Association. She had trained at St Thomas' Hospital with Isla Stewart, a major – some say necessarily despotic – activist in national nursing politics. So this First Lady of Haslar, the top hospital, was part of a new wave thrashing out a suitable shape for nursing to come. Her political acumen must have had an impact on the navy's medical branch, but is not in records.[4]

After Benin and the Boers

As formally accepted members of the greater defence medical team, nursing sisters could seemingly be allowed near military conflicts. However, they were varyingly protected – when possible – from danger. In the next decades Isabella Smith and Eva K'eogh were the first two NNS members to go to war at sea. In the punitive 1897–8 invasion of Benin, they served in the requisitioned P&O liner-turned-hospital-transport, SS *Malacca*.[5]

Miss Smith returned, replacing Louisa Hogg as Head Sister at Haslar, in 1899. Naval hospitals increased from five to 13. NNS officers were welcomed at naval hospitals but 'by the end of the century they were not a panacea for all that was wrong' in naval health care. Nursing sisters had to be just one part of the wider process of finding solutions at home and abroad. (Two apiece were based at Gibraltar and Bermuda, usually for two-year periods.) Female naval health care staffs appear to not have gone overseas in the Boer War (1899–1902), unlike their army counterparts.

The service had 29 members by 1900, as the changed twentieth-century navy emerged with its steam-powered battleships carrying torpedoes, its submarines and its new alliances and enmities globally as the empire waned. Angry suffragettes that decade torched public buildings for the vote and upended all notions of seemly female behaviour. Suffragists called for world peace. On the other hand, bands of patriotic women literally played to the navy's tunes, not least the 'delightfully cerulean', Royal Navy Ladies' Orchestra. Others in the Navy League pushed for deadlier vessels, the mighty Dreadnought battleships.[6]

Queen Alexandra (the Princess of Wales in Fig. 2.2) was one of the people seeking to rationalise navy and army nursing services, just as her husband (soon to become Edward VII) was controversially pushing for military and naval reform after the Boer War revealed

PUNCH, OR THE LONDON CHARIVARI.—NOVEMBER 22, 1899.

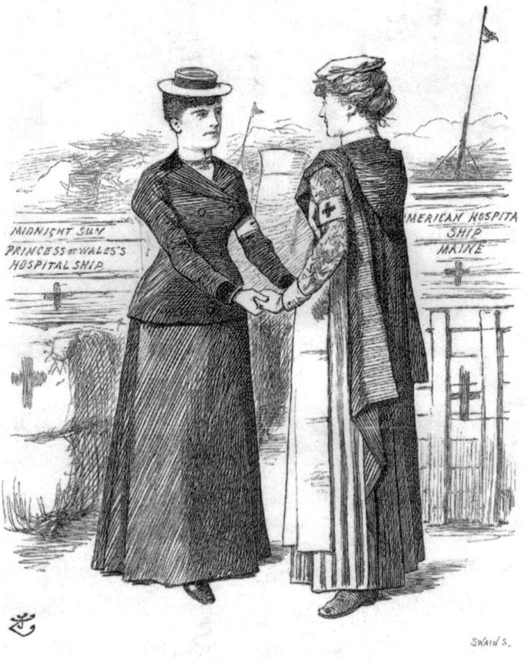

SISTERS OF MERCY.

THE PRINCESS OF WALES (to COLUMBIA). "THANK YOU, SISTER, FOR YOUR FRIENDSHIP AND GENEROUS HELP."

Fig. 2.2. In the Boer War, ladies' roles in defence included fundraising for sailors' and soldiers' wellbeing: 'Sisters of Mercy', *Punch*, November 1899.[7]

room for improvement. In 1901 her wish for such amalgamation 'as soon as possible' was opposed by the Admiralty, which was embroiled in clashes about revolutionary internal change. Grounds for this refusal were incompatibility: naval pay and allowances were less than the army's and very few naval sisters were liable for foreign service. However, soon after the queen was rejected a reorganisation of the 31 naval sisters' conditions meant they were brought up to the level of their 67 army counterparts. Both were better paid than their civilian equivalents.

Lord Selbourne, the First Lord of the Admiralty, whose mother was a vice admiral's daughter, acceded to Queen Alexandra's easier request: The *'great wish* of my heart has *always* been to have the Navy Nursing Department also under my *special charge*, and that it may likewise bear my name', this daughter-in-law of the then recently deceased Queen Victoria wrote. As a result in 1902 Queen Alexandra's Naval Nursing Service and Queen Alexandra's Imperial Nursing Service were born. Continuing royal patronage made patriotic members of the services proud and established the corps' unimpeachable stature.[8]

The Matrons' Council of Great Britain and Ireland in 1902 publicly criticised the navy for failing to move with the times. These 'outsiders' stepped into the reform fray and urged that QARNNS members be given both power and 'the clearly-defined professional status of the Army Nursing Service'. It is likely that Louisa Hogg was the worm in the navy bud here, because her friend Isla Stewart was a leading light of the council. The matrons:

> urged the formation of a Nursing Department in affiliation with the Medical Department at the Admiralty, superintended by a fully-trained and administrative Nursing Officer ... It is noticeable under the present regulations that ... the Nursing Sisters are still under the control of the Medical Officers not only in relation to the care of the sick, but also others to their personal discipline and the regulation of their hours on and off duty. The highest possible efficiency will never be obtained until the personal control of the Sisters is placed in the hands of a [Lady] Superintendent of Nursing.[9]

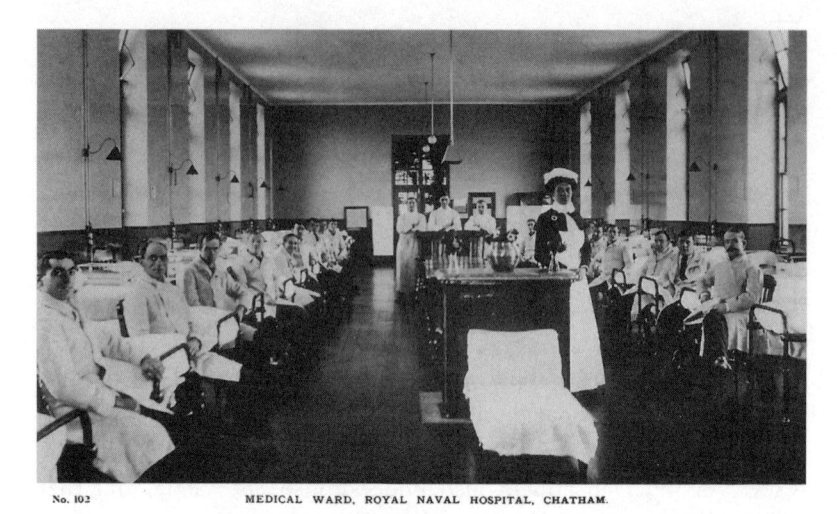

No. 102   MEDICAL WARD, ROYAL NAVAL HOSPITAL, CHATHAM.

Fig. 2.3. QARNNS sister, well-disciplined patients, sick berth staff, and no MO: Chatham Royal Naval Hospital, c. 1912.

'Veiled warriors' throughout Britain were fighting on three fronts, according to nursing historian Christine Hallett: the fight to save their patients' lives, the battle for their professional status and the complex, deeply revolutionary struggle for their rights as women. In addition, defence nurses, although loyal, were slightly challenging hyper-masculine tradition. They were clearly about to be involved on another battlefront too: the coming war with Germany.[10]

Reserves and VADs rush to the rescue: 1911–14

Rumours in 1909 indicated a reserve of 300–400 'nurses are to be commandeered for service in the Navy Reserve'. The *British Journal of Nursing* commented tartly that the coercion was: 'just as 100 years ago men were gagged and compelled to serve on ships by the notorious "press-gang"'.

In fact, willing hands were coming forward nationwide – but not always being welcomed by armed forces leaders. The (all-male) St John Ambulance Brigade Royal Navy Sick Berth Reserve had begun in 1905; the Territorial and Reserve Forces Act of 1907 brought about the all-female Territorial Force Nursing Service; and an army nursing reserve had begun in 1908. In addition, civic-minded women were flocking to the British Red Cross Society and the Order of St John. In 1909 these popular organisations, fired by lofty ideals of self-sacrifice, had founded the Voluntary Aid Detachment (VAD) system. Volunteers (two-thirds of whom were female) began training for roles in hospitals, including auxiliary nursing, cooking, clerical work and driving. Some male VADs served with the army and navy.[11]

The Admiralty announced plans for its medical branch in August 1911. Nursing reserves were to be found by asking civilian matrons to deliver the required number of action-ready but non-combatant nursing sisters, on demand. They would not be trained by the navy in advance. This subcontracted recruitment process saved the navy's time and gave civilian women managers, not MOs, the crucial power of selection. By early summer 1914 a reserve of 102 existed. Like the 50,000 VADs nationwide they were ready to rise to whatever was required of them.[12]

Some volunteers welcomed the prospect of being able to contribute to the war effort, as well as the opportunity to travel. It seemed 'emancipatory'. The many suffrage campaigners joining all-women organisations such as Scottish Women's Hospitals overseas units are proof of that. For the majority their readiness was simply part of the new 'natural' militarising of civilian life. Few sheltered women would have been able to comprehend the unimaginable tragedy ahead. QARNNS regulars anticipated a marked extension of naval nursing.[13]

Nursing for the wartime navy: 1914–18

Warriors of the wards

World War I began for Britain on 4 August 1914. The strategy of the Allied Powers was to blockade the Central Powers (principally Germany) by sea, and stop that blockade being broken. The Royal Navy was the key organisation in this. At its peak 450,000 naval personnel were involved. Three-quarters of seamen were regulars or former regulars. Two-thirds of nurses looking after them were straight from civilian hospitals, so there was some degree of cultural mismatch. Reserve nurses were welcome 'visitors' without knowledge of naval ways and language.[14]

Over 300 women were QARNNS or QARNNS(R) – reserves; 1918 was to be the peak year with 279 in the combined regular and reserve force. The nurses' role was to deal not only with the wounded but also those made poorly by common problems such as tuberculosis, falls and poor basic health caused by pre-war poverty. Depending on pressures, usually there were two nurses and ten aides per 100 beds. They were 0.15 per cent of the navy's health care complement, as the majority of nursing personnel were (male) sick berth staff. Later the QARNNS members were joined by 534 VAD (RN), as naval VADs were called. QARNNS sisters were said to look 'charming in their dark blue uniform faced with scarlet, and spotless kerchief caps'. In popular culture wartime nurses were portrayed as nobly

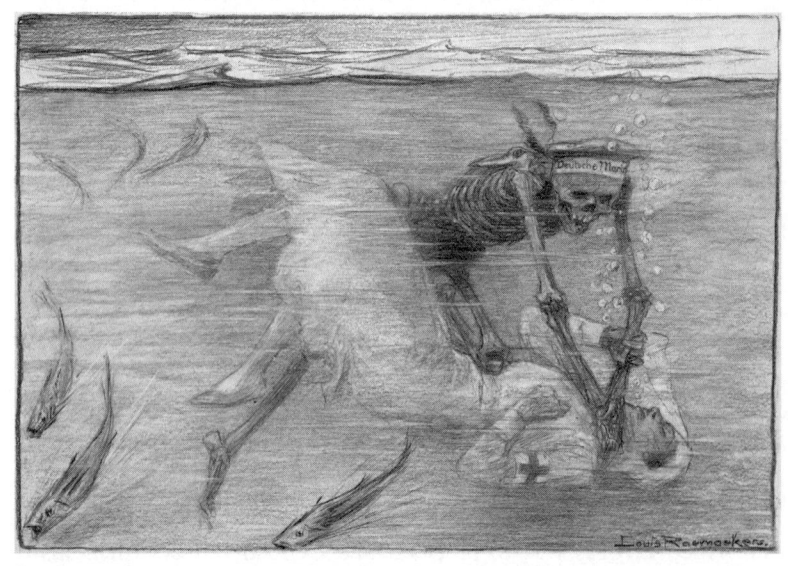

Fig. 2.4. Red Cross nurses were often shown as the most upsetting victims of German atrocities in World War I. Coloured chalk drawing by Louis Raemaekers, 1918.

self-sacrificing. When these 'angels' were attacked by the 'beastly' or caddish enemy, therefore, there was more public outage than for attacks on male health care personnel.[15]

Both navy and army had their own separate health care teams and systems. The navy had no matron-in-chief, unlike the army. Instead it had head sisters at the various hospitals. About 100-odd regular QARNNS were working in the 17 Royal Naval Hospitals (RNHs) used in wartime: Haslar, Plymouth, Chatham, Dartmouth, Osborne, Queensferry, Deal, Shotley, Portland, East Pilton, Granton, Haulbowline (Cork), Lambert, and Peebles. Naval auxiliary hospitals (RNAHs) were set up. QARNNS sisters, and from December 1917 VADs, worked in these RNAHs which included Southend-on-Sea, Hull, Chatsworth and Truro. On the Isle of Bute a volunteer, Marchioness Augusta Crichton Stuart, nursed in her own converted home, Mount Stuart.

For most of the war QARNNS regulars were outnumbered twofold by the reserves. This was especially the case at Haslar,

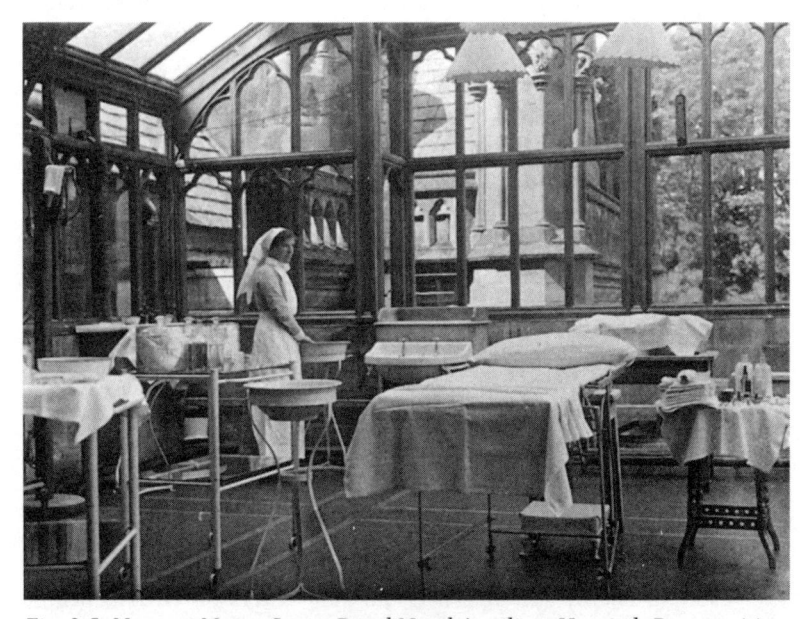

Fig. 2.5. Nurse at Mount Stuart Royal Naval Auxiliary Hospital, Bute, waiting in the operating theatre, which was the Marchioness's former Horoscope Room.

where there were as many as 47 reserves to the 14 regulars in 1918. Regulars were spread thinly because they were supervising newcomers. Under five worked on each of the nine naval hospital ships: *China*, *Delta*, *Drina*, *Garth Castle*, *Magic II*, *Plassy*, *Rewa*, *Soudan* and *Somali*. His Majesty's Hospital Ships (HMHSs) acted as casualty receiving stations and transports for evacuating injured personnel. In addition, two sisters worked on the naval ambulance train. Seemingly no women served on His Majesty's Ambulance Transports (HMATs), the floating ambulances which were not protected by the Hague Convention.[16] Hospital ships of every nation supposedly had international immunity under the Hague Convention of 1907. They were safeguarded from attack, in theory, by their white hulls, lights and huge green crosses.

Initially two reserves and two regulars sailed together in each ship's team, then the ratio declined to one regular and two reserves per ship. Presumably by then experienced sisters had handed on the baton to reserves, so were less necessary. Not only did sailing mean risking death, it also meant being intermittently underutilised and therefore frustrated. This is because casualty receiving facilities are necessarily situations where the flow of patients stops and starts.[17]

Angels in action at sea

Naval nurses were roughly ten times fewer than army nursing personnel. They travelled far less. Army sisters were near the action, in France and Flanders, then Gallipoli in 1915, Salonika and Macedonia after 1916 and in northern Russia in 1918. QARNNS members carried on serving in two of the three overseas hospitals, Gibraltar and Malta ('the Nurse of the Mediterranean'). In 1915 the 11 regulars working overseas were trebled by 27 QARNNS (R). Numbers overseas then stayed constant throughout the war, rather than swelling.[18]

Most of the QARNNS' drama was in home waters and not always the result of enemy action. Three nursing sisters on HMHS *Rohilla* survived its sinking in a storm off Whitby in October 1914, as they set off to bring the wounded back from Belgium. Tragically, three partying sisters from the HMHS *Drina* were fatal victims of a Christmas 1915 explosion in the Cromarty Firth. The HMHS *Rewa* was torpedoed off the north Cornwall coast but the four naval sisters on board all survived. Reserve Louisa Chamberlain died when her hospital ship *China* struck a mine in Scapa Flow in August 1918.[19]

Royal Navy battleships played one of their most important roles when they supported the amphibious invasion of Gallipoli. Ships waiting just offshore then took some of the 73,485 casualties to Egypt and Lemnos. Around a score of QARNNS members were involved in that terrible campaign from April 1915 to January 1916, at a distance. Lillian Phillips (born 1884) had one of the most action-packed of overseas wartime careers. She had entered Haslar in 1913 and then her various moves included: in 1914, fetching the wounded across the Channel; in 1915, again in HMHS *Plassy*, taking the Gallipoli wounded from Lemnos; from November 1916 to Spring 1918 in Mediterranean waters in the hospital ship *Karapara* and at RNH Malta.[20]

Fig 2.6. QARNNS sisters in lifejackets enjoying their veils being blown in the wind. Capes and veils could be an occupational hazard, especially for lightweight women in strong gusts, caught up almost like kites.

Changing the organisation

Wars' twists and turns often force attempts at fast changes. In naval nursing two key organisational moves occurred. Firstly, in 1916, after yet another German declaration of unrestricted submarine warfare, the Admiralty ordered that in UK naval hospitals nursing sisters should gradually replace male SBAs 'as far as practicable'. That meant SBAs could go and serve in warships (where women would never have been allowed). It presaged the later WRNS slogan: 'free a man for the fleet'. For some men, this official move brought a most unwelcome release into danger.[21]

Germany announced it would no longer respect hospital ships after February 1917. QARNNS sisters afloat were supposed to be replaced by SBAs. However, they often were not. This was probably either because of SBAs' opposition or people being too busy to rearrange satisfactorily settled teams.[22]

The second move, that December, was that the navy did what the army had done two years earlier. It realised that, in the absence of enough professional nurses, they could not do other than take up VADs. In this way, naval VADs emerged. Four lady probationer VADs had begun in 1915 but no others. Now, in December 1917, the new large intake of 'Very Artful Darlings' and 'Virgins Awaiting Destruction' worked in naval hospitals, including the naval auxiliary hospitals, such as the Hull naval wing developed by Marjorie, Lady Nunburnholme.[23]

The Commandant in Chief of the British Red Cross Society Women's Voluntary Aid Detachments, was someone who had always wanted to be sailor: Katharine Furse (1875–1952). From the first months of the war in summer 1914 this widowed mother had enjoyed being 'something of a volcano in the [British Red Cross Society] offices'. In November 1917 she switched to leading the navy's new female organisation, the Women's Royal Naval Service (WRNS). So, entirely coincidentally, the VADs she had commanded now entered naval life in two ways, as naval VAD (RN)s and as Wrens.[24]

Naval VADs were placed by their county directors, who acted somewhat as matrons had done, allocating women to the navy or army, rather than letting women choose. Some were General Service

VADs working as cooks, maids and clerks, not Nursing VADs. No naval VADs served on ships in this war. This is probably because the usual substitution level ashore was two VADs to one nursing sister, meaning under-experienced VADs would have taken up too much space aboard. Also, they were only on six-month contracts, which would have caused administrative difficulties. Ironically, those short-term contracts had come about during Katharine Furse's reign as a way to retain army VADs who were too prone to walking out in protest at military hospitals' strict regimes. Naval VADs were used until the war's end and after.[25]

Back to almost normal

The war ended, suddenly, in November 1918. Hospital ships' nursing sisters decreased from a peak of 35 in 1916 to just three in 1919. Similarly, on land, reserves went back to civilian hospitals. Just 14 reserves were left by 1919. Reserves had more than doubled from the start, from 102 to 227. Regulars in the QARNNS usually carried on; Lillian Phillips did so until 1946. The force numbered 77 by 1920, only three-quarters of the 1914 level.[26]

Women's role in health care had been large, but restricted by the gendered limitations the navy imposed. In 1918 of the 6,569 medical staff 12 per cent were women: 831. Despite their late start, almost double the number of VADs to QARNNS members had served, albeit only some had nursed, as opposed to supported, in hospitals.[27]

Counting the costs

In terms of human costs, ten QARNNS sisters were casualties; five of them reserves. No naval nurse was killed in combat. The ten constituted 3 per cent of the naval nursing team. Six VADs died. The total naval medical officers and nursing staff who died in World War I were 1,503, or 22 per cent of that branch. By contrast approximately 23,527 naval personnel died. In all 505,519 cases were dealt with.[28]

Nurses were extensively praised after the war. The Archdeacon of London commemorated the HMHS *Rewa* survivors as 'heroic women who were the worthy nurses of a Sea King's daughter'. Some 67 nursing awards were conferred upon women who came in the category 'Admiralty'. Nurses were honoured with the Royal Red Cross (RRC), a special nursing award begun in 1883, which is still spoken of with awe. Others were proud of being awarded the new, but slightly less prestigious, Associate of the Royal Red Cross (ARRC). Very exceptional feats were recognised by the RRC Bar. Awards also went to 20 nursing staff from civilian situations, such as Miss Edwardes at the RN convalescent home in Great Malvern. Nurses also received campaign medals – Lillian Phillips was awarded three. VADs were awarded VAD decorations and campaign medals too.[29]

By the war's end at least 1.3 per cent of people paid to work in naval services were women. Members of the newly formed Women's' Royal Naval Service were the greater number, then naval VADs, then QARNNS. Unlike QARNNS, Wrens were newcomers to the navy; not necessarily professionally qualified to do their specific job – but sometimes overqualified; and did an enormous range of tasks in far more places. A smaller percentage went overseas and none worked on ships. Wrens were not similarly cast as angels although some of their officers were regarded as tartars and others as potential sweethearts. As Chapter 3 shows, WRNS members had a very different war to health care personnel.[30]

CHAPTER 3

Wrens in World War I

We have the biggest chance women have ever had, and we mean to be worthy of it.

Katharine Furse, 1918.[1]

Better late than never: November 1917

Katharine Furse, World War I's most important naval woman, later hoped her 'grandchildren may be interested in the fact that a woman among their relatives held that rank of a Rear-Admiral'. It was an unthinkably high and unusual role for a woman at that time. As a girl, she had dreamt of being a midshipman. As the first director of the Women's Royal Naval Service, she surpassed that dream, not least because she was such an instinctive organiser. Her joke was: 'If I saw a child being run over by a tram, my first reaction would be to organise somebody else to rescue it.' As it turned out, she organised thousands of women to rescue the navy and nation.[2]

The WRNS she led was 700 times the size of the QARNNS, and more visibly managed by the Admiralty. It was a more mixed population, with several tiers and roughly ten ratings to every officer. By contrast, all QARNNS members were officers. The ratings they supervised were from other bodies, such as SBAs and VADs. Also the WRNS was initially a temporary measure that lasted only two years. QARNNS was and is the continuing permanent service, not a

Fig. 3.1. Katharine Furse in tricorn hat, the first director of the WRNS.

worrying new phenomenon nor seen as a possible dilution of proud naval masculinity.

A women's branch of naval services had been considered as early as December 1914. Acting Vice Admiral David Beatty, the controversial wartime leading light, had written to Ethel, his wife, about the rumoured move, saying he had 'never heard such nonsense'. There was already plenty of work for women that men could not do. If women were married it was 'enough to look after their homes and children', he declared. Nothing had come of the planned corps. Probably this was because the need for civilian women's help was not yet seen to exist; his colleagues shared his views of women's natural places and getting on with the war at sea had priority.[3]

However, three years into the war, the Allies were struggling and the burden on the navy was immense as it struggled alongside the army. German U-boat attacks increased, and needed countering. Battleships were providing support for convoys of merchant ships as well as troop carriers. Campaigns were being waged in Italy and the Middle East, as well as in France and Flanders. More naval personnel were essential. The only possible way forward was that women would substitute for men wherever possible, freeing men to work in ships and submarines, as well as on land. In the end, the number of extra men in the submarine service alone was to amount to the entire number of wartime WRNS.[4]

Women's help was less unthinkable in late 1917 than in the war's early days. Various rounds of male conscription in January 1916, April 1916 and April 1917 had meant women increasingly did 'men's jobs' on land, from chimney sweep to temporary heads of their husbands' businesses, as well as leading and staffing the many women's war organisations, and serving as Women's Legion army cooks. Public feeling was moving towards seeing women's contribution as essential, rather than worrying about possible loss of femininity.

A specifically naval precedent had existed since 1915 when women were allowed into Admiralty clerical work, even Intelligence. Other women were working in naval dockyards and naval barracks by September 1917. Moreover, in March 1917 the army began setting up a women's service, the Women's Army Auxiliary Corps (WAAC), so a template was in place. There was urgency, too: the War Office had not replied to a navy request to share WAACs.

An auxiliary of women, which the navy could use as it saw fit, must have seemed an inevitable choice to Eric Geddes, the innovative new First Lord of the Admiralty. After all, his sister happened to be Chief Controller of the WAAC. Dr Mona Chalmers Watson (1872–1936) had since 1916 been pushing for the greater use of women. Brother and sister and Dame Katharine would ideally have liked a common pool of female labour. It would have been more useful and flexible, and meant that women were not having to break into an established organisation. Such a combined female service did not seem likely to happen soon, so an immediate navy-only women's force was needed. The push came from a civilian male, rather than being triggered by a later cocktail party suggestion made by the enterprising Lady Rocksavage – as a WRNS myth claimed.[5]

The aim of this belated move was to free naval men to go to sea. A small ancillary team of women would do a limited range of non-combatant work, just in Britain. It would be focused on ports and probably staffed by the wives and daughters of naval men. So, although a new initiative, it would feel like a body safely within the wider naval family. It was like extending a boundary, embracing 'our own' women naturally rather than letting in a fresh and therefore unpredictable force.

This Women's Royal Naval Service turned out to have three stages in its two-year life: designing and setting up (November 1917 to February 1918); settling in and expanding (March 1918 to November 1918); and a post-Armistice existence until 1 November 1919. There is no record of whether it was expected to be like the QARNNS, or if the matron-in-chief was asked for advice. Despite inter-service rivalry, the navy wanted it organised 'along the lines of' the army's women's auxiliary. It would fit around the Royal Navy's patterns and be informed by knowledge gained in setting up the temporary, peripheral but crucial VAD in the last few years.[6]

A 'Second Sea Lord for the ladies'?

Who was to be the females' mini-counterpart of the Second Sea Lord (the person responsible for naval staffing matters)? What wizard could quickly establish and run an impromptu dovetailed women's organisation from scratch without fussing? It had to be a female because it was a tradition that women were managed by women – in organisations such as prisons, the Post Office, Civil Service and naval nursing. Edith Bass, the Admiralty's Principal Lady Superintendent, supervised female personnel such as typists. Possibly some naval officers' wives thought they would be right for the position of director. However, at this late stage, they were already leading naval welfare work, including with Agnes Weston's Sailors' Rests and the SSFA. For example, the well-networked Amy, Lady Drury (1863–1953), an admiral's wife, was a committee member of Royal Naval Friendly Union of Sailors' Wives and Chairman [sic] of the Ladies' Advisory Committee of the Navy League Overseas Relief Fund.[7]

As luck would have it, one person was already tried and tested as suited to harnessing the energies of thousands of women newcomers on the margins of the armed forces: Katharine Furse. Dame Katharine was not an obvious candidate for the leadership of such a naval body.

She was not an aristocrat – and Dr Chalmers Watson had nearly been rejected by the army for not being one. No naval background prepared Katharine, although her son was a naval cadet. However, throughout the first three years of the war she had been Commandant in Chief of the British Red Cross Women's VAD. She was friends with the key women founders of the new Department of National Service, so she knew the issues. Even better, she was known and trusted by the WAAC leader, having shared Somerset House premises. Better still, Dame Katharine and her top echelon were available; they were about to switch horses in mid-stream, leaving the VAD because of 'irreconcilable differences'.[8]

On the eleventh day of the eleventh month, 1917, over lunch brokered by Dr Chalmers Watson, Sir Eric asked their guest the head-hunting question Mona had already tipped her off to expect. Would Dame Katharine lead 'a new Naval organisation of women?', his bombshell to galvanise useful action in a navy he saw as rather sclerotic and desperately short of hands. Yes, she would.

So the Women's Royal Naval Service, mark 1, was a hybrid born of several 'parents': the navy's need and patchy new willingness; the army's parallel acceptance of female civilian 'outsiders' as substitutes; the 70-year battle of women for the right to be citizens and professional health care workers; the QARNNS' and their army counterpart, Queen Alexandra's Imperial Nursing Service's impressive example of the part women could play in defence nursing; and the long-established principle that women, like camp-followers, could be expected to readily meet men's non-battle needs as and when required.[9]

Setting up: November 1917 to February 1918

Dame Katharine went to the Admiralty to start the ball rolling the very next day. 'I was asked to "put in a scheme" ... They were extraordinarily nice ... I was embarking without a chart, on a new voyage, knowing nothing of the seas ahead.' She was to be formally appointed on 23 November but began work at once, despite being exhausted from the VAD internal struggles.[10]

Her task was to work out what such a naval women's force would be, within the parameters set down by Admiral Sir Herbert Heath, the Second Sea Lord. Sir Eric Geddes had emphasised 'the necessity for accepting the Admiralty point of view ... which, thanks to my faith in my naval colleagues, I could agree', she wrote. In days her friends did what, today, would be called developing the concept – with metaphorical towels round their heads, Katharine joked. The classic *Kings Regulations for The Navy* 'became our "bible"'. They had no naval aide, and did it in the comfort of a friend's flat, not an Admiralty office.[11]

The plan was that women who actively wanted to work in this new naval service would begin as soon as possible. They agreed to serve 'for so long as his Majesty shall require your services i.e. for a period of 12 months or for the duration of the war', whichever is the greater. Lord Derby, the Secretary of State for War, and the husband of one of Queen Alexandra's Ladies of the Bedchamber, had instructed Mona Chalmers Watson that the WAACs would not be enlisted. Certainly they would not be conscripted (conscription for men was unpopular). They would be *enrolled* voluntary female members. Similarly, Wrens would be enrolled. As the navy was a more elite organisation than the army, WRNS members were expected to be even more decorous, not

Fig. 3.2. Cooks were some of the first women to be taken up by the WRNS. All Wrens were seen as daughters of the Senior Service.

versions of Jack Tar or Tommy Atkins. Members of the WRNS would be properly waged, on a par with the WAAC. High pay was expected to woo high-calibre lively women who were already wage-earners, such as teachers, who had previously been revolted by the idea of wearing uniforms and been unable to afford to work for volunteer-level honorariums.[12]

Women's temporary and instant tasks would be the traditional sort: domestic and clerical work. Similarly, the WAAC's four categories were cookery, mechanical, clerical and miscellaneous. This meant no costly training would be involved at this cash-strapped and urgent juncture. WRNS members were initially expected just to be immobiles, living at home, mainly in naval ports. Their official motto was to be *Never at Sea*. If women were mobiles the navy would be responsible for their accommodation needs and act as parents to potentially gallivanting hoydens. To the Admiralty instigating such mobility must have looked like an administrative job too far, when their business was winning the war. The army, by contrast, always intended women to go to France. Indeed just under half served overseas, as did army VADs of both categories: nursing and general service.[13]

Despite the navy's early wish that all women would be immobiles, it quickly became clear there would have to be mobiles too, especially among officers. Dividing women into stay-at-homes and rovers was as crucial as organising status. The WAAC leader had been instructed that her members should not have any military ranks in case it upset the army men. Women were called just 'officials' and 'members', with civilian-sounding titles such as 'administrators' and 'forewomen'. By contrast, the WRNS used naval terminology as in 'officers and ratings' but also called women 'members' and used civilian terms for ranks such as 'Principal'. WRNS officers included former VAD leaders; Sir Eric had asked for as many as possible to switch allegiance. Naval men would be the women's ultimate authority in work situations. However, off duty, the mobiles in their hostels (there was to be nothing as unladylike as barracks) would be controlled by female officers and petty officers.[14]

Clearly, the service's name had to include 'women' and 'Navy'. Silly acronyms for VADs had 'made us sensitive and wary'. Dame

Katharine's team rejected various names, such as Women's Auxiliary Naval Corps (WANKS). 'Wrens' – innocuous small birds – was acceptable. Dame Katharine had to plead with the navy for the 'Royal' aspect of the name. It certainly gave the new service more status, linking it to the 'Royal' in Royal Navy, as well as to the QARNNS' and QAIMNS' links to Queen Alexandra. It *sounded* more dignified than its army counterpart: WAACs was pronounced 'whacks'.[15]

This new women's naval force was to look after its members in every way – training, food, clothing, welfare, pay – and, it turned out, career progression and eventually overseas postings. Wrens were treated as daughters of the Senior Service. This patriarchal approach maintained the 'men are warriors/women are home-makers' way of thinking, so the status quo looked safe, whatever the realities. In fact the two women leaders saw their forces as offering bigger

Fig. 3.3. Even before the war women enjoyed dressing up in sailor kit at photographic studios (left). In the war, some Wrens actually wore a version as uniform (right) and looked like counterparts of their brothers and sweethearts.

possibilities for women's own growth. Mona Chalmers Watson regarded the WAAC's creation as 'an advance of the women's movement'. Similarly Katharine Furse, a reader of transcendentalist poet Walt Whitman (himself a former volunteer defence nurse), indefatigably idealised her organisation as an opportunity that would enable women's spiritual, personal and physical development as citizens. 'We have the biggest chance women have ever had, and we mean to be worthy of it.' On 29 November Admiralty Office Memorandum 245 formally announced the establishment of the WRNS this crucial late-stage add-on. The necessary wheels were turning well.[16]

Looking shipshape: December 1917–January 1918

What would these WRNS members look like? The Admiralty wanted to know early on, 'but we pretended not to be interested in this, because we were very anxious that the usual remarks should not be made that women think only of dress,' Dame Katharine recalled. This top-to-toe kit would have to assert women's association – but not quite equivalence – with the Royal Navy. 'We ... wanted to copy naval uniform in all *essentials*' (author's emphasis). One of the advantages of this approach was that jackets had a flattering shape, without the lumpish breast pockets the WAAC and later WRAF had. Edwardian women at that time did not have brassieres with two supportive cups, but light, darted bust bodices which created a mono-bosom above their heavily boned corsets. Outerwear was somewhat based on VAD women's uniforms. The Treasury was opposed to the 'wasting' of expensive gold lace (the braid on sleeves). Instead, the WRNS chose *royal* blue lace. They accepted 'without regret' the lower-status colour 'because gold lace was definitely the prerogative of the men', Dame Katharine said.

Uniforms did not arrive immediately, so initially WRNS personnel were to work in mufti or a mix. This must have hindered their integration. So too did men's practice of calling women 'Miss', rather than by rank (because it seemed rather rude and anomalous to chivalrous ears). Wrens themselves called each other by surname, for example just Smith, not Alicia, Miss Smith or Wren Smith.[17]

When Herbert Heath approved the laurel wreaths round the anchors on Dame Katharine's buttons as she gave him the requested viewing in the First Lord's room, he told Sir Eric she was entitled to them because she was the 'equivalent rank to a Rear-Admiral for certain purposes'. However, her pay, £500 pa, was less than half the rear admirals' £1,095 pa. The discrepancy was presumably partly due to lack of seniority, her not being liable to serve at sea, and the usual pay gap based on the idea that women were not the family breadwinners. In fact this widow had two sons to keep and was also looking after her widowed mother.[18]

A staffing structure emerged to support her. Finding the right women for the most senior roles was the first step. Most were ex-VADs already known to the director. Remarkably few were from naval families. Less senior officers were selected from applicants not necessarily already known to the VAD or navy. The main officers were quickly placed by mid-December. Headquarters first was within the Admiralty in Westminster. It grew so quickly it had to move. Dame Katharine emphasised that their new Mayfair base 'was not too far away for us to keep in close touch with the Admiralty of which, we were, of course, an integral part'. However, the severing must have made a difference to the easy daily neighbourliness.[19]

To be manageable the organisation was subdivided and subdivided again. The WRNS structure was based on geographical regions and occupations, rather as the VAD was based on counties and the navy on 'commands' (areas), as well on branches and specialisations. Eventually around a thousand women were to be in each of the seven geographical areas. The size depended on the busyness of the location and on senior male officers' willingness to employ females; Scotland was not keen. Each WRNS division had around 20 sub-divisions, under a principal officer. Divisional officers' teams looked after not only women's workplace situation but also their entire lives, especially if they were mobile ratings. Some served in small units of 20, which could be women only. There were to be ten categories of jobs for officers and 21 for ratings by the end of the war.[20]

WRNS members' terms of service were fuzzy. They were formally civilians who could not be made to stay on, nor court-martialled for desertion. The director found: 'If most of the naval officers in ports ... could have had their way, our service would have been brought under the Naval Discipline Act.' She herself wanted this 'but the Government would not face public opinion in this direction, or had not the time to get the necessary Bill passed'. Such exclusion made Wrens seem somewhat exceptional to the navy rather than part of it, unlike the WAAC and WRAF, the other two auxiliaries.[21]

Yet Wrens proudly felt themselves to not be civilians but 'in' the navy. The official documents they signed certainly made it look as if they were in it. If they breached their contract they rendered themselves liable, 'on conviction by a Court of Summary Jurisdiction, to be sentenced to imprisonment with or without hard labour for a term not exceeding six months'. In fact, such harsh punishments never happened – partly because there was no need, said Dame Katharine, who saw no crime and little insubordination. The few small problems 'could be dealt with in sundry other ways by our officers with the help of naval officers, who often bluffed the women into believing they could be dealt with under naval discipline. They needed very little bluffing, because they loved playing the game of being in the Navy.'[22]

Matching women to situations in 'the game': January 1918

Potential officers' applications were processed in late December 1917. Reference-seeking did not stop for Christmas festivities. Were potential officers 'likely to be just and humane?' it was asked – an indication of Katharine's values. Individuals' records show ex-VAD interviewers were wary of *grand dames* with little ability to be flexible. Experience in managing servants was not a valid qualification. Successful WRNS officer applicants had to be white British and not to be 'common' or possess any slight regional accents. Applicants like Barbara Craster, who later became Principal at the WRNS College, were ideal on paper and in actuality. Bengal-born, her father was a colonial judge. She had been a VAD for two years, and her reference was from the head of the Royal Naval College, Dartmouth.[23]

Some WRNS members began training on New Year's Eve; officer training proper began one week later. By 18 January the first officers had been appointed to bases and stations. When they settled in, their next step was to find out just how women should substitute for men. How many would be needed where, doing what, and when? Officers also had to make sure the stop-gap facilities were right. These included hostels with 40 square feet (3.7 square metres) per woman, plus in some cases work areas with a rest room, canteen and separate female toilets. In one of the rare references to menstruation adequate incinerators for used sanitary towels were stipulated.[24]

Dame Katharine felt as they met naval officers that winter that they were truly leaping straight into the deep end of the navy's pool:

> there was so much to learn and so little time to learn it ... we realised that they were very impatient of anything that was not strictly naval. They seemed to expect us, as soon as we appeared in uniform, to know all naval customs and to adhere to them; we were perfectly delighted to try to do so, but it was sometimes a little difficult to know by instinct what was the right and wrong way of doing things.[25]

Ratings were recruited through the Ministry of National Service, at Labour Exchanges (job centres). They had two weeks' basic training, then skills-related training of varying lengths. Experienced naval men trained the women until WRNS instructors gained enough knowledge. There was no mention of women being free to refuse to do unsuitable jobs. Nor did anyone raise the possibility of crèches. In the early days, women with dependants were not encouraged.

Working fine ... with tensions: February–November 1918

Supply, demand and discipline

Naval officers formally knew that the WRNS was there and that Wrens would try to help, not hinder, because on 4 February Admiralty Weekly Order 414 was circulated. Basically, it summarised Dame

Katharine's team's initial WRNS scheme. It clued up senior men as to what new sorts of personnel they might be able to incorporate.

In early February, Dame Katharine demonstrated the management style to which she wanted her officers to aspire. She printed a Whitmanesque booklet, and sent around a moving high-minded essay, *The Beloved Captain*, too. She entreated her officers to behave nobly: 'To be beloved by the women entrusted to our care by the Country and to help them to win the finest possible reputation for our Service should be our ideal ... You are Pioneers and as such you must necessarily start off to discover possibilities and to create a service out of nothing.'[26]

In reality, the immediate struggle was to ensure the right kind of women were trained and standing by to be delivered to the right kind of jobs, and to find them decent facilities. Her principle was that it was the WRNS' role to 'put a round peg into a square hole' – a view that did not wrong-foot women as square-shape misfits. Applications by such round pegs with a wide range of war experience were piling in. 'The popularity of the Navy gave us the pick of the women volunteering for service because "every woman loves a sailor" holds true,' Dame Katharine said with uncharacteristic simplicity. Women also loved the idea of the sea and the hats. Those weary of war service fancied a new organisation. More wanted to join than were accepted.[27]

Loving sailors in fact was a problem. One of the elephants in this room was sex. Any woman away from home, working alongside men, had to be careful about her moral reputation. In the VAD, Katharine Furse had argued that if her members were seen as 'prigs and prudes' or 'the perfect ladies' that was better than the opposite. So too in the WRNS. The challenge was not only the disciplinary one of stopping service personnel having intercourse out of wedlock: an ambition as vain as Canute's. The navy, specifically, needed to protect naïve women from being taken advantage of by men whose testosterone levels were high and who felt a duty to keep up Jack's stylish reputation for having 'a girl in every port'.[28]

Concern was practical too. Defence recruitment would dry up if fathers feared for their daughters. Pregnancy and sexually transmitted disease would waste valuable trained personnel. Dame

Katharine was determined that her charges should be not seen as morally lax as WAACs were rumoured to be. She urged women to be 'visibly good' but enlisted Herbert Heath to adjust male conduct too. On 20 February he wrote to all naval commanding officers asking they help ensure women 'were seen in the right light ... they ask only to be treated with that courtesy and respect which their sex demands'.

The basic idea was not that there should be no discrimination, but that there should be – females were a special species, to be treated chivalrously. Such gendered standards are most humorously illustrated by Dame Katharine's story that she occasionally suggested that the WRNS should adapt the navy's jovial toast 'to our wives and sweethearts – and may they never meet!' and drink to '"to [our] husbands and sweethearts and may they never meet" which was invariably received with [by naval men] shocked reserve, no twinkle being allowed to penetrate.'[29]

Can she do that? Yes!

Personal attitudes apart, more and more Wrens were swiftly and deftly segueing into the necessary work. Naval men's acceptance of women varied by location and situation. Helen Beale, the Divisional Director at Devonport, left a diary that indicates that a mix of both push and pull determined the degree and range of women's new naval roles. She interviewed naval officers in her area to see, in effect, what gaps they had or could place on a wish list. Officers like her also used this opportunity to understand other ways in which women could assist. As the months wore on a mix of naval need and WRNS ability meant it was clear that the range of jobs could be widened.[30]

Behind some male resistance to women employees is also a fear that civilian females might be useless, present a security risk or be too disturbingly alluring, and even an irrational terror of the archetypal feminine (which is said to stand for dark enchanting mysteriousness, the unruly forces of nature, being uncannily foresightful and having the power to produce life). Male ratings in cosy sinecures were

Fig. 3.4. Wren ratings lining up by the sea, summer 1918.

sometimes unhappy at being 'freed for the fleet', because that might bring disruption and even the risk of their death.

Similarly, Wrens resisted work in the less glamorous fields, such as cooking. The most readily accepted Wrens ratings were in traditional women's roles, doing menial tasks men were happy to offload. Mobiles were increasingly needed to fill gaps, including at remote locations.[31]

Women were attracted to roving work such as riding despatch motorbikes and driving officers in flashy limousines. Among the more technical jobs for ratings were those concerned with the machinery of war such as priming depth charges, maintaining searchlights and repairing hydrophones. Small numbers were in ship repair work which had been broken down into less-skilled tasks. Electrical and engineering roles including welding and operating lathes were allocated to women. Occasionally, 'natural' graduation occurred, for example some of those constructing anti-submarine wire net were fishing community women used to mending their husbands' nets. Although women shipyard workers had been incorporated into the WRNS, surprisingly few did women's traditional shipyard jobs: only seven were draughtswomen, 14 were sail makers and one an upholstress.

Officers worked in branches including office-type work such as accounts, administration, cypher, fleet mail, intelligence, secretarial and pay, but also anti-gas, quarters and signalling. Some even trained male ratings. They fitted in, proudly and politely.

Their director gloried that:

> we undertook every form of service ashore which a woman could perform, wherever the Admiralty appointed us ... we staffed hush-hush listening stations in remote places and fitted depth charges and paravanes in ships ... We baked, painted, cleaned ... and last but not least, we felt proud and pleased to be allowed to take our part in whatever had to be done wherever it was possible for women to do it.

Table 3.1 shows that 52 per cent were doing clerical and domestic jobs. Part of the reason women did not initially do much 'men's work' – say, wireless telegraphy – was that it involved being sent away for training, which delayed the start of their usefulness. However, shortages soon meant women simply had to do 'men's jobs'. A Wren might have several positions and locations throughout the war, in response to changing naval needs.[32]

Table 3.1 **Top five roles for WRNS ratings in 1917–19**[33]

ROLE	NUMBER	PERCENTAGE
Clerk	1,140	17%
Steward (assistant)	856	12%
Cook	574	9%
Shorthand typist	504	8%
Domestic worker	424	6%

Given that WRNS ratings were supposed to be substituting, did they do so on a one-for-one basis? Sometimes, but there was great delight if women found that, say, three could replace four men. However, it was difficult for them to learn quickly that which men had been trained to do for years. Other jobs were too heavy. It was feasible to be porters in victualling stores. But stretcher-carrying required that more than two women would have to be substituted for each pair of males; it was not cost effective. Tall and a trailblazing skier, Dame Katharine commented that:

> it has always seemed to me stupid to try to prove that women are in all ways equal to men; the sexes are different ... women's minds may equal men's ... but women are seldom as strong muscularly as men. Being very strong and muscular myself, this is one of the places where I feel entitled to be emphatic.[34]

Wrens of all strengths and abilities were not only in traditional locations but at Royal Naval Air Service stations too. The Royal Naval Air Service and the army's Royal Flying Corps were uniting at this point to become the Royal Air Force, meaning that Wrens already working in RNAS stations transferred into the Women's Royal Air Force, which had begun on 1 April 1918.[35]

Summer expansion

The WRNS had shifted dramatically in six months from expecting women to simply be immobiles in home ports to recognising they could serve overseas. By May plans were afoot to send the first – and only – Divisional Director to head the first WRNS overseas unit. Ida Jermyn was in the navy's Mediterranean HQ by August and some 'especially good' WRNS went too to Malta, Gibraltar and Genoa. Was allowing Wrens to serve overseas an expression of naval approval, a sign of urgent labour needs, or both? The latter: Dame Katharine rejoiced to Miss Jermyn that 'the Navy is so splendidly broadminded and shows no jealousy with regard to trusting us to share the confidential and more important work.'[36]

All women's services were seemingly set for a long and ever-expanding existence. In June 1918 WRNS officers were told to start thinking about giving leave to those who had worked flat-out to meet initial needs. At least five new hostels were opening, especially at air stations. Women doing naval work as non-service personnel started

Fig. 3.5. Arguably the most fortunate WRNS personnel: those in Malta, late 1918. Ida Jermyn is in the centre.

to be absorbed into the WRNS; by 1 June all women employed in naval, as distinct from civil, establishments were absorbed, almost overnight. Some, apparently, did not even grasp that they were now officially Wrens. Dame Katharine saw the period as a pinnacle of the WRNS' success. After 300 Wrens paraded along with other defence personnel for the Queen and King's silver wedding anniversary, on 6 July, Sir Herbert praised her in tellingly proprietorial terms: 'I hope you will let it be known ... how proud we of the Navy felt of our Wrens.'[37]

In August there was a new wave of officer appointments. By September the WRAF's senior management problems were no longer besetting WRNS officers, so WRNS leaders could get on with expanding the service that could be offered the navy. Finally, in October 1918, WRNS were included in the *Navy List*. They were truly there.

Fig. 3.6. WRNS posing on surrendered German U-boat, *U-123*, probably at Cowes, 22 November 1918.

What does a temp do after an Armistice?

Unexpectedly, on 11 November 1918 came the Allied victory. WRNS driver Enid Bell had the thrill of being the only woman present at the surrender of the German U-boat fleet on 21 November. Others were posed for photographers on a captured U-boat. Those en route to Bizerte had to stop midway.

Wrens celebrated and wondered what would happen next. It was not a matter of naval men immediately taking up where they had left off. Relieved female stand-ins did not straight away take off tricorns and overalls. Men had died and more personnel were still needed. Servicewomen were still essential, not least because they could be paid less than civilian women. They were relaxing company for war-weary men too, especially in the Mediterranean. Duty still called. Dame Katharine acknowledged: 'The Navy needs the Wrens standing by indefinitely and I would not fail them for anything in the world.'[38]

Demobilisation is necessarily slow and veterans often have many feelings including regret and dread of life outside the institution. In World War I WRNS' case some wanted an end to the confinement. The director herself wrote three days after the Armistice: 'These are very blessed days, but the wanderlust they bring is almost overwhelming.' However, most Wrens did not seem interested in quick demobilisation, unlike exhausted male combatants. As women they were not at risk, had not served long enough to be fed up, usually did not see their future as female civilians as appetising and above all most were enjoying the camaraderie and opportunities WRNS life had brought. Ida Jermyn was one of the many who did not want to come home, not least because there were no interesting jobs for her to return to.[39]

Dame Katharine wrote that in winter 1918:

> very soon we realised that, as women, we had only to help wind down the business of war and with as little elaboration as possible. When we saw there was no hope of even a nucleus of the W.R.N.S. being maintained, I wrote a Minute to the Second Sea Lord ... suggesting the completion of our demobilisation with as little delay as possible, giving as my reason that the men who were returning ought to fill all openings available. It seemed to be a courteous way of proving to the last that we women had no wish to take advantage of the welcome which had been shown to us by the Navy and that we realised that our employment in the Service was due to a war emergency.[40]

In fact the WRNS continued for another year as the demobilisation process rolled on. The records suggest that this was a period when the service really got into its stride. 'No sooner was the Women's Royal Naval Service through its "Trials" and in good working order than the war came to an end,' the director had remarked. Wrens carried on maintaining that good working order in a slightly more euphoric climate. Pushing for victory was no longer a pressure, which meant service life could be enjoyed by the victors. It became a time of chopping and changing, being almost sent somewhere to do one task then sent somewhere else. Great flexibility was required of the women in winter and spring 1919.[41]

Fig. 3.7. Wrens marching in peace celebrations, Portsmouth, 1918.

From Devonport, Helen Beale wrote wryly 'the joke is that down here lots of the men in charge of the offices have been groaning at having [had] women at all (what is the use of these people et cetera. Et cetera.!) But when it comes to taking them away, they [Wrens] suddenly seemed to be too valuable to part with!' On the other hand, some returned men wanted women out fast, to free jobs and housing for male family breadwinners. Demobbed servicemen were feeling so insulted by women being in men's places that Helen gave the instruction that her Wrens could wear plain clothes off duty. 'They are having, I'm afraid, an unpleasant time in the streets just now.' Uniforms made them a target. The WRNS director felt it was it 'a great pity that after the way men and women have worked side by side to win the war, men should at present be showing such an extraordinarily antagonistic attitude.'[42]

Dame Katharine and other women leaders of organisations such as the Women's Legion and the YWCA were trying to organise the next stage for released women. Sorting out a domestic service agency to match housemaids with potential employers and trying to make spinsters' emigration easier, through the Society for the Overseas

Fig. 3.8. Stewards (General) demobilising in 1919. Would they become housemaids or emigrants?

Settlement of British Women, were two key attempted solutions. Few British opportunities existed for the newly empowered women in search of a satisfying life.

A permanent service or not?

In the bittersweet summer of 1919 there was some discussion that the WRNS might continue as a permanent, if small, peacetime corps. Hopes were raised, dashed, then in May 1919 raised again when the navy told the director to make recommendations in case her corps was re-established. Then came a time of waiting, while Admiralty ambivalence and accelerated demobilisation continued. Some of the remaining Wrens marched in debonair naval style in the 19 July 1919 Peace Parade as if there was no sword of Damocles above them.

In response to Wrens' pressure the director tried another tack: a reserve, not a continued service. She asked the new second sea lord to allow a reserve attached to the Royal Navy Volunteer Reserve. It would be organised along the VAD lines and its members would include recruits from the Girl Guides. The Admiralty refused. Herbert Heath's letter of 2 August seemed to accept a fait accompli: 'it is so sad to think of the demobilising of such a splendid force'.[43]

Demobilisation carried on. On the one hand, women were honoured and petted. Awards included four Commanders of the British Empire. On the other, they were sloughed off. WRNS historian Ursula Stuart Mason found: 'One gets the impression from notes in files that the Admiralty found them uncomfortable company and wished them gone.' The navy set the WRNS official demob day for 1 October 1919 but some anomalies went on until 11 November 1919. The 'heart-breaking' severing of the WRNS limb from the naval body was made somewhat acceptable because of continued idea of separate spheres for women and men. As one anonymous WRNS member had written about the polarisation:

> The Wrens are as one with the Navy, as one both in spirit and mind... .
> Now the Wren must work for the Service, with the heart, the head and the pen,
> for the Wren belongs to the Navy, and the Navy belongs to the Wren... .
> The Navy must go into battle, must watch o'er the crested foam,
> But remember that Man is the fighter, that Woman must battle at home.[44]

However, some believed a new war would begin within two years and so, of course, a women's naval service would be needed again.

Wartime WRNS appraised

Statistics vary but it is commonly agreed that around 7,000 women had joined. When war ended the WRNS comprised 5,054 ratings and 438 officers. At least 73 had honours conferred. In all, 23 Wrens had died, though none were killed in action. The only fatality on active service was in October 1918: shorthand-typist Josephine Carr died when the Kingstown to Holyhead ferry, RMS *Leinster*, was torpedoed as she sailed to begin serving.[45]

All the terrible years of war had brought tragedy, but it also equipped women to lead new post-war lives, some connected to the navy. War may have changed them, but surprisingly 60 per cent of ratings had remained immobiles living at home. On joining, only 10 per cent of the 543 recorded officers were married. A handful were widows. Some married while serving. Others were widowed by war's end. They had seen their children serve, as Dame Katharine had. Leaving naval services in 1919 could mean beginning again with a changed and depleted family, as very different sort of women from their 1917 selves.[46]

An unattributed newspaper cutting found in Dame Katharine's archive, possibly by her, reads: 'The new women's Naval Corps existed only for the purpose of taking a very small share of the lightest part of the Navy's burden.' It indicated that cultural ideas about suitable activities for women had reduced the scope of Wrens' potentially huge contribution. Had the WRNS (and naval VADs) been in place from 1914, they could have played a greater part, as well as been more integral, just as the QARNNS had been.[47]

The director's determinedly upbeat account is the fullest available today. Few personal stories remain. Some, like Helen Beale's, speak of cultural mismatch, which both women and men dealt with in a range of ways including staying diplomatically silent, learning hard, cracking jokes to alleviate tension, being generous with each other's foibles and putting the greater good before personal feelings. Many internal documents show the WRNS to have been a well-organised body that rose to an extraordinary challenge. It did so rapidly, harnessing administrative skills learned elsewhere and always responding to the needs of the navy. These women's achievements left proof of how ordinarily and extraordinarily useful they could be to any future navy prepared to accept them – even as co-warriors o'er the crested foam itself.

CHAPTER 4

Nursing in the Peacetime Navy: 1919–38

The frantic babel of flooding blood
gave way once more to the ordered round.
We healed the boys who merely fell to mundane flukes,
Returning them to warily placid berths.

Anon

The interwar world

The QARNNS and WRNS were such separate worlds that their members seldom knew each other. They only met when a Wren needed nursing. Olga Franklin (1895–1987) did something highly unusual: she crossed the bridge. Born into the navy (her father was secretary to the Superintendent Devonport Dockyard) she moved

Fig. 4.1. Olga Franklin: from VAD to QARNNS.

from being a VAD cook, then a coder in the WRNS, into the navy's proud permanent band of nursing sisters. Then she rose to become the QARNNS matron-in-chief.[1]

If any woman wanted to continue in paid work in a naval service in the years 1919 to 1939, joining the QARNNS was the way to do it. Throughout the interwar years QARNNS sisters were the steady and sole beating heart of female naval service. Just as before the WRNS existed, the QARNNS was again *the* women's naval service. The service was small – under a hundred women. However, it was there in unquestioned place, not a make-do adjunct. By contrast the WRNS was now out of the official naval picture until 1938.

Interwar *Navy List*s give the most striking visual proof of women officers' absence from naval life. It is a bit like looking in a phone book where the Smiths and Jones have all been omitted. The only visible women were QARNNS; Edith Bass, the Principal Lady Superintendent; and Mrs Picton-Warlow, the Admiralty Inspector of Children's Welfare, by 1925.

Male personnel in the depleted and changing navy dropped to a quarter of the peak number – just 118,500 by 1922 and 97,000 by 1930. As well as facing poverty and unemployment, naval families at home were also dealing – without a national health service – with the individual impact of war's damage including wounds and mental ill health, and then later pay cuts.

Grievances grumbled on as naval attention turned from the wartime main task of opposing the German Grand Fleet to new theatres. QARNNS planners must have been aware they might need tropical disease skills to help support naval men in the Malta-based Mediterranean Fleet and the China Fleet, based in Hong Kong, Singapore and Wei Hei, as well as in the Atlantic/Home Fleet. Naval nursing sisters were in some of these locations and naval wives were in most of them. QARNNS sisters nursed such 'accompanying wives' and their children in Singapore and Malta, which meant navy-linked women were, unusually for civilians in the period, getting free health care.[2]

Naval ships were in the Baltic supporting anti-Bolshevik forces attempting, unsuccessfully, to crush the Russian Revolution from 1919–20. Britain was standing by to attack the new Republic of

Turkey's expansion in the Chanak Crisis in late 1922. Naval attention was focused on China and Hong Kong, standing by to protect Commonwealth assets and evacuate British citizens, following the 1923 termination of the Anglo-Japanese Treaty. The navy was a reluctant and under-equipped pawn in the mutual 'call-my-bluff' game that Britain and Italy were involved in, following Italy's invasion of Abyssinia and the Italo-Ethiopian War of 1935–6. Finally, the navy was involved in patrolling the Spanish coast in the Spanish Civil War of 1936–9. A 70-strong destroyer flotilla was gathered in the western Mediterranean and World War II seemed likely to begin in 1937, not 1939.

Every woman interested in the navy must have wondered 'what next?' Would it be a war in Europe against Germany and Italy? Or would it be war in the Far East against Japan? Danger grew as Britain joined the international arms race and developed King George V-class battleships, Illustrious-class aircraft carriers and Tribal-class destroyers. War was looming, and pro-war sympathies were polarised. Women were certainly cast as inherently peace-loving, but reality became more complicated when loyalty to a nation and to military relatives got in the way.

The very first woman MP to take a seat – Lady Astor, in 1919 – happened to be passionate about the navy because her constituency was Plymouth Sutton, and Plymouth was one the navy's three principal areas, along with Portsmouth and Chatham. 'Women have got to make the world safe for men since men have made it so darned unsafe for women', she contended, but also told Parliament:

> what a good thing it would have been if there had been a woman at the Admiralty twenty years ago. She would have saved the Navy a great deal of trouble. She would have told them that if there is a contented Service, particularly as far as the women are concerned; it is the basis of an efficient Service.[3]

Her point was that women had intrinsic and overlooked abilities. In actuality the nearest thing the navy had to 'a woman at the Admiralty' was a top QARNNS officer, who had health on her mind, and not the power or knowledge to determine naval strategy.

Fig. 4.2. MP Nancy Astor dancing with a sailor on Plymouth Hoe.

Nursing in a changing profession

The interwar QARNNS was the steadfast continuing female presence in naval service. The remaining VADs were reorganised, and continued to do supplementary work in service hospitals such as Haslar. Today the naval VAD interwar story seems to be lost. However, these volunteers were, like Wrens, categorised into mobiles and immobiles. Probably some living near ports were immobiles and members of naval family networks.[4]

QARNNS members enjoyed clear structure and roles alongside the equally established naval medical service. Sisters were respected for not having flinched from risk in the war. They were in a profession where status was a key issue in the interwar decades. In the 1920s the *British Journal of Nursing* repeatedly protested against the Admiralty's 'lack of consideration', including QARNNS members' omission from war bonuses: 'They have shared with our sailors all the horrors and perils of "unrestricted kultur" on the high seas. They have ministered unceasingly ... And what are they got for it?' The *Journal* quoted *Truth*, which had referred to 'the consistent official neglect' but said that nurses' struggles for fair compensation despite being civilians:

have not been entirely fruitless. The Admiralty have decided that members of this class are entitled to a war gratuity. That there should ever have been any demur upon this point is astonishing, but coming as it does in the middle of the sudden zest for economy, this concession indicates a belated consciousness of shabbiness.[5]

A select band of navalised civilians

Between the wars the QARNNS was a small service of between 81 and 87 members. It fluctuated each year, probably because of service needs rather than women's availability. They were all single (it was understood that anyone who married would thereupon resign from the service). Unlike Olga Franklin, they were not necessarily from naval stock, although often from armed forces and clerical families. Upper age limits varied but usually no-one over 35 was allowed to join; Olga was 32.[6]

In theory, a QARNNS member could walk out at any time. As a civilian, formally, she was not under the Naval Discipline Act. In practice, some made it a lifetime career, retiring in their early fifties. Leaving before the agreed contract period ended was not counted as 'deserting', as it was for SBAs. Misdemeanours in this period are barely discussed, but they include failure to report for duty. There is no indication that anyone was pregnant out of wedlock. Sairy Gamp-style tales of over-familiarity with patients, stealing and being drunk were long gone, because these were proud officers. Like doctors, it was unthinkable that they would collude with or abuse patients. 'Starchy' was a word SBAs sometimes used to describe nursing sisters. However, this is partly an expression of the rivalry from men who were less trained and had less authority but enormous practical experience.

Becoming a naval doctor, by contrast, was not seen as a possible career move for women, as in the civilian world. The navy had no women medical officers and the WRNS' Dr Dorothy Hare had moved to Civvy Street. She was now working in politics and setting up hostels for ex-servicewomen with sexually transmitted diseases, as well as becoming one of the first women registrars, at the Royal Free Hospital.[7]

Nursing sisters' mobility was geographical rather than social. Kathleen Harland, the QARNNS expert, reports that 'The appointing of Sisters reflected the needs of the Navy and ... adaptability would always be an important characteristic of any Sister. Many must have served out their careers in south England, at the three main naval bases [i.e. Portsmouth, Plymouth and Chatham] with perhaps a tour in Malta and Hong Kong.' No typical deployment pattern exists, according to the QARNNS sisters records. Typically, the navy moved people every couple of years. However, the duration of QARNNS' appointments varied, for example at Haslar Kathleen Hickey was head nursing sister for ten years, from 1912 to 1922 but Mary Clark succeeded her for only seven years.[8]

Table 4.1 shows where QARNNS members were based in a fairly typical year.

Table 4.1. **QARNNS locations in 1930**[9]

HOSPITAL/SICK QUARTERS	QARNNS
UK	
Haslar	19
Plymouth	18
Chatham	15
Portland	4
Dartmouth	4
Shotley	3
OVERSEAS	
Malta	10
Hong Kong	3
TOTAL	76

They were not in interwar hospital ships, which were few or at times non-existent. RFA *Maine* was the only hospital ship at that time. (The RFA was the Royal Fleet Auxiliary, the navy's civilian-staffed support service.) Usually cruising with the Mediterranean fleet the very elderly *Maine* was staffed by male health care staff. By contrast their army counterparts in QAIMNS served on troopships taking personnel to overseas bases. The limited range of overseas options for QARNNS members was caused by two factors: the navy's closure of auxiliary hospitals such as 'Wedgewood Castle', Gibraltar's picturesque blue RNH; and the Admiralty's (unexplained) choosing to exclude nursing sisters from some shore establishments.

Changing on the way to new war: 1933–9

In the interwar period major changes were taking place in the wider nursing world and in defence nursing. From 1919 all nurses had to be registered. Reshaping in army nursing in 1926 altered the defence nursing climate and probably helped lead to QARNNS gaining a national leader in 1927. Margaret Keenan (1869–1939) became the first head sister in chief. While training at Barts, this war veteran had been in the orbit of Matrons Isla Stewart and Ethel Bedford Fenwick, leading figures in pushing for better training and for all nurses to be registered. That meant Miss Keenan brought political knowledge to naval nursing.[10]

Slowly the QARNNS was moving away from total naval control of all its minutiae. In 1928 it was agreed that the power of veto in interviewing new personnel should shift from the medical director-general to his deputy and the head sister in chief jointly. A QARNNS consultative board began, and included civilian members like Lady Betty Pound, wife of Admiral Sir Dudley Pound, nicknamed Winston Churchill's anchor. From 1933 to 1935 more changes were made following the 1930 Warren-Fisher Committee on Services. A new ranking system to include senior sister and matron-in-chief roles evolved, plus mandatory State Registration certificates for newcomers, and better pay, allowances and pensions.

In addition, the problem of women's retention was addressed for the first time in naval women's history. A medical director expressed concern that a long-service system should exist because: 'it would be impossible to maintain the discipline and nursing efficiency of the Naval Hospitals if any large proportion of the Sisters' establishment were filled by individuals having no intention of making their life career with the Navy.' However, changes were hard to achieve. This was partly because of Treasury poverty but also because the QARNNS was governed by the old Civil Service rules from 1883 rather than by naval rules. Treating female personnel as civilians was exactly the problem to be faced just a few years later in the new WRNS as war loomed.[11]

Under the new matron-in-chief, Bertha Martin (1883–1963), a war veteran, the QARNNS moved towards World War II. Her director, Surgeon Vice Admiral Percival Nicholls, in November 1938 announced plans for the new Naval Nursing Reserve. No longer would civilian hospital matrons tell a batch, in effect, that 'you and you, you're volunteered' as in the previous war. Instead the required 400 State Registered Nurses were to apply individually and directly, just as prospective Wrens were to do.

Emergency Medical Service Hospitals and the Civil Nursing Reserve (CNR) were set up by the Ministry of Health early in 1939. They were designed to meet the likely high rate of civilian casualties and consequent need for 100,000 nurses. Immobile VADs were to work within the CNR while mobiles would serve in service hospitals, including naval ones overseas. The Admiralty initially decided that QARNNS sisters should not be afloat on the navy's hospital ships then changed its mind. Women's presence was thought worth the effort for the way it increased men's morale: 'female nursing staffs must be carried in the interests of patients', naval decision-makers agreed.[12]

Although the QARNNS was the navy's female service, and had been working well for 65 years it was not used as a model for the new Women's Royal Naval Service that the navy was establishing. QARNNS members were to *nurse* Wrens (and, of course, men). However, they were not quite to be the WRNS' sister service in this biggest temporary and partial feminisation of naval services ever: World War II. Female auxiliary incomers were about to become 9 per cent of the navy. By contrast, female nursing officers had been fewer than 1 per cent of 'the Andrew'.

CHAPTER 5

Naval Women Win World War II

> *It still seems wonderful that the Royal Navy, the very heart of the British tradition and probably the most conservative institution in the world, should have opened its door to women.*
>
> Vera Laughton Mathews, Director WRNS[1]

'Skipper' Vera Laughton Mathews (1888–1969) made her way from Trafalgar Square tube station through Admiralty Arch, on Wednesday 22 February 1939. '[M]y heart thumping against my ribs ... It is the custom in the Navy to jeer at the Admiralty [as a brake, but] to me the Admiralty seemed holy ground.' It happened to be Guide Thinking Day, which mattered to this lively leader of the Sea Rangers, led as it was by so many guiders and former Wrens.

With Second Sea Lord Admiral Sir Archibald Carter ('to me he seemed like a god') and others in the naval secretary's room, plans for a possible new naval women's auxiliary were discussed with VLM (as she was usually called) and a Mrs Wyatt.[2] VLM had no idea that this was, in fact, her interview for the role of director. On 31 March Mrs Laughton Mathews, aged 49, mother of three school-age children and daughter of the navy's foundational historian, Sir John Knox Laughton, was formally invited to become the nearest thing to a female admiral. Her new life was to begin from 11 April 1939 – and two decades of women's quiet but sturdy naval-minded effort had preceded it.

Fig. 5.1. When the navy opened its doors to women Wrens were 'almost sailors' but did not quite share sailors' vicissitudes, such as carrying heavy kit bags and sleeping in hammocks that bowed their backs. 'Bent to it. Oh yes, just like the men, in hammocks....', Joseph Lee, *Evening News*, 24 November 1942.

Fig. 5.2. Widowed Vera Laughton Mathews, Director WRNS throughout the war, with her children in 1946.

Women move towards the navy again: 1919–39

Naval praise for World War I Wrens had not led to any vestigial WRNS continuing. However, since 1919, ex-Wrens kept the spirit alive with two organisations that needed no naval sanction or funding, and which flourished because of women's networking and some extra-mural naval cooperation. The twin pillars were the Association of Wrens and the Sea Rangers. The AOW, which still continues today, is the veterans' body. Sea Rangers were an adult, sea-focused version of the Girl Guides (of which Dame Katharine Furse had become an international leader). Both the AOW and the Sea Rangers were founded in 1920. Vera, formerly Miss Laughton, had been a wartime trainer of new Wrens. Subsequently, despite marrying and becoming a mother, she had headed the Sea Rangers and also edited the AOW journal, *The Wren*. She was an obvious choice for a future leader.

Women and girls had stayed quietly but firmly sea-minded throughout the interwar years. For example in 1934 HMS *Victory*, named after Nelson's flagship, had a Girl Cadet Corps. Sea Rangers adventure novels for girls, which were a genre like can-do boarding school and early career stories, peaked in the 1930s (see colour plate 10). Public-spirited, and, since 1928, now fully enfranchised women were active in welfare and campaigning organisations such as the National Spinsters' Pension Association. By 1935 women leaders nationwide were planning organisations to assist in the coming war. Two years later defence staff were discussing whether to have a combined services women's organisation or a separate women's corps in each of the services. Throughout 1937 and spring 1938 Dame Katharine, in her capacity as President of the AOW, along with other ex-WRNS officers, repeatedly offered their services to the Admiralty.

Only in summer 1938 did the Admiralty consult Dame Katharine about how many women would be needed in wartime, and begin planning an outline of the possible future organisation. The Board of Admiralty agreed on 25 July 1938 that about 3,000 would be needed.[3] These women would be doing domestic and clerical work, so they would not need expensive training. Even more costs could be saved by employing them as civilians within the Civil Establishment of the navy: they would not need uniforms. Immobiles living at home in ports would save the public purse from having to pay for accommodation.

Mr C. M. Bruce, the retired civil servant brought back to plan the new WRNS, had consulted naval commanders in chief at the various ports as to what types of role the new temporary workers might play. He had also asked Dame Katharine for suggestions as to who might lead the new service (she herself felt she was too old). Instead she suggested team members to do the preliminary organisation. VLM later surmised that the lack of take-up on this was because Admiralty people senior enough to take such decisions were too busy with looming vast problems of war to even think about a women's service: 'What they were looking for was someone on whom they could dump the whole thing and leave her to get on with it' that summer.[4]

After Munich it gets serious

In response to the Munich Agreement of September 1938, a women's naval auxiliary service was agreed on 22 November. Although just 3,000 personnel had been thought necessary at least 15,000 applied for further particulars. Finding a person willing to handle this huge number of responses spurred the Admiralty into action as someone was needed to reply to these applications. Vera Laughton Matthews was summoned over five months later in spring 1939 and asked to work full-time setting up the service then go part-time, keeping a finger on the pulse. Pay would be like all servicewomen's, two-thirds of men's. In her case she was the equivalent of a rear admiral.

Her acceptance letter declared 'I ... will do my utmost to help in building up a Service that will be a worthy auxiliary of the Royal Navy.' She had not then grasped the entire significance of 'the unborn fledgling' being placed within the Admiralty Civil Establishment Branch. Essentially Wrens were to be nested like civilians such as typists, not proper Royal Navy.[5]

She was to be employed full-time for three months to work on this new service-that-might-be-needed. Angela Goodenough (1900–1946) helped as the deputy director WRNS who had been appointed even before her. The Admiralty's chief woman officer, a successor of Edith Bass, Angela is of especial interest in this history. She was, like Olga Franklin, someone who was born into naval life, and first worked in one part of naval services then switched to serving the navy to another way.

It was on Angela and VLM's fact-finding trip to Portsmouth, aboard the venerable training ship *Implacable* 'which I knew so well from Sea Ranger days ... sitting in his [Colonel Wyllie's] cabin that evening that we unexpectedly heard the broadcast announcement of the revival of the Women's Royal Naval Service,' recalled the director.[6]

'With sinking heart'

Finally it had happened. Flurries of media attention followed. Back at the Admiralty Vera and Angela got stuck into the Herculean task. Early applicants asked why they had not been taken up. Still more applied. VLM consulted Dame Katharine's 20-year-old dusty papers 'with a sinking heart', looking for precedents. 'But conditions had so changed there was nothing in the old papers to build on ... her recommendations that the WRNS should be 'a real part of the Navy ... [were] already forfeit. Indeed, the new Service had retrogressed' because it was not under the Second Sea Lord but part of the Civil Establishment department. 'I had no idea at that time what a handicap it would be; I merely knew it was the wrong status.'[7]

Setting up the basic outlines for a small force of immobiles for an undefinable period, the new director shook at her 'temerity' for three nights. Then she decided to start afresh. She wrote her own plan, telling herself she did not have to be perfect nor fill Dame Katharine's shoes. Key officers were selected: 'they would be the great arteries of the service to come'. Uniforms caused no controversy. They were just 'a modernised version of the 1918 uniform' and braid was again blue, not gold. Yet even as late as July 1939 'the Admiralty were still oblivious ... that there was a W.R.N.S.', VLM bewailed.[8]

At that pre-war stage VLM's team were officially required to just prepare for 'a Service which would work on voluntary lines in peacetime' with few staff and no training to be done. However the director started 'secretly and guiltily' making plans and interviewing potential mobiles in case war came. This indomitable newcomer, nicknamed Tugboat Annie because she was big and unafraid to argue, had very little contact with her superiors all this time. 'I never even knew if I was doing what was required of me.' At the Admiralty, 'the root of the matter was that we were dealing with [civilian] people who were not concerned with the detailed manning problems of the Navy, and had no idea of how urgently and how soon the W.R.N.S. would be needed.'[9]

The war begins: 1939

Finally, the arbitrating axe fell at 11am on Sunday 3 September 1939. VLM was at home reading the newspapers in bed before church. Angela was on duty. When 11 o'clock struck in the First Lord's Admiralty office, she was bowed to and told: 'Miss Goodenough, I have the honour to inform you that we are at war.' How would this hastily designed new women's naval corps cope?[10]

Firstly, very competent senior officers were found to administer the well-thought-out but still flexible new machine. Most were in the mould of the leader. Just as Katharine Furse's key officers had been VADs whom she trusted, so initial World War II pillars were officers who had been in the WRNS before, or were inspired by sisterhood in the women's rights struggle, Girl Guides and Sea Rangers. For example Chief Officer Dorothy McKenzie had been a Girl Guide Commissioner. Second Officer Betty Archdale was the daughter of VLM's friend from suffragette journalism Helen Archdale, and her forebears had backed women's university education. Fervently (and tactically) these leading women embraced traditional naval values.

WRNS officers began their training at Greenwich Naval College. VLM had seen how WRNS officer training was physically marginalised in the previous war, in a women-only suburban house. This time around they were housed with elite males in the august institution that had been at the heart of naval induction since 1877. On the first night VLM addressed people in what was to become her haven. It was 'surely the first speech ever made by a woman in the Painted Hall' where Nelson's body had once lain in state. She thanked Admiral President of the College, Charles Kennedy-Purvis, for being such 'a broadminded man ... who could welcome women into such a sanctuary of naval officers of naval officers without thinking that the world was coming to an end.' He admitted the inclusion was going against the traditional naval grain but 'I've always been a bit of a Bolshie.' Being proud of making bold innovations was to be one of the ways men handled the inclusion of women.[11]

Secondly, there were so many applicants for so few places that the *crème de la crème* could be selected. In autumn 1939 the growing HQ team asked some of the thousands of waiting applicants to come forward. It was pell-mell, because there never was a Phoney War for the navy: action was immediate as the Battle of the Atlantic began, with naval ships escorting merchant convoys to combat the German U-boat menace. Would-be Wrens flocked in – or tried to – despite the organisation not being quite ready for such an influx. As the title of a compilation of Wrens' memoirs much later made clear, some women 'only joined for the hat' unlike the less stylish women's auxiliaries.[12]

Round pegs are readied for a range of holes

Applicants were enormously diverse: young and old, single and married, navy-minded and shoresiders, well-travelled ex-pats or stay-at-home innocents. Some had silver spoons in their mouths and some had quickly eradicated nits. Prime Minister Winston Churchill's daughters had influential strings that they tried to pull, as did some Sea Rangers. They were almost invariably white British nationals, although some had grown up overseas, such as the daughters of planters in the empire's colonies.

Regulations stipulated that applicants had to have one British parent. Somehow this appears to have become muddled with whiteness and loyalty to the crown. Sylvia Jensen, the daughter of a Danish father, made a fuss about being rejected. The response by VLM, whose mother was Spanish, makes clear that although formally the Admiralty said it would investigate individual cases, in fact dealing with such anomalies took up valuable time. As the WRNS already had sufficient applicants, it made sense to sidestep such cases. It was more straightforward to take on the women whom sailors joked were 'Daddy's an Admiral' types. Indeed, 49 per cent of WRNS officers initially were closely related to naval men. All chose this service over any other (unlike the more reluctant women put in the army's Auxiliary Territorial Service, the WAAC's successor).[13]

Interviews and entry procedures were set up. 'Officer material' women had their talents spotted and were marked out for elevation. Room was found. Hotels, mansions and boarding houses were requisitioned for what came to be called Wrenneries. Sometimes home was an icy Nissen hut hastily erected in the back of beyond, which Wrens made homely, for example by polishing black Pitchmastic floors with shoe polish bought with their precious ration coupons. Socially and physically spaces were devised in existing offices. In workplaces what were seen as crucial facilities – ladies' toilets with cubicles, rather than urinals – were created. Uniform manufacturers worked flat-out to produce clothing including that navy blue coat and skirt, with black tie and white shirt, which Churchill approved as 'practical and dignified', or even the right sort of apron. Many under-equipped ratings just wore a WRNS armband over their civilian cardigans in those initial winter months.[14]

'Jenny Wrens' completed two weeks' training on entry, initially in ports, later at central depots. It was a version of boot camp involving learning how to deal with gas attacks, keep fit, march, scrub stone steps, absorb naval lore and behave appropriately. This was their first encounter with naval language: a building was a ship and outside was ashore. A floor was a deck; a toilet was a head. Officers were 'Ma'ams' not 'Madams.'

At the end the 'newly feathered' were able to choose what they wanted to do, within limits, and had to pass a test as to their suitability for that role. Demand for domestic Wrens, especially cooks and stewards, was even harder to meet than in the previous war, as Hollywood had raised many women's expectations and women had become too proud to be skivvies. Then, fledged, they were sent out the establishments which had already made specific requests for this or that sort of Wren.

At that stage there were two categories of work: specialised (such as cooks, cypherers, drivers) and general (which included stewards, maids, messengers.) Later there were four branches: domestic, clerical and supply, technical and communications. The key needs were to fit these round pegs into square holes (as was again said) as soon as possible; arrange somewhere acceptable for them to live and work; and make sure they looked like part of this team. Newcomers increasingly entered as mobiles, in search of adventure – preferably sea-related. The demand was too great for Wrens to remain immobiles as initially envisaged. Administrating (drafting) was easier if you could just put a woman where she was needed.

Fledglings start flying high and wide: 1940–1

Hard-pressed managers had started seeing the unexpectedly impressive things these hastily imported 'Jennies' could be asked to do, for example, women replaced men entirely as the much envied, leather-jacketed Triumph-motorbike-mounted despatch riders at the Admiralty. From January 1940 the director pushed through schemes for specialist training. Some were put on WRNS courses taught by the usual civilian women in local colleges. Others were trained, and trained to become trainers, on naval premises by men. Teleprinter operators, for instance, were taught at the Admiralty by naval officers.

In May 1940 Germany attacked France and the Low Countries. The Allies had to evacuate. From 23 May to 4 June during the Dunkirk evacuation Wrens were involved in many roles, including as coders in Portsmouth encrypting directives about what the rescue ships should be doing. Few Wrens were based in the small Dover Command area (where the Dunkirk evacuees landed) as Table 5.1 shows. However, they were proportionate. Everyone available worked as motor transport drivers, communications staff and supply ratings who kitted the rescued men. For nine days they were improvising and organising flat-out, providing welcoming food and makeshift bunks for fatigued men. Women were doing the supportive work that officers' wives like Agnes Weston's helpers would have done 60 years earlier. They did so this time as nigh on insiders. 'Dunkirk was a milestone in our life as a naval establishment ... We were almost, not quite, real Navy. Gone were those happy, crazy days of plain-clothes Wrens when the war was far away and ... we could still send the messenger out to buy bars of chocolate,' as Ramsgate's Chief Wren Powell said.[15]

Table 5.1. **Numbers of WRNS members by year and area in World War II**[16]

LOCATION	Jan 1941	Dec 1942	June 1944	June 1945	Dec 1945
Portsmouth	2,739	8,666	16,434	13,937	7,653
Western Approaches	2,648	9,663	15,583	17,242	n/a
Nore	2,417	9,981	18,891	15,687	11,314
Rosyth	2,553	4,264	6,841	7,454	6,252
Dover	296	507	1,278	805	n/a
Plymouth	–	4,845	5,014	7,307	6,769
Orkney & Shetland	–	459	1,370	1,325	n/a
Overseas	0	952	n/a	5,718	4,437
TOTALS	10,653	39,337	More than 65,411	69,475	More than 36,425

New sorts of jobs and dangers

New courses began, including for supply ratings learning about how to kit the navy. Despite the need for more hands, the Admiralty decided all Wrens should be on two weeks' probation initially. It was a way of avoiding the expense of taking on people who proved unsuitable or quickly left. Some 18 new types of ratings' work were added to the first nine from 1940, and then another 15 in 1941. The number eventually rose to 125.

This year was significant because women took on non-traditional jobs that brought them much mobility. Such trail-blazers included

Fig. 5.3. Ruins of the bombed Wrennery in Queen's Road, Great Yarmouth, 18 March 1943.

maintenance ratings, who learned on the job but became so good that naval officers fair-mindedly pressed for some to become 'Maintenance Qualified' with specialised pay. Wrens were slotted into many new situations that were suggested by the navy, not initiated by the WRNS. Varying degrees of cordiality greeted them as they freed men for horrors at sea or arrived with irritatingly inadequate training. Their enthusiasm, and willingness to shoulder burdens fairly, quickly mitigated this.

Now in all but the most intransigent situations they were working against an escalating background of danger. The Battle of Britain waged from 10 July to 31 October 1940 and the Blitz lasted from September 1940 to May 1941. Wrens' lives – especially in Portsmouth, Plymouth, Bristol and London – were coloured by bomb-dodging, sirens wailing and their hostels and offices being destroyed. Nazi Germany's Luftwaffe was intent on invasion, which truly felt imminent as the air war intensified. Women and civilians were always aware, as Vera Laughton Mathews reflected, that however traumatised their lives, 'it was a soft life compared with the lads up there' – those in the British fighter planes whose radios women would soon be servicing.[17]

Beyond Britain's walls

Such cushioning for women was changing slightly as the need grew for Wrens to do what had been unthinkable: fight this now very apparent enemy by serving overseas, or indeed – if they were over 21 – serving anywhere where the navy pleased. Over 4,000 were ready to leave UK shores. Betty Archdale headed the first overseas draft in January 1941. Initially Wrens went to Singapore, the crucial home of the Eastern Fleet. The second batch, comprising eight cypher officers and 12 Chief Wren special wireless telegraphic ratings, were sent to Gibraltar in August 1941. Tragically their ship, the *Aguila* was torpedoed and all the women died when it, and its rescue ship too, were sunk. Other Wrens quickly volunteered and were accepted, because the need for staff was so great. WRNS members were permitted to travel on armed naval ships after that. Some carried out midshipman

Fig. 5.4. Probably women's most daring image of the war: 'Wrens climb from the quarter boom, "Thirty seconds from deck to deck", Scotland 1943', by Lee Miller.

duties on a destroyer. WRNS units were also set up in Washington and other places as needs expanded in 1942 and women sailed despite the U-boat wolf-packs' effectiveness. A third batch was headed for Alexandria but en route Commander in Chief Mediterranean Fleet Admiral Sir Andrew Cunningham made half of them return home because he thought 'women could not stand up to the rigours of a war zone'. However, as he admitted after seeing many Wrens in Alexandria and the Middle East later, he had been wrong: 'they could and did'.[18]

Some Wrens took to British coastal waters in small boats from October 1941. These much-envied boats crew Wrens ferried naval men from shore to moored ship, as did Stoker Rozelle Raynes for real and Deborah Kerr in the movie *Perfect Strangers*. Never numbering more than 575 at their peak, they developed a tough culture, taking delight in 'drinking tea from a bucket in a broken cup to the accompaniment of unmaidenly language' and being able speedily to climb up huge ships. The role was so popular that petty officers gave up their status for the chance to be boats crew Wrens. However, initially at Dartmouth, said Florence Hayes, one of the first 12, 'we were not made welcome'. Typing and cooking were more acceptable activities.[19]

A servicewoman's place

Should a servicewoman have the same status as a serviceman? In 1941 an administrative conflict blew up over the question of inclusion under the Naval Discipline Act. VLM, like Dame Katharine, wanted it. Incorporation was not about the practical matter of how Wrens would be punished. Rather, she said, 'the point at issue should be *what is the proper legal status for a Women's Service*. I have always thought it should be an integral part of the Royal Navy and that it is wrong for its members to be legally civilians' [author's italics]. The War Office wanted to put all the Women's Services, including the QARNNS, under the Act, as some army women moved to semi-combatant status, such as gun site teams.

However, Admiral Charles Little, the Second Sea Lord, thought inclusion in the NDA was simply not needed as the WRNS was 'the smallest Service with the fewest difficulties'. VLM politely agreed that 'the disciplinary position in the WRNS did not necessitate any changes in status': Wrens were indeed well-behaved generally. The point was about belonging and equality, she explained. However 'the shadow of the court-martial loomed large in the minds of the tender-hearted naval officers who shrank from the painful thought of a little Wren in the dock.'

There was no shifting. This pivotal anomaly was to rumble on for over 30 more years: 'the only major matter of policy for the WRNS on which the Admiralty did not take my advice', thought the director, as she faced all the other less foundational challenges in helping the navy win the war.[20]

Adventuring: Orkney, Italy and more: 1942–3

> Gather round while I tell you a story
> of a lass who develop a yen
> for a life of adventure
> she signed her indenture
> joining up as an overseas Wren.[21]

So wrote an anonymous member of that growing breed in WRNS history, women who travelled abroad (a thousand-fold increase on the tiny number of their World War I counterparts). As the campaign in North Africa built up throughout 1942 Wrens were sent out East to work in naval units in a range of roles including cyphering, administrative duties and secretarial work.

Senior Wrens were also battling internally with the Admiralty to ensure the WRNS was really part of the navy. From 1939 the WRNS had worked frustratedly at the problem that they were organisationally positioned as part of the Civil Establishment. It reflected the way of thinking that 'Jennies are civilian ladies', almost visitors, which lay behind the idea that it was wrong to count them as part of the military by putting them under the Naval Discipline Act.

After two years' battling, in 1942 VLM won, partly because stripe-conscious naval men's confusion about equivalent ranks was

Fig. 5.5. Protecting females from marauders: Wrens at the Aviary camp on the road to Cairo.

inhibiting co-operation with females. The 'C.E... . surely let us go without a tear', she celebrated. At last the WRNS was, administratively, among the naval departments, 'which was what it always should have been.' WRNS members were also enjoying an updated image: society portraitist Cecil Beaton photographed them in the extremely stylish new WRNS uniform that year, which meant they could feel even more proud.[22]

However, the navy was still grappling with the problem of where Wrens should be on the spectrum between protected lady and brother-warrior. Combatant status became more and more a grey area as war hit civilian women. After Alexandria had to be evacuated in June 1942 the Admiralty decided its policy was that Wrens 'should not be sent to stations where there was considered the possibility of their falling into enemy hands'. However, 'in the event of things going wrong, women should remain at the post of duty in circumstances where this would be expected of men.'[23]

Any hands, including Wrens', were needed overseas as war escalated. The USA joined the Allies after Japan's pivotal assault: the bombing of Pearl Harbor. Malta was under siege at Christmas 1941 and Singapore fell in February 1942. These were such serious losses that from March the National Service Act (2) insisted all unmarried women between 21 and 31 had to do war work. At times this brought bottlenecks which led to the expansion of WRNS premises, including decamping from Greenwich. However careful selection continued: the right sort of women had to be taken on, including for the crucial but often boring code-breaking work at Bletchley Park and Bombe outstations in Eastcote and Stanmore, where Wrens were about a fifth of the personnel.[24]

Overseas service

Mobile Wrens, not local female civilians, were also in units throughout the Mediterranean where they supported the preparations for November 1942's Operation Torch. In early 1943 there were two

Fig. 5.6. Second Officer Kalyani Sen visits Rosyth, with Chief Officer Margaret L. Cooper, Deputy Director of the Women's Royal Indian Naval Service (WRINS) in June 1945. The WRINS began in 1944.

main clusters of action that determined Wrens' location. The Allies invaded Sicily from North Africa as a way north via occupied Italy. Wrens were allowed in Italy when it became safe. On the other front the forces were building up for the invasion from England's south coast of occupied Normandy. This plan meant Wrens were moved to the south coast to support what would be an enormous movement of ships, taking personnel and equipment across the Channel.

More hands were increasingly needed, globally and at home. Women's naval services like the WRNS began in South Africa, as they had in Canada and Australia the year before, and in the Netherlands and India in 1944. (The US equivalent, WAVES, begun in 1942, did not really use the British WRNS model. Also VLM did not approve of its exclusion of non-graduates, women with children under 16, or those who could not be completely mobile.)[25]

Fig. 5.7. Pioneering WRNS air mechanics at the WRNS-only technical training establishment Mill Meece, Staffordshire, September 1943. Air Mech (A) Peggie Morris (later Carmichael), who kindly loaded this photograph, said when asked if was she the star sitting on the plane, 'I wish I was'. Instead she is far left on the third row.

New technical windows open

The most 'superior' group of Wrens 'and they had every air of knowing it ... in boiler suits [and] a smart sailor cap' were the radio mechanics like Win Cluny. Her war included making test flights in Barracudas and Fairey Swordfishes. From 1942 they did nine months' training in maths, physics and electronics, then three hard months at Warrington's HMS *Ariel*, training alongside men before moving to naval air stations. Win later made the point made by so many Wrens when explaining matters to modern listeners: that their male classmates were usually pals, not rivals, not least because traditional pink and blue ways of behaving continued.

> I have to say that although we lived close together, there was no harassment of any kind. This may be unbelievable by today's standards, but true all the same. We sewed the men's badges on, we repaired their pullovers, and they would give us their rum rations when we had colds.[26]

In the UK more Wrens trained in this year, 1943, that ever before: 4,000. Ratings' centralised training facilities expanded rapidly, at Mill Hill (which took 900), Tullichewan Castle (650, in huts) as well as the original Westfield College in Hampstead (housing 450). Before that new Wrens were trained and held in the local training and drafting depots in each Command. Fledged Wrens had more chance of serving in unfamiliar locations now, if they were doing the right kind of work, such as communications. Destinations included Orkney, where numbers were to treble. The types of possible jobs now numbered 53. They included women working in meteorology and aeroplane repair at the naval air service stations, just as their port-based sisters were now working on torpedoes.[27]

Overseas and on the sea

In March 1943 one of the 14 female MPs, Thelma Cazalet-Keir (1899–1989), in parliament asked about the WRNS' position. Richard

Pilkington, the Civil Lord of Admiralty, was able to proudly tell the Commons that 'of the existing number of Wren officers two-thirds are doing non-administrative work, which means that they have, in fact, relieved naval officers.' As there were over 700 WRNS officers at that point, it appears that around 460 naval officers had been freed to sail.[28]

Could not WRNS serve on ships too?, he was asked. 'If, when and where it is found practicable to employ Wrens that will certainly be done,' he replied. It turned out to be practicable on the converted passenger liners which were sailing as troopships. Relatively luxurious vessels such as the *Franconia* had plenty of women's bathrooms, plus separate sleeping spaces which could be guarded at night. At least 30 Wrens served at any one time in the much sought-after roles as cypherers and coders, including handling messages for the top brass being taken to the Quebec and Tehran conferences of Allied leaders. However, unchaperoned Wrens, including boarding officers, tended to visit naval ships only briefly. All-male enclaves were no-go zones for ladies.[29]

Fig. 5.8. WRNS boarding officer in unwise but regulation summer gear, climbing an unknown ship to deliver confidential information, 1943.

Allied successes meant even more Wrens went overseas in 1943 and 1944, including to India and Ceylon, Africa, Palestine and the Persian Gulf. The decisive defeat of the Axis powers in North Africa in May 1943 had created a new climate of optimism and determination. Now the focus was on Sicily and Italy. Cairo Wrens typed the secret invasion plans and replaced the male headquarters staff. Novelist Barbara Pym enjoyed the Versailles-like Caserta Palace headquarters near Naples. The first draft of Wrens since 1919 went out to Malta now that the siege had been lifted.

Their director affirmed that at this point, 'The WRNS was completely absorbed in the naval pattern; there was no longer any doubt as to how they would do or how they should be treated. They fell into place and were taken for granted.' In the midst of war few men had time to cavil at their essential colleagues, rather than appreciate them. A senior naval officer at Greenock admired Wrens for not only absorbing naval tradition but also creating their own. Some were in awe of how stalwart these young female newcomers were, even when torpedoed. However, as the WRNS director pointed out, 'even the best men find it difficult to expect the same high standard of duty from women'. Sometimes shrewd Wrens used men's attitudes towards women to get their own way, for example by turning on tears or sending their prettiest blonde colleague to wrest a favour on their behalf.[30]

From D-Day to Hiroshima: 1944–5

Wrens contributed in larger numbers than ever before as the war was reaching its climax in 1944 with the escalation of the war in the Pacific and the great organisation of the D-Day landings. Every Wren who could be spared was drafted to free men for the sea. Portsmouth was an especial focus. Supply Wrens there substituted for men by 100 per cent. The victualling stores employed 70 per cent Wrens, not 55 per cent as had earlier been expected. Many Wrens handled top-secret information about the invasion, scotching the myth that women were dangerous gossips who jeopardised security.[31]

1. Hannah Snell, cross-dressed marine, c. 1750.

2. Women nursing the wounded during the Battle of Trafalgar, 1805. Detail from Daniel Maclise, *The Death of Nelson*, 1859–64.

3. Women were part of waterfront life and traded goods, including sex, with seagoers. *Portsmouth Point*, etching by Thomas Rowlandson, 1811.

4. Sex industry workers and alcohol were rowed out to moored ships. The women sometimes worked and partied aboard for several days: *Exporting Cattle not Insurable*, by William Elmes, printed by Thomas Tegg, 1813.

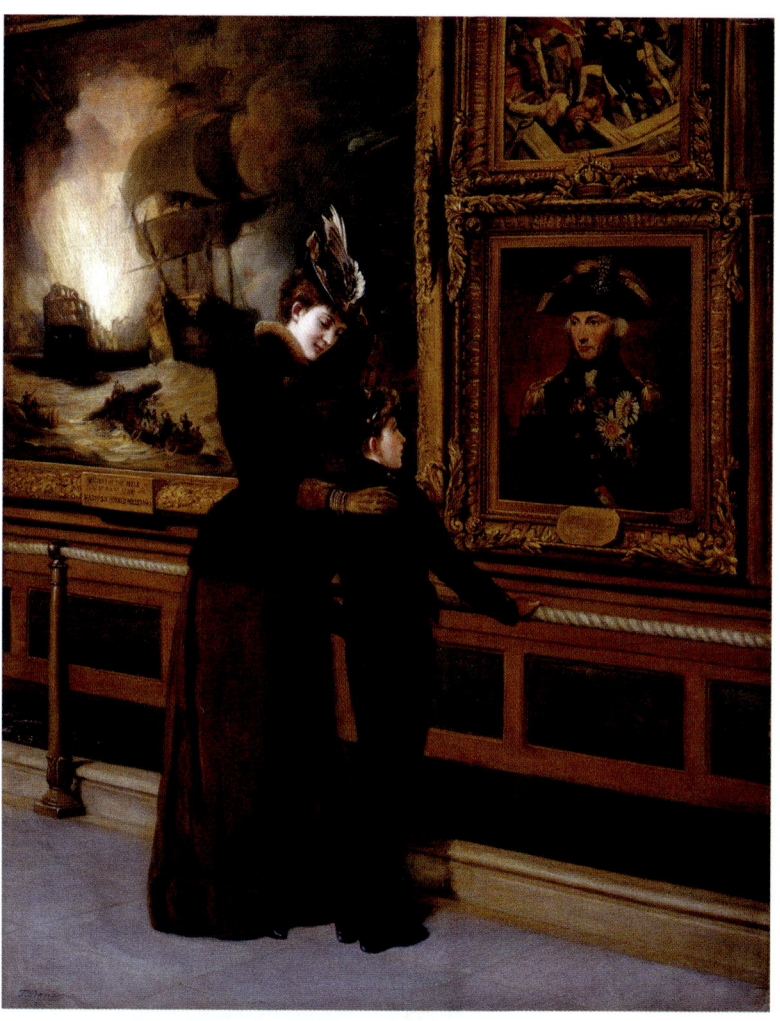

5. Women and men alike joined in the admiration of the nation's greatest naval hero, Nelson: *England's Pride and Glory*, by Thomas Davidson, 1894.

6. A sailor takes his girlfriend to pay homage to his hero. Postcard, undated but *c.* 1900.

7. World War I WRNS recruiting poster by Joyce Dennys, 1917.

"MY GAWD! AND TO THINK I JOINED THE NAVY BECAUSE THE WIFE MADE ME SCRUB THE FRONT DOOR-STEPS!"

8. Decorative Wrens at the waterside: *WRNS Officer and Ratings: Boat-cleaning at the Coastal Motor Boat Base, Haslar Creek, Portsmouth*, by A. D. M'Cormick, 1919.

9. On ships men and boys did 'women's work'. Postcard, undated.

10. Girls in novels and reality learned about the sea as Sea Rangers and Girls' Nautical Training Corps members, sometimes as a prelude to joining the WRNS or reserves. Detail from P. B. Hickling's cover of *Sea Rangers at Sloo*, Blackie & Sons, 1948.

11. World War II recruiting poster, undated.

12. Recruiting poster of the 1960s inviting Wrens to serve 'with', not 'in', the Royal Navy.

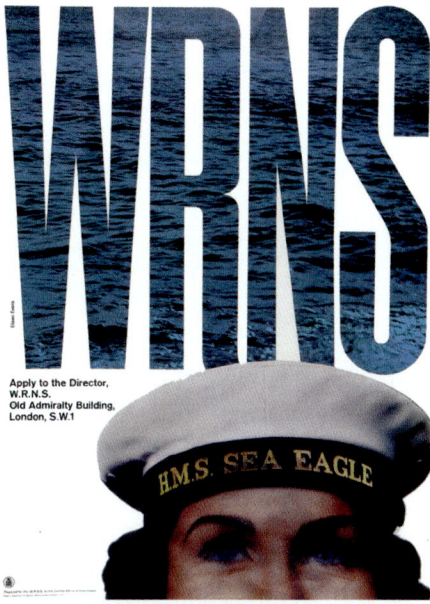

13. Leading Wren Margaret Young, the WRNS' only female blacksmith in World War II. She is working here as a moulder's mate.

14. Leading Wrens on a survival course at HMS *Dryad*, 1960s.

15. WRNS stewards give finishing touches to the dining tables at RNAS Culdrose, Helston, Cornwall, 1985.

16. Cleaning materials being given to a Wren, probably by a Wren steward, 1970s.

17. Naval women undergo Tarzan assault course at Royal Marines Commando Training Centre, Lympstone, Devon, 1996.

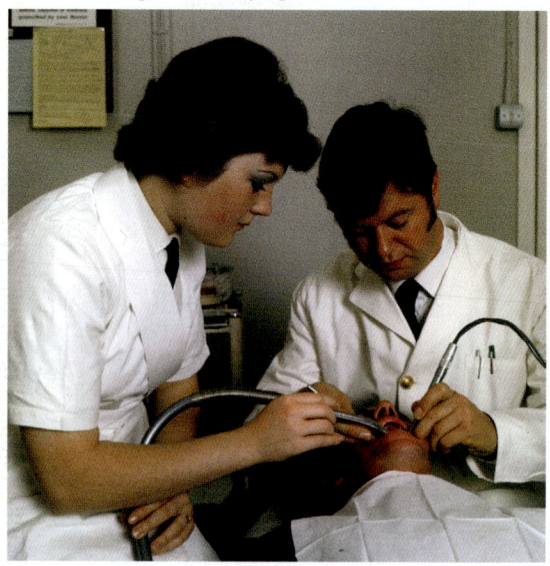

18. One of the many Wren dental surgery assistants playing a key role in the delivery of dental services, 1970s. Dental surgeons were rarely females at this point.

19. Naval women on the firefighting course which all personnel have to undergo, 2001.

20. Marine engineering artificer apprentice Liz Meggit using a pillar drill at HMS *Sultan*, in 1993.

21. Leading Steward Teisha Freckleton on HMS *Somerset* takes part in a refuelling at sea operation with a Royal Fleet Auxiliary ship *Fort Victoria*, 2001.

22. The Royal Navy's leading women. Commodore (then Captain) Inga Kennedy (left) and Captain (then Commander) Ellie Ablett, 2013, Portsmouth.

23. Former navy LGBT activist Mandy McBain (left) and Sherry Conway, a serving RAF squadron leader critical care nurse, enjoy a mainly female guard of honour after their wedding in April 2016.

24. Combined Services co-operation on HMS *Illustrious*'s sickbay in a Role 2 Afloat training exercise, 2012.

25. Women and the Royal Navy exhibition, National Maritime Museum, 2017.

26. Sailor relaxing by her ship: unnamed naval woman from HMS *Sheffield*.

27. Royal Fleet Auxiliary CDT(X) Laura Frudd taking a reading with a sextant on the bridge wing of RFA *Fort Victoria*, 2010.

Most Wrens were in offices, not on boats or in ships, when the long-awaited landing on what was coded as 'the Far Shore' began on 6 June. For weeks all leave had been suspended. Working hours were lengthened. Security was tightened yet further. The Wrens learned new codes. Other services and even Americans became fleetingly part of the team: typist Ginger Thomas was loaned to the army's General Morgan, the original planner of Operation Overlord. She enjoyed the way he always addressed her as 'sailor'. The bated-breath work environment was stressful – but she found it exciting too.[32]

Then, overnight, all the vessels were gone. Feeling left behind, anxious and proud, some Wrens watched the stunningly empty harbour through windows. They felt such aching concern, and some envy, for their male colleagues as well as the brothers, boyfriends, husbands and fathers who were involved in the landings. Three-quarters of the communication staff left that day were women (1,088 women by contrast to 252 men). Some boats crew Wrens were on small vessels flying the kite balloons and acting as pilots taking smaller ships across the Channel.[33]

When the ships returned from Normandy, WRNS techies fixed the damaged ones. Cooks prepared food for men on fast turnarounds. Elsie Horton was working in the signals distribution office in Fort Southwick's underground complex. She said that, amazingly, after a few weeks, life settled into a routine of vessels and planes to-ing and fro-ing to France. The struggle there went on for nearly another year.[34]

Of the naval women's services it was the QARNNS who were first to cross to Normandy. A little later, on Friday 15 August, the first party of Wrens went over, to Courseulles-sur-Mer, Normandy. The picture on the cover of this book shows Wrens like these as jaunty victors, on the day that the invasion of Provence also happened to be beginning. These Wrens were followed shortly after by the first party to Arromanches. Then more, including teleprinter operator Laura Ashley (as she became) went to Granville, then on to Paris, then Brussels. Some were in liberated Europe for many educational – and euphoric – months. The WRNS, at peak membership that autumn, was able to send more women overseas. Others were switched in batches, say from Ceylon to Sydney, as new naval needs became imperative and as trust in their ability to deliver – in some permitted roles – was now beyond question.[35]

Handling victory and counting the cost

Wrens' focus in 1945 was both on winning the war in France and the Pacific, and wondering about post-war life. Demobilisation had begun in March 1945 – married women first. It stepped up as Wrens in some jobs were told their categories were redundant. Many wanted to stay on, as they had in the previous war. As now-expert supporters of naval operations Wrens were still needed, for example in Kandy at SEAC (South East Asia Command). There the focus was still on victory over Japan, and then on the military governing of the now-anti-colonialist countries such as Burma, Malaya, Singapore, British Borneo, Sarawak and Sumatra, Indochina and Indonesia. Some Wrens were allowed to apply for extended service. In the UK it was not too late for young women to join: new, short-term opportunities were available, not least as the return home of men overseas was slowed down by POWs having priority.

The end of the war in Europe was marked in the courtyard of Queen Anne's Mansions on Tuesday 8 May 1945. Second Sea Lord Admiral Sir Algernon Willis addressed WRNS, navy and QARNNS in a thanksgiving service. Later that day the Admiralty lauded the director, now *Dame* Vera, for the part Wrens had played 'in support of the Fleet and in the Naval Commands ... they have shared the burdens and upheld the traditions of the naval service.'

Air mechanic Peggy Morris found 'the girls were not allowed in pubs', so they danced at Edinburgh Castle and devoured dried egg and chips in the NAAFI. Down by the sea in Dartmouth, Second Officer Patricia Thornycroft could not find the right mood to celebrate, because she had lost two brothers, a fiancé and many friends. Adrenaline was overcome by war-weariness. Instead she greatly enhanced her popularity by offering to take over all possible duties in the operations office while others went out to celebrate.[36]

July brought the war's end after the USA bombed Japan. The formal conclusion came on 15 August. An unknown WRNS rating at Kuruengala, Malaya, typed out the Allied terms of acceptance of the Japanese surrender. Wrens worldwide on 2 September celebrated with rum on VJ Day. Orders were to 'splice the main brace', meaning officially issue extra celebratory rum or grog (diluted rum). This was on top of the rum tot routinely issued every day at 11am, until 1970. Wrens normally got a cash allowance in lieu but this time they were allowed to take their tot of rum (which was usually watered down for boys and women).

Although hostilities ended, work had not. Many Wrens were needed in post-war Germany, including as teleprinter operators. Wrens wanted to carry on with that shared shouldering of the navy's burdens, although some were also relieved by the end of being bound to self-less duty. A telling 10 per cent of ratings and 26 per cent of officers waived any priority rights for immediate demob (for example, being married actually entitled them to early emancipation from service). They waited until all the other people in their group were released too. Strong members cried on being told they were to be 'disowned' in effect. These sisters in arms had enjoyed new freedoms, exceptional mobility, camaraderie and a proud sense of having contributed. The Royal Navy and the WRNS communities (the two were not necessarily synonymous) had become their families, and not necessarily in an institutionalising kind of way. The life had brought many fringe benefits. For Patricia Thornycroft, the harbour view from her 'cabin' in a Dartmouth cottage had given her something she could not explain. She thought it strengthened 'my belief that goodness must prevail, and [it] gave me the courage to return to such a shattered world.'[37]

The fatalities caused by 'freeing a man for the Fleet' were relatively few. In total 303 members of the WRNS had died. The fallen are recorded in the WRNS Book of Remembrance which, in 1984, the director Patricia Swallow carried to St Mary Le Strand church from Greenwich; her late mother's name was one of those inside it. They are still commemorated every year by the Association of Wrens. Many less serious losses had long-term repercussions too; Peggy Morris was injured in a hangar but did not know she was entitled to compensation: 'No-one mentioned it when I came out', and she was later involved in an MoD appeal to secure it.[38]

Honouring Jenny

In all, 116 awards were made to some of the 100,000 wartime WRNS. Others were recognised for being in a particular service or campaign. Indeed some were decorated by the country in which they had served. The USA gave First Officer Eileen Gifford Trubody a Bronze Star for her SEAC work. Formal British recognition sometimes did not happen, so one of the frequently asked questions on the WRNS Benevolent Trust website is 'How do I apply for a UK Armed Forces Veteran's Badge or Campaign medal?' Today heroine-seeking media still flock to meet driver Beth Booth, who in 1944 was awarded a British Empire Medal for bravery. The citation declared she had 'helped drag a Fleet Air Arm observer away from the wreckage of his crashed Swordfish biplane, while explosions inside the aircraft scattered burning debris all around them.'[39]

Oddly few awards were given. In 1943 Prime Minister Winston Churchill had told parliament 'There will be no sex distinction where the conditions [for giving awards] are satisfied.' However the honours

Fig. 5.9. Wartime service meant Wrens could now be boys' role models: Frank Reynolds' cartoon from 17 January 1945.

system was poor at recognising women and support work. Four decades later a House of Commons Select Committee still found 'race and gender can determine whether (and what kind of) an honour is received'. Also women in that war were, protectively, seldom allowed into positions where they could be the right sort of brave. Sometimes recognising one woman's valour would have meant revealing that many women with her had been at risk too, potentially triggering public outcry. It was also, more puzzlingly, imagined that recognising women's feats would somehow detract from the significance of men's brave sacrifices.[40]

WRNS members' awards process was additionally hindered by tardiness and allocation quotas. The director remarked with astonishing mildness, for her, that 'it was a pity recommendations for awards to the W.R.N.S. did not start earlier'. Also each year only a limited number of awards were allowed. So the delay in starting meant that 'the end of the war found many more recommended than could be honoured'. An unknown number of deserving candidates did not get the recognition they merited.[41]

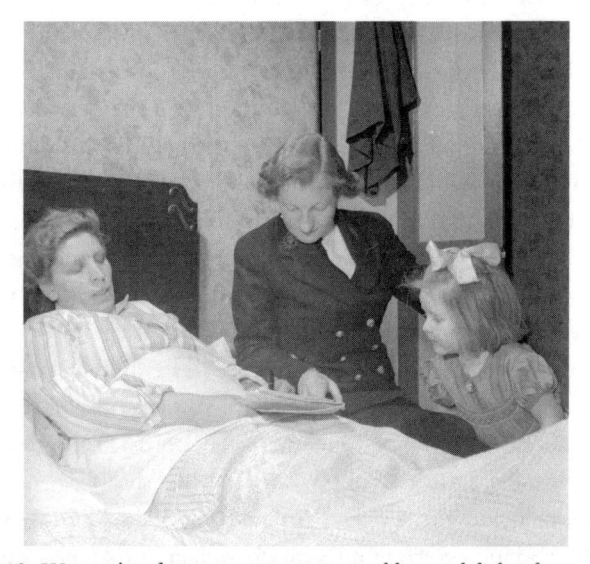

Fig. 5.10. Women's valour was not recognised by medals but by practical support. Chief Wren Nye, Naval Family Welfare Service, arranges for children to be cared for until the poorly sailor's wife can resume her family duties.

Moving on to Civvy Street

Peace brought even more wedding bells, although an unknown number of Wrens had wed too in wartime. Often they borrowed one of the trove of aristocrats' donated gowns Polly Cartland assembled for the purpose. Of the 30 WRNS members sent to the Far East with Betty Archdale, 11 had wed quickly, six to navy and Fleet Air Arm men. Other Wrens had held off from marrying in wartime but now felt they could relinquish their dedication to service and feel confident that they would not be quickly widowed. Leading steward Lois Price walked up the aisle on VJ Day. Wedding photographs in newspapers show a high number of husbands were naval officers. Molly Shakepear's marriage to the submarine ace for whom she had been secretary was attend by five admirals; one declared her war record was 'almost as distinguished' as her husband's.[42]

Former WRNS press officer, and then radio personality Nancy Spain felt able to come out as a lesbian to her intimates and live circumspectly with the female partner of her choice, Joan/Jonnie Werner who had been a former WRNS driver. In fact almost no record of wartime Wrens' same-sex relationships exists despite the statistical likelihood of affection deepening into more. The main, slight story is Cynthia Gilbert's diary of her feelings for Lilian, a local woman in Alexandria (and her friendly family). 'I knew we just adored each other and always would, ours would be one of those friendships that never ended.' Many non-sexual female friendships did indeed never end. Numerous Wrens became the favourite aunties and godmothers of their wartime friends' children. Camaraderie was all the more appreciated as post-war civilian life proved far less matey.[43]

What next, work wise? 'Some of you will be quite certain the one thing you want to do is get back to where you left off before the war', thought one early demobbed cinema projectionist. Others struggled with the mundane after living a wartime life that was 'much more varied, more colourful, richer than anything we had known before'. Many who had joined straight from school had known no other work. Finding jobs for so many newly released personnel is always a feat. Mary Talbot, who was to become a very ground-breaking Director

WRNS much later, was one of the WRNS education and resettlement officers helping people make the transition. It was hard for women whose expectations turned out to have been rather fruitlessly raised, especially if seeking mechanical work. Air mech Peggy Morris used her skills as Singer's first roving sewing machine 'repair man'. 'The school teachers loved it', because she showed them they could understand the technology and solve minor faults by themselves.[44]

Many went home and looked after shattered households. Some women 'remained steadfastly reticent' about their wartime exploits. Others, acting with a newly learned sense of their own power, drastically changed course. Torpedoed Wren Freda Bonner retrained as a doctor: 'Was it the memory of the naval doctor swimming from raft to raft [helping full out for two days before he died] that led me to make this choice?' she asked herself. Dorothy Runnicles, still only 20, went on to university from the remote Scottish RNAS Fearn, 'run almost entirely by women ... We had a chief officer woman, all the mechanics were women' to another women's world. At Bedford College for Ladies she joined the university women's boat club. Hating the war 'because it was so awful, a ridiculous slaughter of people, I joined the Peace Pledge Union.' She later demonstrated at Aldermaston and Greenham Common.[45]

Some of the luckiest Wrens went on to work at sea, as lady assistant pursers on commercial liners. WRNS training had made many ideal employees for a variety of jobs – if only they could settle. Boat-minded veterans became leaders of the Sea Rangers, which the Admiralty had formally recognised in 1945. They also led the Girls' Nautical Training Corps, which had started in 1942, been halted and then flourished again after 1949.

How did it work?

Cords connecting Wrens and their navy are multi-stranded, often contradictory and unevenly spliced. Most working together was done in crises which sometimes gave women and men alike too little time to think about what they were doing, so they just utilised the situation as best they could. At times Wrens were cynical that men only let them in nicely when they wanted something out of them. The WRNS, as an auxiliary organisation, had to play its part on men's terms. With all her experience of fighting for woman's rights Vera Laughton Mathews, however, tried to ensure matters were dealt with on her terms as much as was practicable. Her success looks extraordinary when examined closely.

The Royal Navy did change (but mainly temporarily) because of the WRNS' advent. Servicewomen were so useful that they implicitly forced new recognitions of female potential. Did members of the WRNS change? They gained huge confidence in what women could do and be. So could they not carry on assisting the navy, fully integrated with male colleagues, and in a permanent capacity, to the benefit of all, in the new peacetime world?

CHAPTER 6

Women Care for Wartime Patients: 1939–45[1]

> The fact that high standards were expected of a Service with proud traditions ... in no way diminishes the achievement of maintaining those standards. It was not always easy.[2]

Three key people illustrate the three different ways women were involved in naval health care in World War II: Genevieve Rewcastle was the very first commissioned female naval doctor and a married mother of three. Child-free and single, Bertha Martin was matron-in-chief of the QARNNS and Irene Waistell was the tough-talking, motorcycle-riding, elderly commandant of VADs at Haslar.

Over 6,000 women helped naval personnel survive and be well in World War II. The hundred-strong QARNNS was staunchly established as *the* naval nursing service, and still officer-only. Regulars also taught the many desperately needed newcomers. These included the reserves, who brought the total to 1,341 according to some data. Side by side with them were the all-female Voluntary Aid Detachment in which 5,281 members served. Some VADs (RN) were nursing members. Others were general members: support staff including clerks, cooks, telephonists and drivers for hospitals – tasks that Wrens also took on. To the side were the elite: female doctors and dentists, and even the navy's first woman consultant, Louise McIlroy

Fig. 6.1. Out in Alexandria at the naval hospital in February 1945. The women are (left to right): Surgeon Lieutenant Ailsa Whitehouse, Medical Officer in Charge WRNS; Miss K. N. Cooper, Acting Principal Matron, QARNNS; Miss Phyllis Shipton, Acting Senior Sister, QARNNS; and Reserve Miss M. G. E. Maher-Loughnan, Acting Senior Sister, QARNNS. They are being inspected by Admiral Sir John Cunningham, C-in-C Mediterranean.

Fig. 6.2. Varied but united in health care: HMS *Cabbala* Signal School sick bay personnel in 1943. Left to right on back row: the Wren steward who cleaned the ward; two Red Cross VADs; the RNVR medical officer; a St John VAD, Norma Wilson; and the WRNS writer who did the sick berth's clerical work. Front row: a St John VAD and the QARNNS sister.

(1874–1968). All the women were under the umbrella of the medical department, headed by Admiral Sir Sheldon Dudley.[3]

If someone was trying to work out a 'who's what' hierarchy, it might be useful to have the following summary. The largest group were VADs, outnumbering the others by roughly four to one. The most experienced women in naval health care were QARNNS Regulars. The most prestigious were this new phenomenon: the female doctors and dental surgeons.

The cast in health care work

Doc's here – and he's a lady

'A most important landmark in naval medical history was the appointment of the RN's first woman Medical Officer.' Jack Coulter, the war's official medical historian, acknowledged the feat. Some 63 years after women doctors were first permitted to practice in Britain, Genevieve Rewcastle (1897–1951) became Medical Superintendent WRNS in November 1939. Her job, as doctor, was to look after all members of the WRNS, for example inspecting their fitness on entry. Naval doctors, QARNNS and SBAs, would look after sick Wrens. Being a nursing, not medical service, the QARNNS never had a QARNNS doctor (male or female).

Genevieve Rewcastle was not just a civilian doctor working temporarily with the WRNS, as had been Dr Dorothy Hare and Dr Mary Bell in World War I. Dr Rewcastle was the navy's first *commissioned* female officer (meaning officially appointed an officer, unlike petty officers who are non-commissioned) in any branch at all. A woman in such a position was so unusual that she had to enlist the help of the Medical Women's Federation to be paid equally with men of her rank. MP Edith Summerskill commented: 'One of the most significant things is this: the only women in the [wartime] Services who are paid the same rate as men are doctors.' Her point was that women backed by professional bodies were those most able to achieve pay parity, and therefore respect.[4]

The score of subsequent 'lady sawbones' worked with male as well as female patients, although principally with WRNS. Ailsa Whitehouse, one of those pictured in Fig. 6.1, was Medical Officer in Charge WRNS, HMS *Nile*, one of the 1944 intake. Numbers of women MOs swelled from 18 in 1943 to 21 in 1945 (see Table 6.1). The navy's medical branch suffered from a 'numerical nightmare from which it never fully recovered', reported Jack Coulter. This led to the navy opening its doors unusually wide and recruiting doctors from the colonies and dominions in 1944, and women too.[5]

Table 6.1. Numbers of women and men giving health care in World War II, by year[6]

	1938	First few wks of war	1940 (end of)	1941 (end of)	1942 (end of)	1944 (end of)	1945 (May)
FEMALES							
Nursing sisters and reserves	80	222	387	450	658	892	1,095
VADs	n/a	265	500	780	1,587	2,800	3,893
Medical officers	1	1	1	1	2	18	41
Dental officers	0	0	0	0	9	7	n/a
MALES							
Medical officers	800	n/a	1,457	1,705	2,026	2,393	2,535
Dental officers	n/a	123	250	344	461	653	686
SB staff	2,230	3,640	4,300	6,060	8,000	11,000	12,000
SB staff (dental)	n/a	n/a	n/a	n/a	n/a	n/a	566
Total Naval Services incl WRNS, QARNNS & VADs	n/a	162,170	335,150	472,110	613,160	862,050	847,600

Toothwrights emerge

Medical officers' counterparts were dental officers. Britain's first female dentist, Lillian Lindsay, had graduated in 1895. However, dentistry in the navy, not the army, was an all-male occupation. Then seven female dental surgeons entered the navy from 1943. None worked afloat but three served abroad. They were 1 per cent of the dental service at peak, slightly more than women MOs. Like the women doctors, these probationary temporary surgeon lieutenants were officially in the Royal Naval Volunteer Reserve, not the navy's medical branch proper. The arrangement was seemingly in order that they might be equally paid. They wore WRNS-style uniform but with the standard orange 'toothwrights' markings in their lace and hat badges.

Women were dental surgery assistants (DSAs) too. This had been a job for male SBA(D)s. Women who had done that job in civilian life were initially employed. However, they would have had to be paid as much as WRNS chief officers to match usual dentistry wage rates. A cheaper solution was found. The VAD 'lent' 120 nursing members in 1941. They assisted dental surgeons with both female and male patients throughout the war.[7]

Naval Virgins Awaiting Destruction

Commandant Irene M. Waistell (1877–1966) at Haslar, supervising over 70 VADs, was the most famous VAD 'character'. A new VAD arriving at Haslar in 1940 found the intrepid Northallerton-born woman 'fearsome ... a weather-beaten veteran of the First War. [But] her booming voice and constant harrying of us belied the kindness of this wonderful woman ... We adored "madam", and her rare smile was a reward beyond value.' VADs were managed by their own senior officers, including commandants for units of over 30. VADs outnumbered QARNNS members by about five to one. On wards they were very much *under* QARNNS officers, as SBAs had been in peacetime.

They were 'dilutees', in effect, especially as labour shortages worsened. A very socially mixed group of women, often genteel, VADs felt free to leave when they chose. They were also dedicated, despite the military-style strictness of some QARNNS martinets. As VAD Norma Wilson (born 1923), a former mender in Yorkshire textile mills, smiled: 'You were a dog's body and they were the officers. You accepted it.' Another joked that VADs were deliberately put in awful uniforms to make their inferior status clear.[8]

World War II involved 5,281 VAD (RN)s. There were 3,893 at peak, in 1945. At least 800 served abroad, especially from 1944. In the previous war the 'Vivacious and Delightfuls' had been accepted less than a year before the end. In this war they were there at the start and continued long after it ended. Mobile VADs worked in the navy and army hospitals. Immobiles were in the EMHs.[9]

The VADs' role was to do the less prestigious nursing work normally done by male SBAs, whom they were freeing for the sea service. Tasks included scrubbing floors, washing patients and changing dressings, as well as dispensing, clerical work and cooking. As female civilians, these women were paid at a lower rate than male SBAs, yet could be very skilled. By 1943 clinical demands were so great that VADs had to have the same intensive course of training as probationary sick berth staff.

QARNNS

QARNNS regulars were the most experienced women giving health care in naval services. Behind their backs QARNNS sisters were affectionately called 'Dorises' (Doris was a popular name until the 1950s – Doris Day was a beloved superstar), just as Wrens were called 'Jennies'. 'Queer And Impossible, Mostly Not Sane', was the corresponding name used for their army nursing counterparts. QARNNS and QARNNS (R), meaning reserves, members served under three successive matrons-in-chief during the war. Bertha Martin, Doris Beale and then Matilda Goodrich were highly focused professionals in their fifties, unmarried and child-free. Their personal situations were different from male MOs who lived family lives in hospital apartments, not a cloistered female community.

In wartime, former QARNNS sisters had the chance to return and contribute again at senior level. An unknown number of married ex-QARNNS came back when the marriage bar could conveniently be disregarded. QARNNS regulars increased tenfold during the war as the many reserves came from civilian hospitals to help. Similarly, the Royal Navy swelled tenfold with men who entered as hostilities-only

(HO) personnel. In other words, in this war the majority of nurses were new to the navy and so were their patients. Much was unfamiliar and people learned naval culture as they went along.[10]

VAD Beatrice Stobbs was someone who typically found Haslar 'very much run by the naval tradition and everything was shipshape and polished ... should a patient's bed be found with the anchor the wrong way round [on the counterpane] during Matron's Rounds – there was trouble.' The navy's medical department 'appreciated at the outset that women could not be expected to adapt themselves easily to the routine life of a Service essentially male by tradition' explained its historian Jack Coulter. The service recognised 'fundamental psychological differences ... must be catered for if serious repercussions on health and efficiency were to be avoided.' No evidence exists that guidelines or training on this matter were instigated.[11]

Most QARNNS served in the UK in naval hospitals, naval auxiliary hospitals, convalescent units and service hospitals. QARNNS sisters overseas numbers peaked at 219 in 1945. In principle, the most senior QARNNS nurses would, singly, be in situations where they could supervise and train up clusters of reserves, SBAs and VADs, each with their differing levels of nursing knowledge and familiarity with naval medical practices. One reserve apiece, often with two VAD subordinates, worked in sick quarters, where the work was more peaceful and less like A&E in the big port hospitals. In all 1,993 such reserves were anywhere from Oban to Gad's Hill, including in the 100-plus WRNS and RNAS sick quarters from Donibristle to Yeovilton. Few were on hospital ships. Both QARNNS sisters and VADs might relocate roughly six times during their war, according to service needs.[12]

The action

Naval women were looking after matelots, marines, airmen, soldiers and even the enemy, whether they were wounded, injured or sick. Some were close to combat situations and dealt with injuries unknown in the previous war. They were also caring for naval services personnel including Wrens and civilians with ordinary problems. These might range from backache caused by having to switch from civilian high heels to flat uniform shoes, or cooks who developed occupational bronchitis through working in hot and steamy kitchens but travelling on cold pre-dawn buses. Some of the nursing work was crisis care, under high pressure and often working with surgeons in operating theatres. At other times in sick quarters it was more like a GP's surgery.

Shortages of male staff brought opportunities for women. Jack Coulter points out:

> A large amount of clinical and technical work which was customarily done by medical officers was successfully carried out by nurses, W.R.N.S. and VADs ... injections, minor surgical proceedings, blood transfusions and certain routine inspections were entrusted to specially trained sisters and sick berth ratings.[13]

Care ashore

Providing health care very much depended on where the personnel were, which reflected the war's stages. QARNNS sisters and VADs were principally in naval hospitals on land. The UK's established naval hospitals (RNHs) included the big three: Haslar, Plymouth and Chatham, plus the new Kingseat, near Aberdeen. In the UK there were also auxiliary hospitals (RNAHs) created in old buildings, such as Cholmondeley Castle. Broadly speaking, the less onerous the situation, the more it would be staffed by QARNNS Reserves, with VADs' help. Female staff abounded, making naval men's hospitalisation ashore a welcome homelike experience.[14]

Overseas, QARNNS sisters were working in naval hospitals such as Malta and Hong Kong, as usual. They were also at Bermuda, Colombo, Simonstown, the 64 General Hospital in Alexandria and several later ones in Ceylon, Sydney and in Bombay. Sick quarters they staffed included those for Wrens in Durban, Gibraltar, Port Said, Kilindini and Algiers, and five naval sick quarters. The QARNNS'

Fig. 6.3. A VAD wields the willow with convalescent psychiatric patients at RNAH Cholmondeley Castle, Cheshire.

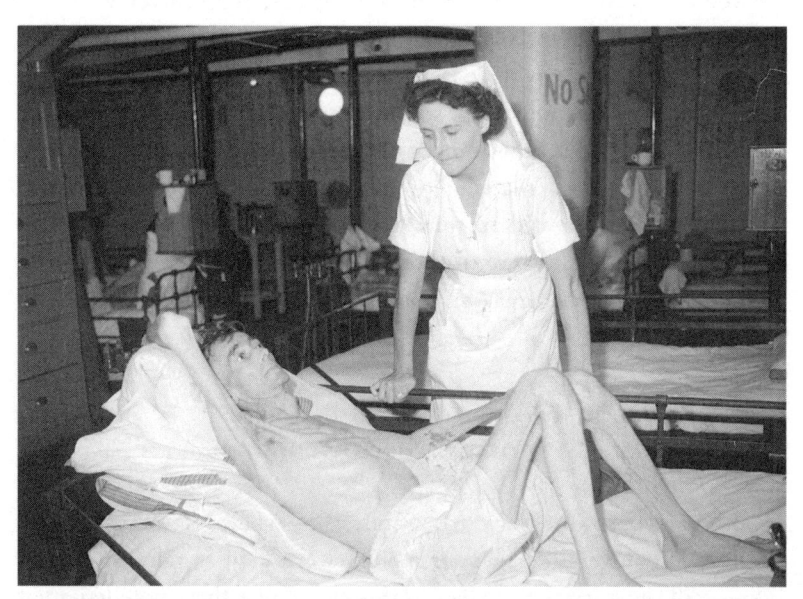

Fig. 6.4. Nursing POWs at sea: Sister S. M. Augustus attends Captain (DO) H. G. Camp, Royal Artillery, aboard the hospital ship *Oxfordshire* in Hong Kong harbour following the reoccupation of the Crown Colony in 1945.

work in Africa, said their historian Kathleen Harland, was 'perhaps less shadowed by the threat of physical danger than that of Sisters in other theatres of War ... [yet] very little let-up in the flood of seriously ill patients.'[15]

On naval ships

At least 81 seaborne QARNNS sisters (not VADs, nor women doctors) were in hospital ships and carriers including HMHS *Oxfordshire*, *Vasna* and *Amarapoora*, *Vita* and the *Isle of Jersey*, plus *Ophir*, *Tjitjalengka*, *Cap St Jacques*, *Empire Clyde* and *Gerusalemme*. No hospital ship was in constant use. Working aboard could be a mix of 'enjoying a foreign cruise' and pell-mell action, even attack. QARNNS sister Bobby Robinson was on the *Tjitjalengka* in the Pacific in 1944 and found it 'tremendously exciting to be in the midst of all the great ships of the American fleet' watching destroyers transfer casualties, by breeches buoy (a zip line between vessels). The later in the war it was, the greater were the number of reserves on board. In 1945, the peak year, seven of the 48 sisters on hospital ships were regulars.[16]

Such women were under fire at times, as hospital ships moved close to action to try to reduce the amount of time a casualty endured between being wounded and treated. No women nursed in the destroyers. VADs were not allowed to serve in hospital ships. However, when the war ended, some were in the three aircraft carriers that repatriated prisoners of war (POWs), possibly because this was also a way to repatriate VADs.[17]

Moving where needed

Health care personnel have to be moved to wherever they are most needed. Whatever their gender medics were kept as safe as possible because of their strategic value. In this global war they travelled great distances, by sea, and were sometimes in dangerous areas.

Supporting the swelling teams in the north and abroad: 1939–41

When war began matron-in-chief Bertha Martin already had 85 regulars primed and 127 reserves standing by. A further 265 VAD (RN)s were ready. In fact in August 1939 55 reserves had sailed off for Alexandria and Ceylon, pre-dating the war's announcement.[18]

In the evacuation of Dunkirk from 26 May to 4 June 1940 VADs and QARNNS members nursed people in the areas nearest Dover. Seemingly none were on the rescue vessels, unlike army nurses. Barbara Greenwood, a civilian nurse who only later joined the QARNNS, found 'It was horrific ... We really didn't stop all night!'[19]

As the military focus on North Africa grew in early 1941, QARNNS officers and VADs – in trousers at times – underwent dangerous voyages to be ready for the casualties. Sister Phyllis Shipton (1904–1982) became one of the first QARNNS heroes of the war when shipwrecked from the troopship *Britannia* off West Africa on 25 March 1941. That August Kate Gribble (1909–1941) was the first QARNNS sister to die. She was accompanying the initial draft of Wrens to go to Gibraltar when their troopship, HMT *Aguila*, was torpedoed.[20]

Any person was at risk. However, women faced additional risks as targets of punitive rape. In Christmas 1941 sexual violence by Japanese army officers seemed imminent in the Hong Kong hospital where Olga Franklin was serving. Rampaging Japanese troops had already repeatedly gang-raped 11 nurses nearby, killing some VADs and massacring patients. When potential marauders arrived at Olga's hospital, her Principal MO successfully diverted them. Later the women became the only QARNNS members to be interned in the entire war.[21]

Operation Torch and onwards: 1942–3

November 1942 was momentous for two reasons. When the biggest invasion force in history thus far invaded French North Africa, a few QARNNS regulars were in hospital ships, embarking casualties and taking them to Gibraltar for treatment. Much inter-service co-operation meant QARNNS were part of a mixed situation, and involved in the subsequent amphibious assaults on Sicily, Salerno and Anzio. Armed forces nursing sisters were in hospital ships as the Allies proceeded north up from Africa. HMHS *Amarapoora* was bombed in September 1943 while supporting the Salerno landings. No QARNNS members were recorded as casualties.[22]

The second significant event was internal, and back at headquarters. However, it was a sign of women being officially moved from the sidelines into the centre and the start of combined services nursing. Finally the matron-in-chief was based at the Admiralty. As early as 1902 the Council of Matrons had suggested this. Doris Beale moved there in winter 1942/3 at a time of salary and uniform standardisation recommended by the Rushcliffe Committee. Like nurses in the other services, QARNNS personnel were given equivalent ranks with the Royal Navy: nursing sisters and senior nursing sisters had the rank of lieutenants; the matron-in-chief herself held commodore rank.[23]

D-Day and after: 1944–5

Unprecedented effort focused on D-Day, the long-awaited cross-Channel invasion of occupied France on 6 June 1944. Extra staff were trained up for Haslar, which was to be a key clearing station. Fortunately casualties in the landing and ensuing hard-fought battles including at Caen and the Falaise Pocket were fewer than anticipated.[24]

This enabled all personnel who could be spared from then on to go out to the new hospital facilities in the Far East, some of which were Combined Services as at Trincomalee, Ceylon. Over 2,000 more beds were created for the possible casualties in the Pacific theatre. VAD Norma Wilson volunteered for overseas service. She became part of the large team in 1945 sent to Australia at the new RNAH *Herne Bay* (nicknamed Hernia Bay) to await massive casualties that never occurred. Cynthia Cooke (who became the QARNNS matron-in-chief in 1973) was among the many in the Pacific looking after evacuated POWs and troops from the Far East from January 1945. Some sailed in homeward-bound aircraft carriers after the war's end.[25]

When the USA bombed Hiroshima in July 1945, Japan surrendered. VJ Day, on 12 August 1945, was the formal end of that war. However health care staff were still needed in the Far East and stayed on. Naval VADs continued too because, as the First Lord of the Admiralty admitted in Parliament, there was 'a severe shortage of [male] sick-berth ratings … and we are having difficulty now in getting them trained.'[26]

Aftermath of war

Wedding bells rang for 327 wartime QARNNS members. The most famous was Sister Mary Parkin who had married Flight-Lieutenant William J. Lynd aboard her hospital ship, *Amarapoora*, in 1944. Marriage meant nearly a quarter of all QARNNS members had to leave the service, as it went back to being a single women's service.

Fig. 6.5. Ceylon, 1946. VAD Enid Crouch and Yeoman signaller Ernie Crouch enjoy the guard of honour at their wedding. Enid's colleagues, all naval nursing VADs, use splints instead of swords. Ernie's signalling pals brandish signal flags.

For other women, sisterly comradeship and professional commitment endured. The navy's first female surgeon, Lieutenant-Commander Dr Rewcastle, left in 1947. Many VADs carried on. Indeed Norma Wilson came back from Australia but then volunteered for Trincomalee, where she served another two years after marrying.[27]

Losses and gains

In those years from 1939 to 1945 impressive feats in naval health care had been achieved in challenging circumstances. Women had shouldered many kinds of burdens. As Olga Franklin said of her nursing sisters, they were 'splendid'. They 'have, at all times, remained cheerful and have made the best of everything'. The only problem, remarked Jack Coulter, was that later in the war inexperienced nurses, hastily trained in civil hospitals, under-supervised, then promoted too early, were sometimes gamely working beyond their abilities.[28]

His official history of medical services in the war tried to sum it all up fairly: 'the work done by naval doctors and nurses, though valuable, should not be exaggerated ... the part played by the Navy was a relatively minor role in a vast medical operational organisation which was essentially a far greater Army commitment once the initial stages had been passed.'

QARNNS casualties were fewer than those of army and Territorial Army Nursing Service nurses. This was not least because so many troopships with army and Territorial Nursing Service (TANS) nurses on board had been attacked, for example the *Khedive Ishmael*.[29]

Of the 1,341 QARNNS members serving, 11 had died. Two had been lost through enemy action: Kate Gribble and a nursing sister flying a patient home. Total naval casualties were 7 per cent, unlike the 0.8 per cent of the QARNNS.

When nurses were honoured, 117 awards were made to QARNNS members: 8 per cent of all awards to service nurses. Naval VADs were recognised by the VAD but also won ARRCs. In the January 1946 honours list a disproportionate 44 per cent of the awards to naval nursing staff went to VADs. Some women went on to interesting careers in very other fields, such as Haslar nurse, Sheila Scott (née Hopkins) who became a record-breaking round-the-world pilot. QARNNS (R) Ann Ramsden, whom Mounbatten liked so much he named his Dakota after her, went on to work in a disastrous Tanganyika groundnut scheme.[30]

Looking back at the scarce and patchy remaining evidence, three main things are striking. War really had given women opportunities to excel in casualty work and gain new skills. Like Wrens, these women had transcended women's traditional physical place and worked overseas and afloat, as well as living in all sorts of unusual or fancy dwellings, including the homes of ejected doctors. Amid all the rearrangements that war caused, they had gained new formal status too as part of the wider nursing world.[31]

QARNNS Sister Polly Dampier-Child was not unusual in her loyal celebration of opportunity: 'I felt very privileged to have served with the Royal Navy and wouldn't have missed my service time for all the rice in China.'[32]

CHAPTER 7

Struggling Seawards: The WRNS 1946–90

In my view the whole period since the end of the war was a gradual process of bringing our Service into line with the Navy.
　　　　　　　　　　　　　　Jean Davies, Director WRNS, re the 1960s.[1]

What does a Wren do when her war ends? Some women certainly tried to carry on as valued cogs in a now dwindling emergency organisation they had come to love. War apart, they were members of a comradely, can-do, female team connected to the navy, which was too good to lose. Initially the post-conflict WRNS was led by one of Dame Vera Laughton Mathews' three musketeers, Jocelyn Woollcombe (1898–1986) from November 1946. Commandant Woollcombe's maturity (she was 48), her 'clear brain and absolute integrity', as well as her naval family background, had been crucial to the WRNS through the hostilities. Now there was a new stage to negotiate.[2]

The question was did the navy want a Women's Royal Naval Service at all? And what use could it be in the new Cold War emnity post-1946? The navy – so underfunded, so often short of skilled personnel, despite men's liability for National Service (1939–60) – struggled with its new role in a nuclear age. Political and military leaders pondered the conundrum of all three women's services (not the nursing services, they were safe). Could ladies in an add-on force aid the professional arms-bearing combatants who went to sea? Slowly the

Fig. 7.1. The joke was both in the ample evidence of naval service and in the wife's presumption that she had really been *in* the Royal Navy, not just part of naval services. Cartoon for the *Ditty Box*, July 1946 by Ionicus (Joshua Armitage).

"*... and can you remember when we were both in the Navy, John?*"

more radical question emerged: perhaps females could even become warriors, although such a word was never used.

Recovering from the war: 1945–9

Cutbacks made the WRNS' future unclear, just as they had in 1919. Costly personnel who could only be used for a few tasks were not value for money. WRNS members could not be combatants, therefore they could not work at sea; as civilians there was a limit to how much coercion was feasible. For example, they could not be made to return if they 'deserted', i.e. left, because they were civilians, not under the Naval Discipline Act (NDA). As it seemed natural at that time for married members to put their husbands' careers first, senior officers saw married women as less reliable than mobile male combatants. They might move where the spouse went, for example. As they were not under NDA this could not be stopped.

Naval men had garlanded the WRNS with compliments. However the Admiralty had given remarkably dismissive evidence to the Royal Commission on Equal Pay in 1945. Women were said to be inferior, and only 75 per cent as good as men in some cases, because they were off sick or absent more than men and they:

> [lacked the] physical strength ... [suffered from] inferior mechanical aptitude, [had] lower capacity for the application of knowledge. [They had the] inclination to get flustered in emergency and [were] more easily discouraged when up against difficulties ... [They were deficient in their] capacity for improvisation; [displayed] unwillingness to accept responsibility and [had an] inability to exercise authority.[3]

A government white paper on the future of the services as a whole emerged in May 1946. Reasons to continue with a WRNS included that it would reduce the need to forcibly conscript men. Women could also be paid less, be sent to isolated places where civilians would refuse to go, and be put to repetitive, fiddly and sedentary tasks. Dame Vera thought that the WRNS was different to the other two women's services because 'the sailor's time has to be divided between home service, foreign service and sea service ... [This] made one hardly dare to hope for a permanent W.R.N.S.'[4]

In essence, the only way women could really work interchangeably with naval men was by being formally accepted as combatants and made liable for sea service. This meant including them under the NDA, which governed the lives of naval men. Dame Jocelyn, while worried that NDA 'should not become a "parrot cry"', also saw that it could be useful for helping a Wren clear her name at a court martial (a very unusual occurrence). Both women and men argued that, as naval women were civilian and special (meaning ladylike, therefore well-behaved), they did not need such a harsh measure. Such idealistic stereotypes obscured a potential view of women as anything like equal. This obstacle was to inhibit progress for the next 30 years.[5]

At least it was agreed that the WRNS, like the other two women's services, would continue as a permanent service from February 1949. The WRNS' numbers would be tiny, ideally 2,300, but with scope for up to 6,000. All ratings would be mobile and prepared to go wherever the Admiralty sent them. Married women would be accepted, providing they were prepared to respect service needs. Dame Vera was the first and last director to be a wife and a mother, although Dame Katharine, a widow, had children. Others married after leaving. Dame Vera thought 'we must accept that the "career" servicewomen would be almost entirely unmarried'. The WRNS was reduced and then started to grow again, as Table 7.1 shows.[6]

Table 7.1. **The WRNS as part of RN services, 1944–90.**[7]

YEAR	Peak year 1944	1946	1950	1960	1970	1980	1990
WRNS	74,635	15,000	5,400	3,100	3,300	3,800	3,600
TOTAL IN RN SERVICES	790,000	788,800	132,500	93,400	86,000	72,000	63,200

In the next few years all servicewomen's pay rose from two-thirds of men's to 80 per cent and became pegged to servicemen's pay, not to that of civilian women. Commandant Woollcombe negotiated fairer pensions in meetings where she was the only woman. When she had pressed for WRNS' rights to a pension after 22 years' service, the other committee members 'at first greeted [this] with incredulous laughter. No woman, they thought, would remain that long'. They went off and got married. Indeed women did not tend to stay long because interesting opportunities dwindled and overseas opportunities were few. WRNS ratings' jobs were reduced from 90 categories to 24. The incentive was that the services helped them leave home and sometimes travel without all the difficulties of organisation that a solo female faced in that stay-put period. Being a Wren meant enjoying a sense of 'family', accessing out-of-the ordinary experiences and doing something worthwhile.[8]

What use are mere girls if Armageddon looms?: The 1950s

Dame Jocelyn, after retiring in 1950, recalled that 'my time as Director was entirely concerned with the conversion of the wartime "temporary" WRNS into the permanent service.'

A changed and anxious world existed in the 1950s. After the Soviet Union detonated an atomic bomb in 1949 the Cold War escalated. NATO began to grow. The number of Warsaw Pact countries increased after 1955. A global nuclear holocaust seemed entirely possible. The situation required defence experts to take new steps, including discerning what women's services might do and how to stop the high turnover, which was costly and undermined operational effectiveness. On director Mary Lloyd's watch from 1950 to 1954, when the WRNS was 3,000 strong, just 14 per cent completed their period of service then left. Another 25 per cent resigned even before their time was up. The remaining 61 per cent continued, however no statistics now exist to show how long they stayed.[9]

The navy needed a reserve too: useful women and men to call in in case of crisis. The Women's Royal Naval Volunteer Reserve (WRNVR) was set up in 1951. Initially, it numbered hundreds, not thousands. It seems that Wrens were not mobilised in close proximity to the Korean War between 1950 and 1953 (where five British aircraft carriers were involved, supplying fighter planes). Nor did Wrens or reserves feature much in the 1956 Suez Crisis. But they were ready.

Mary's successor, Nancy Robertson, another wartime Wren, summarised her 1954–8 period as director as one of 'marking time and settling in'. Certainly, her senior officers' meeting records do not come across as a gathering of defence-focused people in a country rapidly becoming the third nation with nuclear capability in addition to the USA and USSR. They are akin to the minutes of say, a young women's domestic science training college focusing on administrative matters such as recruitment and rationing. One of her main objectives was 'to ensure that there was a worthwhile career open to ambitious and well-qualified girls'. There was also the question of whether enough jobs ('berths') existed at all? Because of new defence strategy,

Fig. 7.2. Limited opportunities for women. Wren Stewards (general) enjoying stand-easy at the Duchess of Kent Barracks, 1959.

'It was a period of withdrawing from a lot of Naval bases, and therefore of Wrens units, mostly from air stations', Elizabeth Hoyer Millar, the next Director WRNS recorded.[10]

In 1957 Minister of Defence Duncan Sandys delivered a pivotal white paper on the future of the military. The preparatory work discussed cutting the WRNS and saving the QARNNS. Neither option appeared in the final version. In parliamentary discussions Plymouth Devonport MP Joan Vickers even wondered 'whether there is any real need for the Women's Services in the future'. Temporary civilian helpers based in YWCA hostels when the need arose would be cheaper than an expensive, 'far larger force of women than is strictly necessary', complete with female officers' servants, she thought.[11]

Despite such views, a continuing, even expanded, women's corps was agreed by July 1957. Could enough long-serving personnel be found? Anxieties about intake levels led to the Advisory Committee on Recruiting. Chaired by Sir James Grigg, it reported in 1958. In the Lords, Baroness Elliot of Harwood (one of the groundbreaking female peers) agreed with Sir James: 'The greatest single deterrent to the recruitment of women is the lack of emphasis on the need for Women's Services in time of peace … when nursing and teaching careers offered appealing alternatives.' Those struggling to retain career Wrens were not helped by his recommendation that servicewomen should be enabled to leave easily when ready to wed. He described marriage as 'a social duty'.[12]

After the committee reported back, there were few steps forward. However, new models of womanhood were appearing in this period. In the long term these were to change everyone's ideas of what servicewomen could do. They led to Wrens sailing, Women's Royal Air Force flying and army women moving closer to close combat. Queen Elizabeth II, the first female monarch since Victoria, ascended to the throne in 1952. This former Sea Ranger and wartime ATS (women's army auxiliary) member wielded a gracious female authority. In business and politics women leaders, including the future first female UK prime minister, Margaret Thatcher, were emerging. This change was in conflict with a climate in which Hollywood movies of the 1950s persuaded women to absent themselves from active public life. Culturally the female role was aligned with Ann Shelton on the iconic forces radio show *Two-Way Family Favourites*, who sang 'Sailor, stop your roaming'. Women were not supposed to actually *be* armed sailors who roamed, or people with the power to determine men's mobility.

Furthermore, male naval officers at that point were largely public school educated; 70 per cent of Dartmouth's intake in 1950 were from this background. Some WRNS officers were sisters of such males and also had private schooling but had obviously not gone to the all-male schools like Haileybury that gave pupils such a powerful boost for a later life of wielding public authority. Male officers were a well-networked elite of alumni sharing a recreational culture that was unlike women's. They used gentlemen's clubs and bonded on cricket fields rather than hockey pitches. They still modified strong language with an 'Ahem, ladies present', because they saw females as such an other species.[13]

"I thought it about time they had something with which to present arms."

Fig. 7.3. Women combatants without arms were increasingly an anomaly. 'I thought it about time they had something with which to present arms.' Cartoon for the *Ditty Box*, November 1945, by Ionicus (Joshua Armitage).

Ladies and teens vs defence needs: The 1960s

Has femininity got to go?

Women and men in political and service life in the 1960s had to work out how to proceed given that the practical needs for women's sections of the armed forces conflicted with deeply polarised ideas of gender. In the musical *My Fair Lady* Professor Higgins sings exasperatedly: 'Why can't a woman be more like a man?' It would be so much more convenient. She could join up and stay 22 years, as men did, justifying the thousands of pounds of training costs. But what valuable 'feminine' traits would be lost in the process, opponents protested.

A solution was urgently needed. Full staffing of the armed forces was becoming harder to achieve because all National Service personnel would be gone by late 1963. There were so many factors against successful recruitment and retention. Defence jobs were not popular. Many older naval men, more than in the army and air force, had spent most of their lives in all-male environments. They had little direct experience of managing a mixed workforce, so how could they know what to expect of this puzzling other species? Politicians did not want to risk public outrage by pushing women too far, too fast, into what was seen as a masculine sphere. Some older Wrens wanted to keep their traditional, unique service. Margaret Drummond, the WRNS director from 1964 to 1967, told a select committee discussing the Naval Discipline Act: 'I considered it to be of vital importance ... that our status was upheld against considerable pressure to bring us into line with the other two women's Services.' The navy had always considered itself special and superior; the WRNS, relatedly, did too.[14]

'Female essentialism' is the term that would now be used for the central difficulty. It summarises the idea that women have innate traits, such as ladylike charm, nobility of spirit or 'natural', 'motherly' revulsion against war. Katharine Furse expressed it in 1939:

> It's not that women would do men's work better than, or even as well as the men could do it ... [It is] simply that they will do, to the best of their ability, that for which, as women, they are suited. It is, I believe, the maternal instinct of women which takes possession of us in an emergency and gives us an enormous desire to do something helpful.

Such ideas still got in the way of objectively appraising all that women might possibly do, on a level and neutral playing field. This way of thinking perpetuated the polarised archetype of noble warrior versus damsel/mother-to-be-protected.[15]

Fun vs service life

A clear strategic progression forward for the WRNS was also hampered because so many left quickly (confirming the idea that women were not reliable stayers). Two main reasons for poor retention were a non-public-spirited culture and lack of contraception, which meant women left disappointed at the lack of lifestyle opportunities, or accidentally pregnant or both. Girl culture generated novel expectations. Helen Shapiro sang 'Don't treat me like a child'. *Georgy Girl*, the seminal 'swinging London' film, offered a vision of a life that was 'fancy free'.[16]

Look at Life – Girls Ahoy, a WRNS recruitment film (1960), shown in every Odeon before the main feature, picked up on the new trend. It tried to show that being a Wren offered freedom, adventure and an end to loneliness. In reality, such hopes could not quite be met because of the disciplinary need of the services. Women joined up but few continued after the initial four years – an interregnum which could be seen as equivalent to the modern gap year. 'Angela Green', a Wren writer of the time, later explained the opposing trends:

> some of us were irked by curfews, officers who seemed too schoolmistressy, and faint hope of jaunting off somewhere exotic. We wanted the wide open spaces of a civilian life, with our own flats and in locations of our choice. Having said that, we made our time in the WRNS work, not least because we were all young, together in a lively substitute family, and away from home for the first time. Being in the WRNS was absolutely wonderful, the best time of my life, despite – not because of – what the organisation officially was.

Indeed anyone reading the two main sorts of writing about Wrens (fragmentary memoirs and formal records) might imagine there were two different WRNS: a gang of young women having a lively time together and a service that needed steady personnel remaining in place for a 22-year career.

Many left to marry – they did not have to resign, but it seemed normal to do so. In 1962–3 a peak of 2 per cent left because of a new phenomenon: they were having a baby, with no prospect of marrying. (Servicewomen were obliged to leave if pregnant, whatever their marital status.)

However, much accidental wastage stopped because the contraceptive pill became available to unmarried women after 1967. Monthly gold blister packs of Ovulen from civilian family planning clinics could be seen as partial saviours of naval services' operational effectiveness.[17]

Young women's desire for more autonomy was strengthened by the passing of the Age of Majority Act 1970 (2). People of 18, not 21 as before, were now officially adults. Servicewomen could stay out later than 'Cinderella passes' had formerly allowed. In the law's drafting process Roy Hattersley, the Minister for Defence Administration, decided that the services no longer acted in *loco parentis* for young women. As a result, naval doctors were permitted to issue contraceptives, even to unmarried women providing they (said they) planned to marry. Not only did this transform Wrens' sexual behaviour. This was also another stage in ending the WRNS' role as a highly moral institution that protected its young ladies. A culture was emerging where Wrens could, if they wished, move towards being laddish like sailors, or like 'Georgy Girls' but without worries about unplanned pregnancy and outdated norms impeding them.[18]

Fig. 7.4. Formality in freewheeling times: a WRNS marchpast at HMS *Excellent*, the salute taken by HRH The Princess Royal, 1970s.

High turnover of newcomers each year wasted resources. Decision-makers could make two possible moves if they accepted that long-term military careers were intrinsically not suited to modern young women's taste. The first, closing down the WRNS, was not feasible because there were not enough good men available to do 'men's' naval work, let alone 'Wrens' work. The other was to find ways to keep women long term. To make conditions more attractive, women and men in Royal Naval Air Stations were allowed to eat together. Others worked and trained together, to some extent. As WRNS director Jean Davies said: 'Conditions for technical training were very often made *similar* to those for the same categories in the Navy' (author's italics). These small initiatives did not go far enough to resolve the problem.[19]

However, interesting work opportunities were emerging in the technical and engineering fields, especially in aviation. Meteorological observers for Fleet Air Arm stations were key new jobs, and much enjoyed. From at least the late 1950s some even went on small arms courses and learned to shoot. Wrens also had access to many sports activities, including hockey, tennis and a lively social life. Outnumbered by men by one hundred to one, heterosexual Wrens had their pick of boyfriends.

It might be imagined that women would now move more into the new submarine-focused naval world. At Faslane the submarine base was opened in 1967, growing to become the biggest of Britain's three naval bases. At that point in the Cold War the site on the Clyde housed the nation's four state-of-the-art submarines carrying nuclear-powered ballistic missiles. The first communication and supply Wrens went there. In fact, they were few and did conventional support work. The under-sea world appears not to have embraced women as readily as the Fleet Air Arm. By contrast, the new units in Singapore and Mauritius, an idyllic sinecure – complete with the picnicking, yachting, partying, social life that the navy was so good at organising – looked most attractive.

Fig. 7.5. Mary Talbot (far right), Nancy Robertson in the middle and colleagues.

Sea service floodgates nudge open: The 1970s

Mary Talbot is hailed as the architect of the big push in this transforming decade of the service's history. The WRNS Director from 1973 to 1976, Commandant Talbot (1922–2012) is remembered as a big woman in every way. Keen on horse racing, she did not suffer fools gladly and paid scant attention to her superficial appearance, such as smudge-free lipstick. She had a vision: that women might one day command warships. Her passion was not so strong that she 'would go to the barricades for it', thought Frank Judd, the Parliamentary Under Secretary for the Navy from 1974 to 1976. However, she had a far more positive view of Wrens' potential than some of her colleagues in the navy, whom Frank Judd saw as threatened 'flat-earthers'. In this decade, when the women's liberation movement brought women's place into question as never before, Commandant Talbot too wanted non-traditional opportunities for women, providing they kept their femininity.[20]

Mary Talbot's momentum increased. WRNS members numbered 3,300 in 1970. They were 3 per cent of the 87,500-strong navy, which was worryingly under strength. High turnover in the WRNS continued, with nearly a third of all Wrens leaving and a third starting every year. They still had a limited role overseas and none on ships. The handful that can be traced include those sent to NATO headquarters in Lisbon in 1971 and the Wren writer in the Naval Attaché's Office in Peking, (soon to called Beijing) in 1975. Because turnover was so high, the possible use of women's labour in the wider defence world was frequently discussed.[21]

Now concentrating on playing a role within NATO in Europe rather than worldwide, the UK's armed forces focused on the perceived – although slightly thawing – Soviet threat to North Atlantic trade. New ships and weaponry were developing. Cutbacks as usual beset plans. The WRNS' future was discussed in relation to all the women's services, including whether RAF women might fly planes and army women could be used in combat.

Crucial change in the WRNS, which aligned them with their sisters in the ATS and WRAF, came as a result of Mary asking for an MoD study to redefine the identity and purpose of the WRNS. This came in 1974 and it was no accident that she made the request just before a major defence shake-up, the Mason Review. The ensuing Pritchard Report was to lead, three years later, to that crucial first step towards women being allowed to serve at sea: the inclusion of all naval services women under the Naval Discipline Act.

Pritchard reporting ...

The MoD study that Mary Talbot had sought, which became the Pritchard Report, aimed to define precisely the WRNS role for the next ten years, examine the organisation and employment structure, and make recommendations. In January 1974 the team began work, chaired by the Assistant Under Secretary Naval Personnel Alan Pritchard, assisted by two WRNS officers and others. The scope was immediately hampered by an undisclosed brief to not discuss the issue of whether women might serve at sea, WRNS integration historian Kath Sherit points out. It was a puzzling omission of what looks now to be the most vital question.[22]

When the Pritchard Report emerged, it revealed that Wrens were not progressing in their careers to the same extent as men. Their training was less rigorous and their non-liability to sea service meant managers tended to underutilise them. Also a tendency to stay pleasantly put meant they did not proceed upward. Wrens were seen as supporting naval men, rather than as themselves being equally deserving of support in careers.

The main recommendations of the Pritchard Report that November 1974 were that women should serve in a wider range of jobs. Training should improve and be more like that of the men. Ideally Wrens would do basic training somewhere better than HMS *Dauntless* which, as new recruits affectionately joked, looked like the kind of wooden-hutted POW camp that celluloid heroes escaped from.

WRNS members should be further integrated with the navy in more areas. Crucially the study recommended they should come under the 1957 NDA that governed the discipline of all naval personnel. Pritchard diplomatically explained why: it would 'stretch the goodwill of the RN' to extend women's employment if the degree of separateness indicated by different disciplinary codes remained. In other words, there needed to be a fair deal; women must not expect to have the old ladylike privileges – although ideally they should remain ladylike in demeanour. An egalitarian culture would not tolerate those much-discussed and maybe mythical archetypes who, to keep their nail varnish unchipped inveigled men into heavy or dirty manual labour. Many change-averse personnel associated such proposals with letting in 'masculine types' of women, which revolted them.[23]

Slowly the recommendations were put into place. Mary Talbot objected to the NDA but accepted it because the Navy Board (the body that ran the navy's day-to-day business now that the MoD had taken over) asked her to do so. It was part of the changing times internationally, as countries such as the USA and the Netherlands forged ahead. Yona Owens, a communications electrician, led a successful 1976 class action lawsuit (group litigation) charging that the US Navy was unconstitutional in inhibiting women's careers by excluding them from ships. Yona's group move became a landmark case worldwide. This kind of focus on rights was at odds with a climate where naval

Figure 7.6. A 'Happiness is Wren-shaped' sticker, which was in circulation in the 1970s.

men, and women too, circulated this sticker.[24] Fleet Air Arm men even ran a 'Fight Tights' campaign after the official 1975 decision to issue Wrens with black tights instead of the voraciously fetishised black stockings. 'This move had a profound affect upon the morale of the Fleet!', teased one FAA officer.

In the UK several barely related events were propelling women closer towards seagoing and integration: tidying up legal anomalies; responding to the new equal opportunities climate; and recognising that shortages of males would necessitate new staffing arrangements. A Wren rating had been treated more leniently than her sailor pals when caught smoking cannabis with them. John W. T. Townsend, the Chief Naval Judge Advocate, checked the WRNS code of discipline and found Wrens had unfair advantages over men. 'I advised that either the WRNS should be subject to service discipline ... or the voluntary code of discipline would require to be rewritten.' The Navy Board chose the former. Moves towards making the WRNS subject to the NDA then began in 1976. Patrick Duffy, the Navy Minister who had replaced the pro-equality Frank Judd, warned parliament that 'increasing integration ... is an area which needs very sensitive treatment. Prejudice and convention can all too easily damage what has been achieved: we need to hasten slowly.'[25]

Hastening slowly

The word 'discipline' misled some into thinking that the NDA was just about policing wrongs – which it was, to some extent. Wrens joked that male 'reggies' (regulating petty officers, the navy's 'police', whose name was pronounced to rhyme with peggies) were vying to be the first to nab a female wrongdoer and then throw the book at her. The change was really, as Mary Talbot pointed out, about emphasising 'a change in our role – our determination to be equally trained and to take on more and more responsibilities within the Royal Navy'. It meant the loss of a proudly separate women's way of organising, and brought gain. The first domino had fallen and started the chain reaction.

Resistance to the NDA principle was not as bad as John Townsend and others expected. On 1 July 1977 female officer cadets at Dartmouth went on parade sporting armbands in pink overlaid with a narrow black ribbon. They did so with official approval and gentle amusement. Rather than being a marker of mourning, Carolyn Stait, a participant, reflected, the bands 'showed a respect for the past, coupled with a recognition that here was a significant change from which there would be no looking back. It was the end of one way of life and the beginning of something that offered much greater opportunity.' They were permitted to splice the mainbrace with tots of rum, at a Black Velvets-fuelled lunchtime ceremony a day later. In the weeks and months afterwards many Wrens barely noticed the different status, except that men now saluted WRNS officers. However, initially 'You can imagine some went to great lengths to avoid passing a female [by] ducking into doorways or suddenly changing direction!' remembered one officer.[26]

As women were no longer civilians, the range of jobs opened up, and not only on the new word processors (later to become personal computers) as routine digital technology came to be categorised as 'women's work'. First Officer Rosie Ball became the first female lieutenant of a naval shore establishment: HMS *Mercury*. Those considering a long career could go on higher courses at the National Defence College: future WRNS Director Patricia Swallow was the first

Fig. 7.7. Wrens lucky enough to be posted to Gibraltar work at the tape relay centre, a form of telephone communication via punched paper tape, which preceded fax and email, 1977.

woman. To save money, certain WRNS administrative tasks such as drafting (allocating ratings to positions) and recruitment were now done by the navy. Mary's successor, the famously charming Vonla McBride, found it necessary to reassure women that this was no naval takeover. She emphasised: 'It is desperately important that integration does not mean a loss of femininity ... We are complementary, not supplementary.' She thought women 'may want to learn to fly Naval aircraft, they may want to serve at sea in a constructive and practical way, but not to bear arms in war. That is not women's way.' In fact that year 100 Wrens volunteered for the ten available positions supporting royal marine commandos in Northern Ireland, where army women had been killed. These WRNS members not armed – that would come about soon. However they certainly were displaying an appetite for action in a war zone, which could be considered tomboyish by Commandant McBride's yardstick.[27]

Officially combatants

Old ideas that femininity was at odds with war were being challenged nationally and internationally. New civil laws in the UK brought forward a fairer situation: the Equal Pay Act (1970), Employment Protection Act (1975) and Sex Discrimination Act (1975). Although women's services were largely exempt from these laws, the legislation both indicated and further created a fresh climate of asserting women's human rights.

In 1976 Frank Judd had formally challenged the idea that women should not go to sea (nor fly Fleet Air Arm aircraft). Suitable non-combatant ships for Wrens were discussed. However, plans were scuppered because no agreement could be reached about which ships would take them. Rear Admiral David Haslam, the hydrographer, opposed the use of hydrographic ships, the obvious choice. Prince Philip, the Duke of Edinburgh, would not allow Wrens on the Royal Yacht *Britannia*. The move was deferred but not dropped.[28]

Another tide began to affect WRNS' progress, too. The 1949 Geneva Convention (Protocol II) was amended to recognise that *any* woman in the armed services was a combatant, just by virtue of being in those services. As from 1 July 1977 a woman now was recognised as having the right 'to take part directly in hostilities', which included bearing arms. Many NATO countries, but not the UK, Germany and Turkey, had trained women in weapon use too. As a consequence, in December 1978 the UK armed services discussed arming all women (to defend themselves, others and property). The navy opposed. In the past, this had been on the grounds that WRNS members were not in threatened locations so did not *need* arms. Admiral Sir Gordon Tait, the Second Sea Lord, was now against arming women because it might lead to 'vocal minorities' pushing for 'wider changes in the employment of servicewomen'. In reality Wrens had been using the navy's guns for over 30 years, although mainly for recreation. First Officer Joan Bolton King had led the WRNS' .22 rifle shooting competition world since the 1960s.[29]

Entering the final furlong: The 1980s

Rosie Wilson, who became Deputy Director WRNS in the 1980s, characterised the period as one in which 'the WRNS were a bit in limbo ... not fully employable'. The prohibition on women becoming combatants affected their gaining of sea experience, which senior positions required. Officers were changing in style but their career possibilities were not. On leaving Dartmouth, Carolyn Stait found that many WRNS officers who had been earlier trained in the genteel atmosphere of Greenwich 'were suspicious and cautious about "the new breed"' who, instead of strolling in the Thames-side park now toiled, in muddy fatigues, over rugged Dartmoor.[30]

Slowly and patchily changes resulting from the 1970s developments were brought in. Navy Minister Keith Speed told parliament in 1980 that 'women will be allowed into more roles, and will bear arms to a limited extent but not be employed in combat roles'. He explained:

> Although the Armed Forces are specifically excluded from the Sex Discrimination Act, we nevertheless try to comply with the spirit of the Act where this is compatible with Service requirements ... Much is already happening.

Women and men began service life together. From 1981 new entrants trained at HMS *Raleigh* at Torpoint, Cornwall. Women were in a female-only block named after their lost, lamented, HMS *Dauntless*. However it takes time to change institutional culture. The navy did not want to alarm its traditionalist members or the public by turning women into warriors.[31]

Two internal reports came out in the early 1980s. Now untraceable, they were referred to by WRNS historian Ursula Stuart Mason. The January 1980 report pushed the door open a little wider, she said, but the April 1981 report was 'predictable but unambitious'. It made the assumption that WRNS members would not serve at sea during the next ten years and that the navy and WRNS would remain separate. Recommendations included that greater employment of Wrens should be explored and that 'men should not be admitted to WRNS-only branches' (such as telephonist).[32]

Exploring new roles

As part of that exploring of Wrens' potential, a handful were, individually, briefly on ships in the daytime. However they were housed safely on land at night, which meant they by missed out on the social evenings in ship's bars when teams were built. This impaired integration. In Mary Talbot's time, potential to train women for the seemingly exciting job of Fleet Air Arm pilots had been on the cards. Rather than being on the prestigious and now rare fighters they were to fly the more workaday helicopters.

The plan was quashed as fixed-wing planes were cut, then later re-emerged. In 1980 16 women began to train for more aircraft-related roles. As a trial, in 1981, four WRNS Engineering Mechanics (Air) were aboard an RFA vessel, *Engadine*, for two whole weeks. They were praised for their work aboard this support service, not proper naval, ship. However they were criticised for not participating

Fig. 7.8. Wren Joan Roberts enjoys photographers' rights to roam on ships, briefly and just in daytime. She is seated on a capstan on HMS *Lion,* a light cruiser at Rosyth in 1973.

in the mess social life, which appears to have been because they did not quite feel welcome in that all-male situation, and did not like the intense cigarette smoke.

That same year Deborah Heesom was feted as the first WRNS members to train as a student engineer officer. From at least the 1970s a WRNS meteorological officer was occasionally aboard ship. A 'Met Wren' was in an Royal Fleet Auxiliary (RFA) vessel in the Falklands in the early 1980s. Wrens counted her 'as somewhat of a blow for the cause of women', found journalist Dennis Barker. On the other hand, Patricia Swallow, the Director WRNS for 1982 to 1985, explained: 'She was good at her job but didn't have the physical strength to open the bulkhead door *en route* for her briefing, so someone else had to interrupt their job in order to open the door for her.' In those early days of equality struggles, such problems were usually seen as the individual woman's failing and not a useful sign that power-assisted handles might be a good idea all round.[33]

Solid objections to integrating Wrens more were that some were physically weaker, did not fit into male lifestyles and a lack of experience could make them liabilities. 'How can you get the experience if you are not allowed to be there in the first place?' was the protest, as women (especially weapons analysts) continued to be allowed only daily sailings. This was not the inclusive and uninterrupted sea service any trainee needed.

The Falklands Conflict in 1982 made visible how much women were expected to stay ashore while a vast fleet sailed, as they had at D-Day, nearly 40 years earlier. Some 40 QARNNS but no members of the WRNS were aboard the Task Force ships sent to the Falklands. This was partly because Wrens were seen as not having enough sea experience to make them useful. They were not even on the requisitioned merchant ships, encrypting and decrypting messages, as they had been in World War II. Wrens in the conflict instead released men to go afloat by doing support work back in Britain, including guard duty at naval gates, supporting the fleet at sea and providing welfare assistance. Four WRNS members were decorated for such work. The conflict does not appear to have advanced the case for Wrens being allowed to go to sea.[34]

Turning the tide

Continued stymying of women's career prospects perturbed Anthea Larken. She can be seen as the Supremo of Operation Seagoing Women, had such a title existed. Anthea, née Saville (born 1938), later became Director WRNS, but in 1979 was detailed to write a report on the WRNS' future. It was greeted by 'vociferous opposition', including from the then-Director WRNS, Elizabeth Craig-McFeely. 'The time wasn't right for women to go to sea, even though so many people in the navy had recognised that seagoing was the way forward,' Anthea found. 'It wasn't so much a glass ceiling. It was a brick wall ... There was a chance of moving along it [that wall] but, unless we could go to sea, employment was limited.' When she became director she brought deep knowledge of both progress being made internationally on integration and of the valuable officers she had trained at Dartmouth, who had left, thwarted.[35]

Using women at sea was not simply a matter of equal rights. It made sense, as the navy was again short of high-calibre recruits. Women were available – indeed, there was a waiting list. Furthermore, 55 per cent of Wren ratings had more than three GCE O-levels

Fig. 7.9. Commandant Anthea Larken in blue, not yet gold, braid, 1988.

compared with 29 per cent of male RN ratings. Would such qualified Wrens stay long enough and justify the expense of training? In winter 1987/8 the Navy Board was concerned that personnel levels were becoming 'critical'. Demographic trends meant that too few young men were joining, which led in turn to experienced older men resigning because they had to put in too much sea time. Long periods away caused stress in their personal lives. Extending women's employment into sea roles would help. If that were to happen, the navy had to reconsider the unpopular idea of expanding the definition of combat roles for women. People feared that 'our girls' would become 'more like men'.[36]

When in March 1988 Anthea Larken became director, matters began moving forward quickly. Carolyn Stait, a high flyer from the training course Anthea had led at Dartmouth, explained how uniquely suited the new director was to the task:

> Anthea had all the grace, elegance and style of the old-style Greenwich-trained WRNS officers but also shared the passion, vision and drive of the new-style Dartmouth-trained WRNS officers; she gently disguised an innate sense of fun, and a slightly mischievous sense of humour too.

Commandant Larken and Deputy Director Rosie Wilson worked towards what was now patently unavoidable: women's sea service. Progress was helped by the success of the few Wrens who had worked at sea for tiny periods. Shipboard communities did not seem to find the odd *visiting* Wren, especially if a reserve, a problem, nor did Wrens themselves. Second Officer Chella Franklin was in the WRNS Reserve and was working at sea far more than others in the late 1980s. She found that the dual standards were getting in the way of change.

> The examples: 'Smith, make the coffee' and 'Jenny, do you mind making the coffee, dear?' are not so far from the truth ... the removal of the intangible benefits that the WRNS enjoy at present would be to their long-term advantage as it would enable them to be treated in a more professional manner.

in HMS *Norfolk*, she explained: 'I get called "Sir" probably half the time, because the majority of the ratings forget I'm female ... I'm there wearing trousers and a tie and doing a job and they don't really think about it.' She solved what seemed to some the symbolic and insurmountable problem of lack of sanitary accommodation for women by simply hanging a sign outside the officers' shower cubicle: 'Out of bounds, lady showering'.[37]

Two motors bring change

By now the need to increase naval personnel by letting in keen bright women was well recognised, though controversial. In summer 1988 Falklands veteran Captain Alan West, Chief Officer Caroline Coates and Lieutenant-Commander Greg Kenyon were appointed to explore women's sea service and integration. They had six months to look at 'current predicted social and democratic trends in society; the need to get the most cost-effective returns from our investment in personnel; what ministerial approval would be needed, recognising successive governments policy that women should not be employed in combat areas.' Evidence about progress, including in

Fig. 7.10. Caroline Coates, at the time of working on the West report.

the Australian and New Zealand navies and the Israeli army (where women had been armed since before 1948 and were sometimes in combat), helped their task.[38]

Their *Report of a Study into the Employment of Women's Royal Naval Service Personnel in the Royal Navy* ('the West Report') appeared in March 1989. Alan West had been expected to take a die-hard position and say women's sea service could not be achieved, so its conclusions were surprising to most naval people. Among the complex findings were that the feminine image of Wrens stopped people understanding the extent to which they were professional experts doing highly technical tasks including in operations; they were not office ornaments in fetching black tights.

Male chief petty officers were the most resistant, including those who worried about the 'emotional clutter' female shipmates might bring. Menstrual cycles were expected to be a problem. In fact, said Caroline Coates, these had already been proven not to degrade women's operational effectiveness. Anyway, so many women were on the pill, which supressed ovulation, that 'proper periods' including pre-menstrual tension were a thing of the past. (Some had no bleeding at all because they took the pill every day, omitting the suggested one week per month break.)

The thorny problems of what to do about 'wastage' of clever, expensively trained personnel caused by pregnant women leaving, continued. Should they be made to leave and reapply? Or should they have as long a maternity leave as they needed? This was an extension of the concern that married women, particularly mothers, in the services would not be able to be single-minded and flexible enough.[39]

Alan West also looked at a core problem – the idea that a different sort of woman would be attracted to a more vigorous WRNS. He explained that hard evidence from other navies showed that their female personnel were not necessarily less feminine. However anxieties about ushering in hard-drinking tomboys, later called 'ladettes', persisted. The prospect was seriously upsetting to those who cherished traditional 'ladies'.

Two main recommendations were made: women should go to sea on non-combatant ships from April 1990; and the WRNS should merge with the Royal Navy one year later. Five ships were designated as suitable for 78 women initially: two survey ships, an offshore patrol vessel, a seabed operations ship and navigation training ship.

These suggestions were not popular. Anthea Larken and Rosie Wilson 'fiercely rebutted' them as not going far enough. They felt clear that far more seagoing women were needed on a fuller range of warships. That was the way to develop a better-integrated seagoing experience. Caroline Coates 'got flak' from some Wrens, particularly older, lower-ranked women, who had no interest in proceeding up a career ladder via sea service. Some veterans also feared that their 'elite identity as highly qualified, well-respected women would be lost in the mass of the Navy'.[40]

Crucially, the West Report impetus coincided with the National Audit Office (NAO) report on MoD staffing, which came out a few weeks later. It said that if the services did not make better use of their uniformed women then it would be more cost-effective to disband the women's services entirely and replace them with civil servants. As almost half of the WRNS posts were not really military jobs, the report found non-uniformed civilians on lower pay could substitute in roles such as secretary and dental assistant. It was similar to the ideas brought forward by the Grigg Report in 1958 and Joan Vickers' recommendations. However, this time around, that important phenomenon, creeping civilianisation, was much more advanced and accepted. This pivotal 'the writing is on the wall' NAO report, together with the West Report, was the impetus needed to jump-start a new way of thinking. Allowing members to go to sea would stave off axing the entire service.[41]

Responses varied, some overlapping. Those supporting women's seagoing roles, even on combatant ships, included a minority of WRNS members and some senior naval officers who had seen the light – even if they did not like it. Against were the essentialists who thought it was plain wrong, almost sacrilegious, because it offended against the natural order of things: women don't go to sea, to war. It's men's work. Traditionalists hated what they saw as gimmicky and hollow public relations gestures and silly political correctness gone mad.

Practical objections included that it would cost a lot of effort, as well as money, to refit ships with separate accommodation. Transplanting women would not solve the problem. It was argued that 3,000 personnel were needed. That was just about the entire number of Wrens in existence, and only a few hundred were likely to be the seagoing sort. One anonymous senior figure, 'Aeneas', told *Naval Review* that as people on ships had at least three subsidiary roles, all of which were physically demanding, 'mixed manning' 'would presumably require one and one third Wrens for every male rating'. This was based on the calculation that women were 30 per cent less strong than men. On that basis, 198 women would be required to staff a Type-23 frigate, instead of 149 men.

Opponents also declared it was impossible to make ships and personnel ready for sea service in only 13 months. No-one had yet resolved whether women would be allowed to stay on ships that were suddenly called into conflicts. Would Wrens be airlifted away to safety? Concerned male officers feared that wives' anxiety about on-board adultery might lead them to pressurise husbands to leave the navy, worsening the shortages.[42]

Some people, including a number of politicians in the ruling Conservative Party, resented the suggestion that women should be at sea at all. Others criticised Alan West for not going the whole hog and saying women should be on warships. Reflecting nearly 20 years later, Alan West dismissed his own softly-softly recommendations as 'pusillanimous', but explained they were what 'the market would bear' then. Today Caroline Coates feels their recommendations were the best that could be done at the time.[43]

A sudden volte face

With this push for speeded-up evolution, rather than revolution, politicians and naval leaders moved to the next steps: investigating whether and how to follow up the West recommendations. In the end, very surprisingly, they went much further. In a major *volte face*, the acceptance that Wrens must go to sea went beyond what anyone thought possible.

Sir Archie Hamilton, the Armed Forces Minister from 1988 to 1993, challenged the navy to substantiate the claim that it was *policy* that women should not be in 'direct combat'. Historian Kath Sherit has found from internal documents that thereafter opponents instead began referring to the 'policy' as just a 'precept'. A wall was weakening. As a result the Second Sea Lord, Admiral Sir Brian Brown, went ahead and presented a Navy Board paper supporting seagoing and subsequently integration. He found First Sea Lord, Admiral Sir Julian Oswald, becoming stronger in his support. 'He was under pressure from his own daughters.'

Rear Admiral Sir Neville Purvis, the Director General Naval Manpower and Training, met individual Navy Board members and persuaded them to support the go-ahead for women on warships. His grounds were that it was better for the navy to 'make this decision on its own terms rather than having it imposed through political correctness'.[44]

Somehow the Navy Board unanimously agreed the paper. Preserving the navy and nation was more important than preserving female and male 'norms'. The navy had accepted many unpleasant political decisions, such as cuts, before. Then the Queen and Prime Minister Thatcher accepted that the 'precept' be set aside.

On 5 February 1990 Archie Hamilton in the House of Commons uttered the momentous words:

> I am pleased to be able to announce that we intend to extend the employment of members of the Women's Royal Naval Service to include service at sea in surface ships of the Royal Navy ... officers and ratings of the Wrens serving at sea are liable to serve there in combat. This represents a change in the long-standing policy that women should not undertake duties that may include direct combat.

He explained that attempting to categorise ships as 'combatant' and 'non-combatant' was 'artificial and misleading'. Modern maritime warfare meant that *all* ships 'will be liable to serve in potentially dangerous waters'. The decision was motivated by concern about lack of naval personnel but also because the decision-makers thought 'the current restrictions on Wrens' employment were in any case ripe for review in the light of developments in other navies and of domestic social trends', he said. It was simply part of widening employment opportunities for the women of the army and RAF too. Furthermore, he agreed to a snappy timetable: 'Our aim is for the first of them to be embarked by the end of the year.'[45]

CHAPTER 8

Women become Doctors and Men become Nurses: 1946–90

If you can treat all sorts of wounds and dressings, yet sympathise and keep the tender touch ...
Yours is the hospital and everything in it, and what is more, you'll be a nurse, my girl.[1]

Nursing Staff

VADs hand baton to WRNS ratings: the 1950s

Bolton-born Matilda Goodrich (1891–1972), matron-in-chief QARNNS, was heading 100-odd QARNNS regulars and many reserves as the war ended and in the transition that followed. All naval health care workers were serving in a new peacetime world while still dealing with war's legacies. Challenges included how to give good care when there was a woeful lack of people to do the less-skilled nursing work. Attracting, training and retaining such staff were to continue to be problems for the next few decades.

Under Dame Matilda regular QARNNS carried on with their defence careers as nursing officers. Some reserves went back to civilian nursing; the National Health Service began in 1948. Scores seem to have become QARNNS regulars in Royal Navy hospitals such as Haslar, after the auxiliary hospitals closed. Much-needed naval VADs such as Norma Wilson carried on and more continued to be recruited throughout the 1950s too. Often very much more than the 'bedpan brigade' (the usual annoying joke name for aides) VADs numbered 3,893 in 1945. Numbers dwindled to 501 in 1949 and to just 94 a decade later.[2]

Cold War conflict brought new opportunities, including proximity to danger. Naina Beaven, a VAD with D-Day experience, volunteered to go out to Hong Kong in 1949. She had a grandstand view, typing up the hush-hush reports made by the stressed HMS *Amethyst* sailors after the pivotal Yangtse incident. International tensions that year led to the navy seeking 500 VADs to form a standing reserve.

A medical branch in the WRNS began too, partly because so few men were interested in being 'poultice wallopers', SBAs. To deal with the shortage, WRNS ratings became SBAs, supporting QARNNS officers and working side-by-side with male sick berth staff. In essence

Fig. 8.1. QARNNS sisters Ruth Stone and matron Barbara Nockolds on hospital ship *Maine* during the Korean War. Ruth Stone is seated on the lowest seat.

the work of these Wren SBAs was similar to that which had been done by VADs since 1939. New (male) SBAs were so hard to recruit that VADs continued to be crucial throughout the 1950s.[3]

Overseas a few QARNNS regulars and VADs were involved in the escalating South East Asia tensions. Regulars Ruth Stone and Barbara Nockolds (later to become a matron-in-chief) went east in early 1950 to work in the navy's sole remaining – and ailing – hospital ship RFA *Maine*. During the three-year Korean War they nursed the many wounded military personnel transferring from Pusan in South Korea to Osaka in Japan. VAD Alfreda Etheridge was one of four replacements for the initial six, just as hostilities were ceasing in summer 1953.[4]

Back home in the UK the Cold War and nuclear threat intensified. Labour shortages in public services led to civilian nurses being recruited from the Caribbean. Similarly, armed forces shortages meant the navy was relying on reserves. More regulars were needed, as was a more streamlined situation. Female naval nursing staff now included QARNNS sisters, Wren SBAs and VADs. They worked with male SBAs, some of whom hated being 'bossed around' by women.

Fig. 8.2. Ann Whatford (right) and some of the last WRNS SBAs play at Haslar, *c.* 1960.

From 1955, SBAs were called medical assistants (MAs), the gender-free term used today. Managing these different categories and their separate hierarchies was a logistical problem. A kind of amalgamation, yet fresh category, was the answer.

New sorts of nurses: the 1960s and 1970s

As a result of the swingeing 1957 'Sandys' Axe', cuts and restructuring were felt across the armed forces. In March 1960 parliament was told:

> the duties previously performed in other hospitals and establishments by Naval V.A.D.s and W.R.N.S. Sick Berth Assistants will in future be the responsibility of the Naval Nursing Auxiliaries, a new section of the Queen Alexandra's Royal Naval Nursing Service.

Newcomers, plus existing naval VADs and Wren SBAs formed a new corps of less-trained and lower-paid female ratings. These 'Naval Nurses' were managed by QARNNS officers. The change simplified personnel management and created an affordable solution to the shortages of ratings in naval nursing. It was hoped that the change would mean women would give years of service and join the reserves too.[5]

Phasing out the roles of W/SBA and the VAD (RN) caused a sense of loss of their proudly women-only communities. W/SBA Ann Whatford stayed on until her four years was up in 1962. Like her SBA colleagues in the WRNS she was invited to become a naval nurse. However, 'I was adamant that I didn't want to go into the QAs. I was a *Wren*!' Instead she left the navy entirely. Other VADs switched. In 1965 the very last VAD, Korean War veteran Commandant Alfreda Etheridge, left aged 70.[6]

From 1962 QARNNS began training women to become state-registered nurses (SRNS) or state-enrolled nurses (SENs). The double-decker system that had emerged throughout the UK from the 1940s embraced civilian and defence nurses alike. These students and pupils (respectively) were on the navy's own bespoke training course, which was governed by Royal College of Nursing standards. Naval Nursing Auxiliary Service (NNAS) students had the pleasure of 16 weeks' training in Malta or Gibraltar. Kathleen Harland points out that taking responsibility for training 'was a major change for QARNNS which had hitherto only accepted candidates already qualified in civilian hospitals.' In 1966 the word 'auxiliary' was dropped from the NNAS: members were simply 'naval nurses'.[7]

As a tiny service with a correspondingly tiny number at its pinnacle, opportunities in the QARNNS were few and striven for. Some variety occurred because in naval bases overseas, such as Malta, QARNNS sisters tended naval families. Working with wives meant delivering babies and giving contraceptive advice, as well as other matters. Opportunities grew, such as specialist training in intensive care and psychiatric medicine. Superintending Sister Nora Miller was a pioneer, going on an exchange to Germany working with RAF nurses and training them in obstetrics, at a time when international tri-service co-operation was new. Shortages of doctors brought increasing responsibilities for nursing officers, including visiting submarines to carry out risk assessment. In this changing world Sister Carole Ralph found her QARNNS colleagues of the time, such as matron-in-chief Cynthia Cooke, to be 'inspiring leaders' who were 'forward-looking in terms of service needs and our professional development'.[8]

In the navy at last: 1977

Under matron-in-chief Patricia Gould, the biggest stride so far in naval nursing history occurred. Like the WRNS, members of the QARNNS and the NNS were placed under the Naval Discipline Act in 1977. Sister Nora Miller remembered 'It changed everything.' QARNNS became properly affiliated to the Royal Navy, although remaining a separate service. They wore a more naval-style uniform with gold braid on their sleeves. When the female nursing personnel came back from their post-NDA course they found some male MAs were quite hostile because the women now had a more naval status. People got used to it.

Kathleen Harland's view was that 'Far from resenting this [NDA], Nursing Officers and nurses seemed to welcome it as being part of the well-ordered world in which they chose to work ... It has helped make nursing in the Royal Navy very attractive, for professional skills could be learnt and exercised in its secure, stratified family-like environment.' Integration seemingly did not bring greater closeness with the WRNS. This was partly because some QARNNS members felt that they had an elite vocation and were in the senior of the two naval women's services.[9]

The 'Fearless Forty' in the Falklands Conflict: the 1980s

Female nursing, but not medical, staff served at sea in the Falklands Conflict from April to August 1982. In the temporarily converted liner HMHS *Uganda*, under Matron Edith Meiklejohn (1934–2008), the 'Fearless Forty' – 15 QARNNS and 26 NNs – formed part of the UK Task Force.[10]

Old and new patterns of hospital ship nursing were visible. As in the past, the ship with its huge illuminated red cross sailed as near as was safe to retrieve casualties. Female ratings were serving for the first time in a hospital ship.

All the naval health care personnel were praised for acquitting themselves creditably. Respect for defence medicine was renewed. Women's role in combat was being discussed anyway at this point and betrousered HMHS *Uganda* nurses proved women could handle combat. Staff Nurse

Fig. 8.3. QARNNS Sister Liz Law at the time of the Falklands Conflict. She became a tabloid heroine because of her engagement, then marriage, to a civilian survivor of the *Atlantic Conveyor*. Liz remained in battle after he had been sent home.[12]

Sally Middleton felt that once HMS *Sheffield* was sunk 'we really got down to business'. Only afterwards did they realise the dangers.[11]

A nurse can be a man, a lieutenant, a mother?

A gender-integrated service began in 1982 partly to rationalise all anomalies. Men entered the QARNNS. Senior Nursing Officer Rajendresen Perusram was the first of 47 male nurses to transfer. The gender-neutral and naval term 'Sister', which was the term used in civilian nursing, was replaced by 'Nursing Officer'. The ranking system changed, meaning, for example, a nursing officer became a lieutenant. Also, from May 1984, ratings' titles changed too, for example 'Petty Officer Naval Nurse Nelson'.[13]

QARNNS sisters were now allowed to stay on after marriage. However, until 1990 they were to experience the same mores as other servicewomen. Being a married woman was acceptable if you put the services' needs first. However marriage 'was viewed as something almost disloyal to the service' said Sister S. Pragnell, who thinks she was the first to stay on. On pregnancy you resigned. Some left the QARNNS for good, such as *Uganda* veteran Head Naval Nurse Maggie Freer in 1983. At least two naval nursing staff took part in a successful class action against the MoD who, it was ruled, had unlawfully dismissed them for being pregnant.[14]

Lack of naval medical personnel brought the final change of this period: a new category called medical assistants (MA (Q))s. Q stood for QARNNS, indicating they were part of the nursing service, not the medical service like SBAs. Begun in 1987, they were successors to earlier Wren SBAs and VADs. MA (Q)s were a new sort, fresh from school and interested in a wide variety of experiences, rather than a professional career ladder. A kind of hybrid medic, in initial training MA (Q)s were, like all females, quartered in the Dauntless block at HMS *Raleigh*. They were uniformed like QARNNS, wearing 'buckets' not WRNS-style 'bottletop' caps. Their promotion structure was the MA, not NN, one. They proudly saw themselves as MAs (like their male colleagues) rather than as QARNNS.

Surprisingly few male MAs resented the new invasion of 12 Rohilla class women (named after the wrecked SS *Rohilla*, a World War I ship – women had been heroic in its rescue operation) and their successors. One of the first MA (Q)s in 1987 thought the male MAs had been somewhat used to resting on their laurels, but were rather galvanised by the women's refreshing determination to get on. Equally surprisingly, some nurses were hostile: they feared the newcomers would take over some of their roles in the coveted sick bays. When women went to sea from 1990, several of that first Rohilla class were assigned (the term was no longer 'drafted') in the same shore–sea–shore cycle as male MAs. That integrated pattern continued.[15]

Women do the doctoring

After World War II the navy's women doctors left. The 20-odd female MOs, such as Ailsa Whitehouse, only stayed on until 1947 at the latest. They returned to civilian life, perhaps affronted by unequal pay prospects: in 1949 the Treasury contended that service 'women doctors are, after all, women and should be remunerated as such'. However, from at least 1954 women MOs did join the navy (not the WRNS or QARNNS). Acting Surgeon Lieutenant Patricia McDonald (later Morley) (1929–2003) was seemingly the first of this new wave. There she met her future husband, then went on to become an internationally famous ultrasound pioneer.[16]

Continuing shortages led to the forces' Medical and Dental Services Committee's Waverley Report in 1958. It discussed new plans to bring in women. This was followed by a recruitment scheme: medical and dental students were offered incentives such as scholarships. Collette Green was perhaps one of those attracted by the new arrangements. They were akin to the US Navy's doctors; women physicians had been quietly commissioned there since 1949. Dr Green was the first woman commissioned as a naval MO for over ten years. *Navy News* in August 1963 announced, 'The first of a limited number of women doctors is to be granted short-service commissions for duty at naval shore establishments in this country and overseas.' The article stressed Collette

Fig. 8.4. Surgeon Lieutenant Collette Green begins her naval training in Portsmouth, July 1963.

Green 'will carry out all the duties of her male counterparts, except, of course, that she will not be appointed to a ship.'[17]

Table 8.1. Women Medical and Dental Officers 1945–89[18]

Year	No. of women medical officers	Total medical officers	No. of women dental officers	Total dental officers
1945	25	2,535	n/a	686
1950	0	365	0	76
1955	1	380	0	89
1960	0	370	0	121
1965	1	390	4	115
1970	7	414	0	118
1975	3	402	6	101
1980	5	283	6	101
1985	6	275	7	92
1989	15	268	6	83

The 1963 UK decision laid the foundation for women MOs' integration into naval medicine. Their numbers increased in the 1970s and 1980s. Collette's successors such as Surgeon Lieutenant Pam

Young were never there to work solely with women. However, not being allowed to work at sea restricted their usefulness to the navy and therefore their potential careers, as with WRNS officers too. This suddenly became evident as a stumbling block at the start of the Falklands Conflict. The only Royal Marines health care team members who were allowed to sail were male, even though female doctors had trained with these reserves. Rick Jolly (Senior Medical Officer of 3 Commando Brigade) summarised a crucial pre-sailing staffing problem from 3–9 April 1982:

> Because we were likely to deploy to war in Royal Navy ships, a really high-level command decision had to be taken on the issue of whether there would be any women in the surgical teams. Nobody had given this matter any real thought in peacetime. If the ladies had to be replaced at this late stage, such an action would remove the female nursing element at a stroke, and would also create big problems in finding suitable male replacements in time. Needless to say, the girls (who had trained hard in peacetime) were a bit upset as well.

Presumably the objections were that women would be in a combat zone and that segregated sleeping accommodation would have to be created. Finally the Royal Marines medical team set off in *Canberra*, 'thoroughly hacked off' that all their female members had been removed. Subsequently the exclusion of a (female) anaesthetist proved particularly hampering. By the early 1990s, however, Wrens, QARNNS, NNs and MA (Q)s were all able to sail.[19]

Enter the 'lady toothwrights'

Barbara Haines, the navy's first woman dental officer (DO) in peacetime, began work in 1955. A few others followed. Their advent was the outcome of the 1951 decision to allow in women and the 1962 introduction of medical and dental officer cadetships (meaning help with study) to attract newcomers. Just ten women joined in the first 18 years to 1973. Usually they had recently qualified.[20]

If QARNNS could turn to ratings for help then so too could the navy's gnasher-bashers. Dental officers' time could be freed up by developing the skills of female support workers. From at least 1960 Wrens ratings became dental surgery assistants (DSAs) in the dental branch. Mary Burdett was one of the early DSAs, in 1964. They were not paired with female dental officers. In her six and a half years, Mary worked with just one female DO, Surgeon Lieutenant (D.) Finnie, who had joined in 1968 a month after qualifying in Edinburgh.[21] Wren dental hygienists were introduced from 1965, after the army and air force had paved the way. They were recruited from both existing Wren chairside assistants and very new Wrens who had done that work in Civvy Street.[22]

DSA Lesley Thomas (born 1956) says Wren DSAs were amused to find they had power. Even the most butch marines could turn to jelly in their presence and faint at the sight of a needle: 'usually they were terrified. You were the one at the other end of the equipment!' The DSA post stopped being women-only in 1977, in line with the integration triggered by all women coming under the Naval Discipline Act.[23]

QARNNS go everywhere

In the years since 1946 VADs, SBAs, NNs, QARNNS, medical officers, dental officers and many others, including radiologists had been part of a fast-changing world of both clinical and social progress. The advent of antibiotics and new psychiatric knowledge had transformed defence medical care. The National Health Service had improved the health of those who later joined naval services.

In surgeries, wards and sick bays, in the *Maine*, HMHS *Uganda* and RFA *Argus*, by 1990 women had contributed much in most areas of naval health care, helping women and men alike during and after the Cold War.

Women's contributions had ranged from looking after casualties off Korea, to giving the pill to naval wives in Gibraltar, to filling teeth at HMS *Daedalus*, to helping save lives in the South Atlantic. Revered matrons-in-chief such as Cynthia Cooke, Pat Gould and Claire Taylor

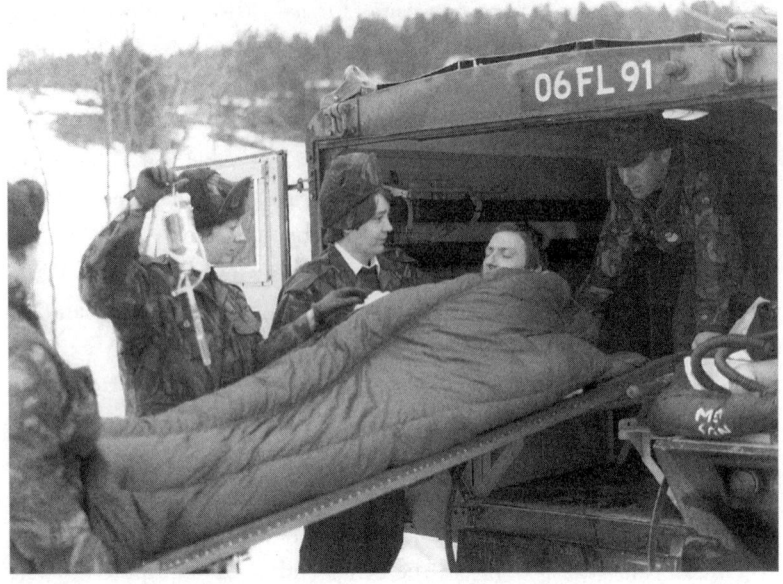

Fig. 8.5. QARNNS increasingly served abroad: a team on exercise load a patient into a Land Rover in Norway, 1980s.

had enabled the professional development of hundreds of women and men. Women in health care served as reserves as well as regulars. Indeed some regulars had their first brief seagoing experiences because they were allocated to work with female reserves on exercises. Among the most exciting signs of progress were individuals' giant strides across status divides. Kay Funnel was the only person to rise from VAD to Superintending Nursing Sister. Falklands veteran naval nurse Sally Middleton retrained and became a doctor.[24]

CHAPTER 9

All in the Defence Medical Services Team: 1991 to Today

Without warning Taliban fighters opened fire... All I was thinking was: there's a casualty and I need to be there... the quicker I get to him the more chance I have to save his life.

Kate Nesbitt

When Commodore Inga Kennedy (see colour plate 22), a former QARNNS sister, in April 2017 became the first ever woman Medical Director General (Naval) this was a telling feat. For over a century the role had only been open to surgeons. Nursing had previously been seen as separate, and stigmatised for being a smaller and largely female force. A woman MDG is still so unusual that the army and air force have not yet promoted a woman to this two-star position.

Aptly, this trailblazer is a graduate of the equally ground-breaking centre for the education of women and district nurses since 1875 – Queen Margaret University College, Edinburgh. Inga Kennedy's recognition is the most significant sign of women's inclusion in the entire history of naval health care so far. Never before the 1990s had a woman been in such a high position.

Today women in the navy's medical services are greater in overall number than the QARNNS. The QARNNS continues as an independent but integrated part of that whole medical service.[1]

Becoming integrated in 1990–2000

Women offering health care in this period included QARNNS officers, naval nurses, medical assistants (the Q was dropped in 1998), medical and dental officers and other staff. New roles were opened to women as part of the general armed forces move towards integration and service in combat situations. Some women felt unhappy since seagoing was not what they had signed up for. However others enjoyed the new eligibility for senior roles it brought.

Change in the QARNNS accelerated rapidly in the 1990s. QARNNS officers came still closer to the navy in 1995 when they adopted naval rank titles and badges, for easier identification. The QARNNS Queen Alexandra's monogram of two As, with an anchor and cable erect was now red (as for medical services personnel) and gold.

Women of the naval health care team were deployed in many conflicts as well as in humanitarian missions, in naval and RFA ships and on the ground, increasingly closer to combat. In the 1991 First Gulf War, when Iraq invaded Kuwait, both regulars and reserves sailed in the navy's own 'hospital ship', RFA *Argus*. The women on board this primary casualty receiving ship (PCRS) included QARNNS sisters, a WRNS dental surgery assistant, an MO and MA (Q)s. Naval attitudes to women's deployment in this war varied. However, one male medic was so proud that the medical branch had 'beaten' the WRNS in having the first women on a ship in an operational theatre that he sent a celebratory signal announcing that to the Senior Officer Middle East.[2]

Women's opportunities were improving. However, the armed services as a whole were undergoing round after round of cuts and closures as a result of the Options for Change programme in 1990 and then the Front Line First defence cost study in 1994. The old idea that women should be sacked or made redundant before men were, as they did not have to support a family was gone, but many QARNNS officers were among the talented people who were knocked back. It is said that when Claire Taylor, matron-in-chief QARNNS in 1994–6, and the Second Sea Lord were discussing which of her prize personnel might have to be let go he looked inside the top folder of her stack and he asked her why someone so good should be made redundant. Captain Taylor reportedly dumped the rest of the files on his desk, saying 'So are all of these too', burst into tears and walked out.

The better news was that in 1996 Captain Patricia Hambling became the first Director Naval Nursing Service to have risen from being a naval nurse. She was heartening proof that high-flyers did not have to start out as officers.[3]

Women doctors were far fewer than QARNNS members, possibly only a tenth as many. Some had brief experiences in ships on exercise before 1991, and slowly they were deployed at sea. In 1996 Surgeon Lieutenant Leslie Sowden (born 1970) became one of the early women seagoing MOs. Sailing in the frigate HMS *Campbeltown* with 291 men she shrugged off a few of the men's difficulties in accepting women's authority; they 'tend[ed] to test you out'. At a time when all women were still being judged by the conduct of one, early pioneers were crucial in proving that skill was the point, not gender.[4]

Defence medics in the 2000s

MA Kate Nesbitt was the first naval woman to receive the Military Cross. Her story highlighted the extent to which women were serving closer to combat. MA Nesbitt (born 1988) is the first naval person – of any gender – to win the award since World War II. She is also the first naval person below warrant officer status to ever gain an MC. The daughter of a marine, she was attached to 3 Commando Brigade in Afghanistan for six months in 2008–9. Near Lashkar Gah, she said:

> Without warning Taliban fighters opened fire, having ambushed us. Within seconds I heard 'man down, man down' on the radio ... [I] sprinted 60 to 70 metres running towards him while under fire. All I was thinking was: there's a casualty and I need to be there... the quicker I get to him the more chance I have to save his life ... I treated him for about 45 minutes ... Bullets were whizzing around my head and shoulders and hitting the ground all around us.

Eventually a Merlin chopper airlifted Lance Corporal John List to hospital. He survived.[5]

When Lara Herbert was training to become an MO in 2007, she 'realised then that I wanted to work as a doctor in areas of conflict.' She had found that 'Most women who join the Navy are sent away on ships, but I wanted to see more active service.' This meant being the medic for 3 Commando Brigade:

> In order to be part of this exclusive club, I had to pass ... the All Arms Commando Course at (CTC) Lympstone in Devon ... [E]leven wet, muddy, gruelling weeks later, I became the first woman to pass ... in one attempt... It was the proudest day of my life ... Over the next few years I lived out of my rucksack, deployed to Arctic Norway, the Himalayas and finally on operational tour to Afghanistan ... with a Royal Marine fighting company.[6]

Kate and Lara's stories are the derring-do end of the naval health care spectrum. Others, such as Jane Risdall (1959–2016), rose to become principal MOs on aircraft carriers such as HMS *Invincible*, in her case, *Illustrious* and *Ark Royal*. Gender became less of a bar to high rank and interesting opportunities abounded in the branch, QARNNS, which had the highest percentage of women in medical service. Figures for 2016 reveal that 66 per cent of QARNNS, and a grand total of 43 per cent of all 1,260 trained regulars in medical branches were women.[7, 8]

Nurses' situation today developed from March 2000 when QARNNS members were officially became part of the Royal Navy. The QARNNS was incorporated, but unlike the WRNS it still had its separate identity. Traditions shifted again when Captain Mick Bowen became the first male director of naval nursing services in 2002. He announced: 'I'm not shy of using both titles [DNNs and matron-in-chief] ... because they obviously have a lot of meaning.'[9]

Table 9.1 shows that women are holding their own, more so than men, despite repeated defence cuts. However, in 2016, only 20 per cent of naval MOs were women by comparison to 45 per cent of doctors in the whole UK.[10]

Table 9.1. **Trained Regulars in Royal Navy Medical Branches 2000–16**[11]

Date	Medical officers Female	Medical officers Total	Dental officers Female	Dental officers Total	Medical personnel* Female	Medical personnel* Total	QARNNS officers Female	QARNNS officers Total	QARNNS Female	QARNNS Total
2000	n/a	n/a	n/a	n/a	n/a	n/a	70		130	227
2005	40	320	20	60	270	730	60	90	140	200
2010	60	360	20	60	320	780	50	80	130	190
2016	60	310	20	50	300+	670	50	80	110	150

Note
* Includes dental nurses and medical assistants.

Health care on land

Women and men alike now work in a changed context. No dedicated naval hospital, nor even an armed forces hospital, exists. In this partly civilianised world of combined services, naval personnel are not nursed by Haslar-bred staff in wards named after admirals. Instead staffs are trained at the Defence School of Health Care Studies, based in Birmingham and

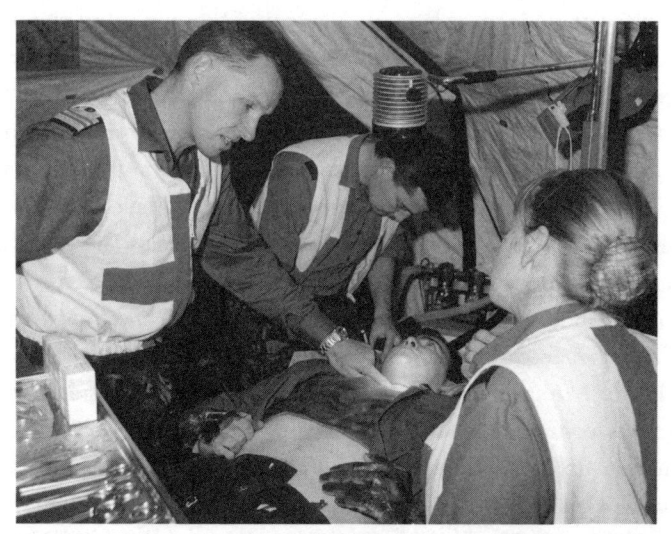

Fig. 9.1. Medical team including QARNNS in a tented unit on an exercise in the 2000s.

work in Ministry of Defence Hospital Units (MDHUs) within several contracted NHS hospitals: Plymouth, Portsmouth and Birmingham, plus Catterick and Headley Court in Surrey. Each person wears the uniform of their own service (which can disconcert patients). Initially unwell naval personnel felt unhappy at civilianisation and combination. Today inter-service co-operation is normal, for example in the 1,000-strong Royal College of Nursing's Defence Nursing Forum (which began in 2005) and the British Medical Association's Armed Forces Committee.[12]

Serving on the move

Sometimes exhilarating challenges face those medics on naval operations and humanitarian missions in the 17 frigates and destroyers. During Operation Telic in the Second Gulf War, 60 naval medics were involved. In the 2014 Operation Weald QARNNS in HMS *Bulwark* in the Central Mediterranean helped save migrants' lives. Some 75 were in the naval surgical team giving front-line medical cover in Helmand, Afghanistan. Women and men are no longer differentiated in the statistics. Indeed doing so is seen as impolite and irrelevant. But it is probable that women made up at least 50 per cent of those in these operations.[13]

Any health care-minded person who wants plenty of seagoing becomes an MA. If she chooses nursing she will be more land-based. In MA (Q) Debbie Hunnybun's case she served three months in aircraft carrier HMS *Invincible*. However when she retrained as a nurse (1996–9) she had no long deployments at sea. When a smaller vessel is deployed on operations, several suitable medics are temporarily assigned to that ship rather than 'belonging' to it. The navy's capital ships (meaning large significant ones such as aircraft carriers) all have their own medical departments with a permanent staff of one or two MOs plus MAs. As well as providing dental and medical care, looking after environmental health and advising on travel medicine, staff also train the ship's company in first aid and stand by to give medical assistance, for example to a distressed nearby fishing boat or oil tanker.[14]

Katharine Cordner, a dental officer, explained the usual pattern for 'Dent Os'. They usually join the navy on five-year commissions.

> In the main, my time in the Royal Navy was spent between the three naval shore bases of Faslane, Plymouth and Portsmouth ... My nurse and I, with our portable dental unit, were flown out to exotic locations [the Seychelles, Gulf and Caribbean] to meet a ship where we would set up in the sickbay and become part of the ships' company for a few weeks ... it was our job to leave everyone on board dentally fit.[15]

The RFA *Argus* remains the vessel which is used when a 'hospital ship' (a PCRS) is needed in an emergency, such as during the Sierra Leone Ebola outbreak in 2014. Currently 238 medical and nursing staff are scheduled to care for patients aboard when the need arises. Royal Marine Band Service women and men act as stretcher bearers. An (atypical) MoD statistical snapshot from August 2016 shows gender patterns on board: five out of 14 MOs, 18 out of the 28 naval nurses, and nine of the 15 nursing officers were female.[16]

Naval women medics are in the air and under water too. In Fleet Air Arm search and rescue (SAR) operations they, like men, take part in medevacs (accompanied medical evacuations). HMS *Somerset* Surgeon Lieutenant Jo Laird in 2014 looked after the patient in a SAR helicopter over Cornwall. Either or both of her two paramedics could in theory have been women, as could the people flying the chopper.

Submarines are the very latest naval vessels to carry women medical assistants submariners (MA-SMs, pronounced 'maz ums'). At least one woman was working as an MA-SM in 2016. The first woman medical officer for submarines was streamed through and given specialist training in 2014. In addition, the first woman to become the medical officer in charge (MOIC) of the Royal Naval Institute of Medicine, Fleur Marshall, was appointed in 2016.[17]

The future for women medics

'Fancy nursing with a difference?' asks the 2017 advert on the QARNNS website, adding 'you could be deployed in combat'. The international political situation suggests that demands on the navy (including its reserve) may be great. Female regulars are to be among the 11 medical staff in the new Queen Elizabeth class of aircraft carriers, scheduled for 2017 and 2020, as well as on existing vessels.

What are the battles naval women still have to fight in health care? Few, seemingly, apart from the general struggle to make an under-resourced service work. Like the transport industry and all the armed forces, the main gender-specific concern is to enable women (and men too) to balance having children and at the same time succeeding in careers that require much time away from home. Given the pattern in wider society that women, more than men, give up careers to do childcare, retention does rely on helping women.

Conclusion: From loblolly boy substitutes to surgeon

Over the centuries women have come far from the time of seagoing wives and mothers like Nelly Giles helping the wounded on ships at sea. Kill-quick Sairy Gamps in quayside boarding houses can never return. Today's naval women have good reputations and access to continuing professional training. They are focused and fully part of the team. Today it would be unthinkable to offer a naval woman MO lower pay than a man's, as the navy did to Dr Genevieve Rewcastle in 1939.

At the National Museum of the Royal Navy's 2017 exhibition of naval women in Portsmouth, a QARNNS sister serving 20 years ago assessed her successors. Carole Ralph finds that now they are 'so professional. They're all over the world. They want to be there. They're able to be there. And they're supported.' As for the wearing of practical scrubs, not iconic white veils, she firmly believes that 'it's what a naval nurse does, not what she wears', that determines how she or he is valued.[18]

For outsiders with a big historical perspective, such as me, it is moving to find continued proof of no-fuss bravery in combat situations. It is clear that women have repeatedly and selflessly risen to do the very best they could to care for the wounded, sick and injured, including their own sisters-in-arms.

CHAPTER 10

On towards Diversity and Inclusion: 1991 to Today

Putting Wrens on ships 'was as big a change as from sail to steam. Men fell on swords saying it'll never work.'

Commander Rosie Wilson[1]

From blue to gold, but red-top spanners: the 1990s

Archie Hamilton's parliamentary announcement that women could sail from September 1990 was the formal start of naval women's future. Hectic months of preparation followed for the WRNS Sea Service Implementation Team. Headed by Captain John Marshall and Commander Rosie Wilson, they worked tirelessly so that women could finally play an integral role in some of the navy's 177 ships. Rosie Wilson reflected later that it was 'a vast undertaking'; there was so much to sort out. 'I don't think that if people had been told that in ten months so much could be achieved that it would have been believed. There was *such* integration.'[2]

It was a twin process: making ready both ships and members of the WRNS. Vessels were selected on the basis of whether their infrastructures could easily be adapted and whether their commanding officers were willing to make a success of integration. Aircraft carriers HMS *Invincible* and *Ark Royal*, assault ship HMS *Fearless*, navigation training ship HMS *Juno* and a number of Type-22 frigates were scheduled to become mixed. Women were going to constitute at least 10 per cent of the personnel on some ships. Such a ratio was thought to be easier. If just a few incomers were trickled in they might have faced lonelier struggles with the institution's teething problems over integration. Ideally they would neither face an intimidating large 'city' afloat nor a tiny established community of 30-plus (as was the case on the small mine countermeasures vessels). About 50–60 Wrens were to sail in an aircraft carrier with its complement of 500–600, and 20 in a frigate with approximately 220 aboard.[3]

Several hundred women were sought. Out of the 3,600-strong WRNS, most had joined with the assumption that the 'Never at Sea' motto still held and would continue. Having their job conditions changed so fundamentally was akin to airport check-in desk staff being suddenly told to become cabin crew, pronto. *Navy News'* front page demanded 'Jennies now able – how many willing?'. The answer turned out to be 'surprisingly few', especially among the much-needed ratings and petty officers. Commissioned officers were keener, but few were required.[4]

HMS *Brilliant* was to be the first integrated ship. Commanding Officers Richard Cobbold, then Tobin D. Elliott, were known to be amenable to the idea of women on ships. They would therefore make the situation work. In any case, the navy prides itself on making situations work. Additionally, the Type-22 frigate was already being refitted, so creating a separate mess for women was readily achievable.

Trouble was expected by some people with deep difficulties in accepting the new, by scandal-hungry media, and by those of any gender who were just plain concerned that seagoing would not be good for women. Cartoons in *Navy News* showed the classic vision of that allegedly impossible pairing: women and warships. A chief petty officer shakes with rage when a weapon engineering mechanic with her gardening trug decorates a huge gun with plants: 'But Chief – it's so much prettier now'. In another cartoon the fictional Admiral Sir Stabme Salthorse roils and steams in his grave. He is in outraged agony over the headline 'No sex please, we're sailors, says Navy. RN and WRNS will advance together to fill sea billets. Aim is equality.'

Some indeed saw seagoing women as being against the natural order of things: lily-ish pink as distinct from proud blue. The twain should certainly never meet at sea. Pessimists predicted illicit sexual intercourse, including adultery. Concerned fatherly men, not just misogynists, worried that women would be proven inherently unsuited to doing heavy tasks, to surviving away from home comforts and to being sturdy, ultra-focused members of the war-ready team. As well as expecting women would fail, some men secretly hoped they would, too, so that the old comfortable status quo could be restored. Some even indulged in petty acts of sabotage to bring that about.[5]

Reality was usually more complex and nuanced. Women had temporarily worked on ships before, without the sky falling in. Also, naval men had mixed feelings: after all, they had talented daughters whose careers they respected. Officers knew they had to put aside old ideas if the navy was to have enough personnel. Richard Cobbold, HMS *Brilliant*'s Commanding Officer, headed the 240-odd primed personnel on HMS *Brilliant*. He later said his attitude towards women

'The Girlhood of Jenny?'

Fig. 10.1. Seagoing women creating a new naval tradition. Smiles' *The Girlhood of Jenny* (February 1991) is a take-off of Millais' 1870 *Boyhood of Raleigh*.

going to sea was 'not particularly simpatico but confident that we would do a very good job ... [and indeed] it all worked well'.

Very quickly the dreaded litmus test moment arrived for *Brilliant*: in January 1991 it was needed in a war zone, the Persian Gulf, as part of the First Gulf War's Operation Granby. Women rose to the challenge. To defeatists who predicted that women would inevitably go to pieces in crisis, Captain Tobin Elliot, who had succeeded Captain Cobbold, praised the way these pioneers coped, including with hours of firefighting in Fearnaught rig: 'So, to all you doubting Thomases – stop doubting. There is no going back. There is no need to.' This was not an experiment that could be shelved. Nor was it a flimsy gimmick to make the navy look correctly touchy-feely equal-oppsy. These women's participation mattered because they were proof of the navy's recognition that it needed combat-ready women if it was to survive in the twenty-first century. Old traditions had to expand.[6]

First steps

Some 150 members of the WRNS were at sea in four ships by January 1991. However Smiles, *Navy News'* cartoonist, was soon sketching senior officers waiting in vain by their warships for more WRNS volunteers to come forward. 'How about a chorus of "There I was – waiting at the church"?' asked a 'jilted groom', looking futilely at his watch as 'brides' failed to roll up for the proffered 'marriages' of WRNS and navy. The number of women slowly increased to over 490 in 1993 and increased again as more vessels were converted.

Willing women were still not always found so sometimes ships that were expected to sail with women aboard did not. Smiles drew disgusted and bemused matelots in a ship's hold unloading the NAAFI's cartons of blusher and tights as the news came: 'No Wrens this trip'. The impression given was of individual women being capricious – again – rather than that a systemic problem needed addressing. Newly entered Wrens fancied heading out to sea, but not many of their more-established sisters were interested. Under normal conditions, about a third of the 60,000 naval men at any time were at sea but at this stage there were far less than a third (1,000) of Wrens afloat.[7]

More and more women pioneers were rising in naval life ashore too. Their advent was often celebrated in *Navy News* in the 1990s. Highlights include the appointment of Caroline Eglin as the first ever woman naval chaplain. Pippa Duncan was appointed the first female commander of a (mixed) shore establishment, HMS *Warrior* at Northwood, Middlesex. Katherine Babbington broke the all-male tradition by being awarded the Queen's Sword for being the best cadet in her year at Britannia Royal Naval College. The ground-breaking female commanders of naval offshore patrol vessels, Suzanne Moore and Melanie Robinson, were feted.[8]

Navy News noticeably carried much less material about trail-blazers after 1995, because the pioneering had largely happened. Gender now seemed a vestigial matter that had withered away – officially. Integration in the UK armed forces meant that women could now do 70 per cent of jobs. Female naval personnel were allowed even more roles: 75 per cent, by 1998. Navy women were involved in the conflict in Kosovo of 1998–9 as well in humanitarian missions such as restoring water to hurricane-stricken areas, and helping evacuate fleeing civilians. As a consequence of studies of women's physical characteristics, the MoD began gender-free physical testing. It was a contrast to the 1980s when women took the swimming test but, unlike their male colleagues, did not have to pass it.

The 'Director WRNS' title ended in 1996 and the role became more honorific. Julia Simpson gained instead, she smiles, 'the rather unprepossessing title of Chief Naval Officer for Women (CNOW)', which was better than the suggested 'COW N'. Annette Picton was the final CNOW, serving until 2005 when the role faded away.[9]

Early adjustments to change

Commander Maggie Robbins, the Deputy Director of the WRNS, acknowledged 'the Navy is without doubt the last bastion of male chauvinism ... when the first women joined ships it was a terrible culture shock for everyone.' Common dits (stories) were like those of Leading Engine Mechanic 'Knuckles' Middlewood who asserted that 'having women [at sea] is just like having flowers on the table. I don't think it's women's place to be on board, and certainly not to be an engineer.' 'It won't work', was the pessimists' chorus. A dit that may have been an urban myth circulated that when one all-male ship's company heard women were coming aboard 'a few guys decided to clear the NAAFI out of sanitary products to see off the Wrens ... it backfired as the lads spent a lot of money on something they had no use for, and the girls ... [had] brought their own with them ... no-one has ever identified the ship.'[10]

Suspicion and sexist resistance in the early 1990s was fuelled by the media who made much of 'girls in stockings and tight skirts being helped by men to climb ladders on board'. Red-topped tabloids sought spanners to wreck the earnest machinery of change. Initially WRNS leaders like Rosie and Anthea dreaded waking up to see what WRNS scandal would be in that morning's paper. In fact only 14 legal cases reached public attention between 1992 and 2015. Ten of these were about naval women's allegations of male colleagues' gendered abuse.

Fig. 10.2. The first Chief Naval Officer for Women, Julia Simpson, stands by the board honouring all the directors who preceded her, 1994.

Renfrewshire midshipman Claire McGarrity of HMS *Brazen* brought the most high-profile case in 1996.[11]

Bystanders' over-focus on teething trouble was worsened again by the speediness with which these new sorts of sailors were enabled to sail. This haste gave adversaries grounds for charging that 'equality' had been imposed without sufficient negotiation with the men who were to be women's shipmates. Some opponents used the word 'fiasco'. A woman midshipman more thoughtfully contended that, because the major 1990 defence review, Options for Change, coincided with this, the policy of sending 'women to sea has often been the scapegoat for what is essentially a period of financial pressure and political constraint'; the navy's frigates had been cut back from around 50 to only 40. In addition the USA's Tailhook Scandal of 1991 had brought a focus on sexual harassment in the services. However, most people in the Royal Navy tended to dismiss this as a US services problem rather than something systemic, widespread and worth understanding.[12]

The unhappiness of female ratings in HMS *Brilliant* hit the TV screens in 1994. Millions of viewers saw a controversial BBC documentary series made by anthropologist Christopher Terrill, which highlighted that some men were still opposing women's presence. In the ribald SOD's Opera (the Ship's Operatic and Dramatic Society show) naval women sang a pastiche of Gloria Gaynor's song 'I will survive'.

> We're not just some little girls/ Who should bow down to all of you ...
> Well, we are sick of all this sea time/ You can sod your life at sea,
> So here we go, out the door ...[13]

Problems and their solutions

Such early problems were monitored in an MoD-commissioned report. Lyn Bryant was part of a team at Plymouth University who from 1991–3 studied sea integration. Cultural change and challenges to perceptions were needed, they found. Their concern included that new ways needed to be found to do physically demanding jobs, rather than women being derided for lack of masculine prowess. Hostile male attitudes such as calling women 'splits' and categorising them as either 'dykes' or 'whores', depending on their sexual availability, needed to be challenged. Men commonly thought women were given chivalrously conceded unfair advantages. A minor example was that women were allowed to wear earrings and pony tails, and have their teddies on display in the mess. Men had teddies too, but had to put theirs away at inspection time. One man lamented 'I still feel embarrassed about going out in a towel for a shower, especially when they [women] are all sitting at the bottom of the ladder.' (Wear a bathrobe, was the practical response.)

Stereotypical femininity/masculinity kept on getting in the way. A female rating felt the navy 'seem to be recruiting a different kind of woman now. This is good because they can go for different types of job ... [on other hand] it's bad because ... they are generally more butch.' Older Wrens think that the women who got on best in this new world of co-educated people who might drink beer from cans and swear were those who had newly entered and expected sail alongside men. 'Outbloking the blokes' was some ladettes' initial survival strategy. Others eschewed bovver boots and tattoos, and enjoyed varying degrees of feminine behaviour, including the navy's makeup lessons by Yardley and Revlon representatives.

Recommendations included the instituting of 'a strongly supported, centrally formulated policy underwriting the provision of equal opportunities and seeking to eradicate sexist and discriminatory behaviour'; doing 'an audit of good practice and policy guides' and improving management training.[14]

Overall, women's integration into sea service was seen as a success despite the odd scandals. Men began seeing the real women beyond the stereotypes. Female leaders gained seagoing experience. They moved on from feeling uncomfortable at the gap between what their stripes said they could do and their actual feeling of not yet being ready to wield shipboard authority. New women entrants took to the life so much that many requested extensions to their sea time.

Unease about women bearing arms lessened, but slowly. Lieutenant Deborah Heesom, a weapons analyst in HMS *Ark Royal*, explained new attitudes to a journalist who asked whether she would shoot someone if necessary. 'If you are trained to do it, it becomes automatic. It's the camaraderie, it's the unit that's fighting, not you as an individual ... but nobody wants to go to war.' Five of the 19 branches open to women were associated with weapons, such as operations missileman.

Women became recognised as valuable additions to ships' companies, not victims of an experiment imposed from above. Carolyn Stait, who was to become one of the first women commodores, found very typically that a 'misogynist' commander on an early ship which included women had subsequently become:

> a total convert who professed that it was somehow more humanising to serve alongside women in the seagoing environment and that the ship became a more effective as a result. The women worked extremely hard to prove themselves. This in turn upped the game of the male ratings who didn't want to be bested by the women on board.[15]

Fig. 10.3. Anxiety about women bearing arms changed: Vicki Taylor RN and her gun in Afghanistan, 2009. Picture courtesy of WRNS BT.

It is widely reported that standards usefully rose, in performing professional duties at the upper level of expectations, and in personal life too. On ship men began wearing deodorant and aftershave lotion, swearing less and seeking to excel in tests. So many women did so well, working with alacrity, that it set the pattern that exists today: anyone who shares the burdens willingly and effectively is welcome, gender apart.

Integration formally set up

In the early years of integration seagoing was something involving less than 10 per cent of Wrens. Yet major steps towards full integration of the navy were afoot. WRNS officers' titles were brought into line with naval titles in December 1990. For example chief officers became commanders. Ratings had already been given equivalent titles to men. Although the term 'Wrens' was no longer correct, except in the early days, for junior ratings, women at all levels continued to be informally referred to as Wrens and Jennies. Newcomers had to be prepared to be at sea for part of their careers.

Braid officially changed colour for WRNS then too. Replacing blue braid with gold was, like NDA in 1977, felt to be both a loss and a gain. The term 'blue Wren' appeared and sometimes the term was synonymous with 'veteran' or even 'proper' Wren. Two distinct sorts of naval women existed now: seagoing, and non-seagoing or 'old-style'. Non-seagoers were of three sorts: those who did not want to take up the option of volunteering for sea service; those too senior to take a step backwards, retrain and sail; and those doing jobs that were not needed on ships, such as drivers.[16]

Motherhood and thorns

While some women were achieving professional success others were achieving success as mothers, but at the cost of their careers. Service women were expected to leave in their sixteenth week of pregnancy. However this was found to be illegal under European Union regulations and some women sued the MoD for extensive compensation. Annette McHugh, a former WRNS petty officer, led the first stage of the ex-Wrens' struggle in 1995. The claimants were criticised by people who felt disabled veterans were more deserving of the money and that women were not playing fair. Pregnant women now had a choice: terminate the pregnancy, resign or take maternity leave (but return within 37 weeks of confinement). Donna Ward, a former steward who had served with

45 Commando Royal Marines in Northern Ireland, was in 1995 the first naval woman to resume her career after being discharged, in 1986. Usually their managers respected compassionate grounds and tried to deploy the woman and her partner helpfully. Being liable for sea service, as well as married to another seagoing matelot, was a thorny matter. Women usually had to defer motherhood, or rely on nearby family members as babysitters, which was harder as kinship networking declined.[17]

Diversity and Inclusion accomplished?: 2000–17

Diversity and Inclusion (the navy always uses the words in the same breath, capitalised, and in that order) became the keywords of the post-2000 MoD. It is now immutable policy that naval 'jobs are open to everyone regardless of sex, race, religion, sexual orientation or gender'. Any discriminatory bullying is outlawed. Navy webpages insist: 'We believe our people should be able to work in an environment free from intimidation, humiliation, harassment or abuse.'[18]

Women's inclusion was evident in the news of pioneers gaining new high positions. They were not promoted in a tokenistic way, but on merit. Quotas were never used in the UK's navy, unlike in the USA. So opponents were inaccurate when they muttered that upstart women were being bumped up beyond their worth just to make the navy look good as an equal opportunities employer.

For the first time there were women commodores (commodores are in the top of the navy's three echelons, just a step below rear admirals). Muriel Hocking (born 1945) had been the first to achieve commodore rank in 1997, but in the reserve. 'Someone said to me "You've broken through the glass ceiling." I didn't see it as that. You just progress,' Muriel considered. Four years later Annette Picton was the first female regular to become a commodore. This was still a climate, though, where Lloyd's List's precedent-shattering 2002 decision to call all ships 'it' not 'she' caused outrage, indeed trauma.[19]

In all 1,145 women were serving at sea in 54 ships by 2003. There were 34,296 naval personnel at that point. Deployed in combat situations, but not expected to take part in ground close combat, women were in many conflicts including in the war in Afghanistan from 2001–14 and the Iraq War from 2003–11. Ideally the navy had wanted 8,000 women to be serving at sea by 2010. Funding cutbacks meant this plan was revised to 15 per cent women (which might mean 3,000, depending on totals) by 2020.[20]

In an institution where nine out of ten are male, the minority group still hit obstacles. However, women took command of larger and larger vessels in higher and higher roles. Charlotte Atkinson was acclaimed the first woman to take charge of an operational UK warship, HMS *Brecon*, a mine countermeasures vessel in 2003. Vanessa Spiller became the earliest female executive officer (the second in command) in the frigate HMS *Kent* that year too. War did not phase them, Charlotte explained, because 'We have the confidence in knowing that everyone has been extremely well trained for the job.'[21]

On land Carolyn Stait became the second female regular to be a commodore, and the first woman to command HMNB *Clyde*, the submarine base at Faslane. 'Military's "brass ceiling" [is] to melt', exulted one headline. The media marvelled that 'the high-flying Wren who has gone nuclear' had charge of an annual operating budget of £190 million, commanded 6,500 people, and was responsible for most of the nation's strategic weapons. 'I hope that if anyone has any doubt about the Navy being a good career for a woman then they might take encouragement from the fact I have been given this job', Carolyn commented.[22]

No-go zones

Although Commodore Stait had ultimate power over eight nuclear submarines, ironically women still could not sail in any. Submarines and the Royal Marines Commandos were the last male bastions. The submarine service was finally opened to British women only in 2011, after lengthy discussion about whether long exposure to submarines' recycled air could damage a foetus. Hot-bedding (sleeping in the bunk of your opposite number while they work) was also seen as undesirable if men and women shared. These problems were eventually resolved, especially as bigger submarines made hot-bedding less necessary. Similarly with the Royal Marines (at the time of writing), within the ongoing decision-making about women's inclusion, a key concern is whether carrying heavy weights may have a long-term impact on female musculoskeletal structure.[23]

Tied in with concerns about submarines and commandos, and sometimes masked by it, was the problem of women in combat, specifically in ground close combat (GCC). To some traditionalists the increasing moves towards GCC seemed like a further step towards 'emasculating' the armed forces and 'masculinising' women. After Acting Leading Seaman Faye Turney's capture by Iranian military personnel off the Iran/Iraq coast in 2007, repeated gendered outrage focused on her behaviour rather than on her male counterparts. A *Guardian* journalist commented 'Unchosen, her fate was to attract a mass of contradictory prejudices about women: working mothers, women at war and oppressive anti-women religion.'[24]

Occasional articles and snarky e-comments from chatroom users reveal that public acceptance of women in the military continued to be problematic. The media inflated those problems with fantasies of ships as a naval version of 'anything goes', seduction-packed cruise ship culture, as in the TV series *Love Boat*. Tabloids carried negative articles about the kind of personal issues taken for granted in any normal modern workplace or community, including adultery and sexual rivalry among colleagues. Headlines included 'A Bun in the Ocean' and 'Navy Love-Boat Probe'. By contrast, veteran blue Wrens regretted the way *their* WRNS was being culturally erased.

Many pages of *The Wren* mourned changes such as the removal of the 'W' prefix before a female rating's rate. Barbara Faulkner wrote a wistful poem:

> 'Women in the Navy' is what they're called now
> I'd thought that's what we were
> how wrong can you be?[25]

Fig. 10.4. Blue Wrens remain passionately loyal via the Association of Wrens. The Yeovil branch of the association visits Somerset's Fleet Air Arm Museum, 2007.

2010 and women going ever upward

In recent years more and more pioneering women have been doing impressive work. The 3,623 women were in a dwindling navy of 35,000 by 2010. Some were breaking through the last few barriers. Becky Frater became the first woman pilot to do stunt flying in the Black Cats helicopter display team, the navy's version of the Red Arrows. Kay Burbidge became the Fleet Air Arm's first ever female senior observer. Kay reflected that 'Joining up as a non-seagoing, blue-badge-wearing Wren, my recent appointment is a true reflection as to the advances in the opportunities available to females in the Armed Forces today.' Much acclaim greeted the appointment of Sarah West (born 1972), the first woman to command a major navy warship, HMS *Portland*, in 2012.[26]

Networking for change – and work–life balance

Becoming an admiral is a dream not yet achieved by any UK woman. Female admirals do exist, such as Michelle Howard in the USA. HRH

The Princess Royal had the honorary rank of vice admiral because she was Chief Commandant of the Women's Royal Naval Service from 1974 until 1993. Today her role is Chief Commandant for Women, Royal Navy. One of the stated reasons why women are not at the very top is that it takes roughly three decades to become a rear admiral; women have not yet been culturally on course long enough. For example, it was only ten years after HRH the Princess Royal completed her education that women were first allowed to study at Britannia Royal Naval College, Dartmouth (in 1977), which her brothers – Charles and Andrew – attended: the fore-ordained rung.

In private some naval women say that women have not benefited equally from the navy's system of fast-tracking promising candidates. According to this view, social prejudice continues to play a subtle part. Women have still not been to the same (male) public schools: Eton, arguably the powerful institution on the planet, continues its 500-year-long exclusion of women, even though they are now 51 per cent of the UK population. Nor do naval women participate as much in the same bonding sports (such as polo and golf, rather than tennis and hockey) as men. However, the moment of women joining the ranks of rear admirals is drawing nearer.[27]

One of the other obstacles is that many women still fall away in mid-career: leaky pipeline syndrome. Reasons include that armed forces conditions do not appeal to young people generally and that women from their early thirties find it hard to combine motherhood with work commitments away from home. Tellingly, only 28 per cent of women in the navy are married. This compares to 42 per cent of men. A total of 88 per cent of armed forces married women have spouses who are also serving, which can mean one or other will be a single parent for nearly a year while the other is deployed.[28]

Ellie Ablett came up with a partial solution to women's work–life balancing act when she set up the Naval Servicewomen's Network (NSN) in 2013. Captain Ablett's aim was:

> to show women, by using positive male and female role models, how they can make different decisions they may not have considered, to still have a personal life and a great career in the Royal Navy. I also

want to demonstrate to naval women how valued they are so they do stay the necessary number years it takes to get to the point where they could compete with the men for those command jobs.

Now well over 100-strong, network members meet annually as well as connect via social media on NSN's own Facebook group. 'Share, Inspire, Empower' is NSN's message. All services also now have *Individual Harmony* guidelines that ensure personnel do not suffer too much 'separated service' time away from home.[29]

Babies in the navy

Pregnancy and motherhood are now taken for granted in the armed forces. Some women avoid pregnancy with the new long-lasting contraceptive injections. Only 6 per cent of all serving servicewomen were pregnant in 2016, which suggests that around 456 naval women may be expecting babies at the time of writing. The modern navy has produced a comprehensive set of online policies and guidelines to support women. Pregnant women are removed from ship as soon as their pregnancy is known. It is for their own good, that of the baby and the situation: warships cannot necessarily afford to put into port to land people needing medical treatment. Expectant mothers then work ashore until ready to take their maternity leave. Armed forces maternity policy now insists 'That no Servicewoman will be treated less favourably because she is pregnant, absent on maternity leave or for any other reason connected to her pregnancy.'

The navy has just issued elegant new breathable maternity dresses and even transferrable plackets so that trouser waistbands can expand. New mothers on leave can pop in on KIT (Keeping in Touch) Days to maintain momentum, and later work non-standard hours.[30]

Humane flexibility about a mum's needs are balanced with necessary strictness about service personnel's discipline. Mothers are made aware there is a likelihood that, 'at some stage in their career, they will be required to serve away from home for a protracted period of time.' Grumbles that women deliberately become pregnant to get out of unwanted deployments occasionally circulate among men who resent not having that option. Now 97 per cent of naval ratings (more than in the air force and army) return after maternity leave.[31]

Seagoing and combatant

Initially 70 per cent of blue Wrens carried on being land-based. Some who have never served at sea still serve. Jacqueline Cartner was one who was initially promised that their careers would not be affected if they chose non-seagoing status. However, this proved not to be feasible. HMS *Collingwood* Chief Petty Officer Cartner fought an anti-discrimination battle with the MoD in 2012 for not promoting her. It looked initially as if it might be a test case for nearly 2,000 blue Wrens. An employment tribunal upheld her claims. However, following the navy's successful appeal no more litigation followed.[32]

Meanwhile the gnawing issue was whether women could really and truly be defined as, and used as, combatants. A tri-service review in 2014 made an interim decision that UK servicewomen could not yet be allowed in situations where the primary duty is 'to close with and kill the enemy', which is how GCC was being defined. David Cameron's Conservative government delayed the final decision until 2016. This was partly because politicians were not sure whether the public could tolerate the idea that women (potential life-givers) were potential life-takers. Also more hard evidence about women's physical strength was needed, and was difficult to find.

David Cameron announced after the 2015/16 tri-service review that the ban was to be lifted, in stages, from summer 2016. 'It will ensure the armed forces can make the most of all their talent and increase opportunities for women to serve in the full range of roles,' he said. Naval personnel are not usually engaged in infantry-style combat so the decision's relevance to naval women is slight. For women who want to join the Royal Marines Commandos, the decision is deeply significant. The feasibility of this is currently being discussed. Clearly, however, naval women have moved forward towards still more equality.[33]

Today and the future

What are naval women today, after all these changes? They are diverse. Few now try to outjack Jack. Any need to prove themselves as good as men has long been superseded. Many officers are what blue Wrens like Dame Vera would call career women. But they now face far fewer barriers. They do not necessarily sacrifice a personal life for career. The short-staffed navy does all it can to help women stay on. Naval women combine partners and children or step-children as well as sport, studying for additional degrees, volunteering for charities and travelling.

The navy's diversity is manifested in other ways as well. Over 7 per cent are black and minority ethnic (BAME) women. Senior officers fiercely ensure the D&I guidelines opposing racial discrimination are adhered to.

In today's tolerant navy women are welcomed regardless of sexual orientation. With admirals they march, uniformed, in Gay Pride parades. Lesbian and bisexual women were often silenced, shamed or even discharged if found out. Mandy McBain, a former lieutenant-commander in Supply, remembers 'friends chose to leave as the pressure was unbearable'. She stayed. Then a European Court of Human Rights decision in 2000, coupled with personnel shortages, led the navy to champion diversity, including work with Stonewall, the Lesbian, Gay, Bisexual and Transgender (LGBT) rights organisation and to champion diversity. Mandy became one of the navy's leading lesbian D&I specialists from 2008, working with management to make it possible for LGBT people to serve with the confidence to be who they are, and be accepted at every level. Her marriage ceremony in 2016 looked both different and similar to most traditional naval weddings. Forces personnel formed a largely female guard of honour with their traditional ceremonial swords.[34]

Some women and men regret what they see as a loss of femininity in naval women, who were until at least the 1980s given official lessons on makeup. A key symbol of that change is women's kit. CPO Liz Howard explains:

Junior Rate women ... [are] no longer issued with a skirt and if they wish to wear one when shore side they have to go to Stores and request one. Senior Rates and female Officers are issued both skirts and trousers with their No. 1 uniforms as we're more likely to have an office-based role at some point. As an engineer I spend most of my time in overalls (which I love as it's like going to work in your pyjamas) ... I very rarely ever wear a skirt.

Some, including veteran blue Wrens, would like naval women to look more feminine. They point out that men have not moved towards wearing less masculine uniforms; women have changed to fit men's styles, which are mislabelled 'unisex'. It makes sense to wear trousers or boiler suits on ladders, but some veterans see ties as masculine apparel which serve no particular use. (By contrast, the air force in 2017 was said to have quietly banned women from wearing skirts on parade. Everyone is required to wear trousers, in order to be inclusive of transgender people. This has not been corroborated.)[35]

Serving women may *look* different to the skirted Wrens of the past but some are still of naval stock and reared in service life. Henrietta Goodrum, a naval writer, was in 2015 celebrated in the *Portsmouth News* as the fourth member of her Gosport family in two generations to join the navy. Her parents met when her mother was serving in the QARNNS. From her birth in 1995 Henrietta has lived in a world where it is normal for women go to sea and have non-feminised job titles.[36]

Henrietta is just one of 2,740 women serving in the navy, as an April 2016 'snapshot' showed. They were 9 per cent of the total. Their work patterns are similar to men's patterns, although 'a big toys for the boys' climate had not yet gone. Of the 7,030 people at sea at that moment, 600 were women – 8 per cent. In the Fleet Air Arm, only ten of the 300 women were pilots although women were 6 per cent of the total 4,490. In the Royal Marine Band Service women were 34 per cent of the total. Table 10.1 shows how much this is still a navy based in south coast ports.

In wider society, pioneering naval women are still being acclaimed, partly as role models to encourage young women to embrace STEM

Table 10.1. Where are they based now: RN women and men in 2016[37]

LOCATION	FEMALE	TOTAL WOMEN AND MEN
Overseas	60	770
London	30	350
South East	1,170	8,970
South West	1,130	13,650
East of England	90	700
East Midlands	~	130
West Midlands	90	320
Yorkshire and the Humber	~	120
North East	~	10
North West	~	130
Wales	~	130
Scotland	160	4,100
Northern Ireland	~	~
GRAND TOTAL	c. 2,740	c. 29,390

NB: the symbol ~ denotes a number lower than ten.

(science, technology, engineering, mathematics) careers. Merlin helicopter pilot Lieutenant Natalie Grainger (born 1988) was named as one of the nation's top rising women stars in the *We Are the City* Awards in 2016. Captain Ellie Ablett has just become the first woman to head training establishment HMS *Raleigh*, the crucial 'front door' of the navy.[38]

Just below her medical services counterpart Commodore Inga Kennedy, Captain Ellie is the highest-ranked woman in the navy. Like Inga, Ellie too is a graduate of a college founded long ago by pioneering feminist educators, Somerville College, Oxford. Currently she is one step away from rising to rear admiral. By contrast, Air Vice Marshall Elaine West at 51 was the first British armed forces woman to make it to two-star rank (the equivalent of an army major general or naval rear admiral) in 2013. Major General Susan Ridge in 2015 became the first Medical Director General in the army.

Women's progress was celebrated in a major exhibition, *Women and the Royal Navy: Pioneers to Professionals*, at the National Museum of the Royal Navy in 2017. Female naval stars of the future will be the first submariners to serve afloat, the first Royal Marine Commandos, the first female Director of Music for the five Royal Marine Bands, the first Medical Director General and, crucially, the first admirals.

Conclusion

Women associated with naval services in Britain have been part of one of the most important organisations in the world. 'In the space of just over 300 years, a small island on the edge of Europe rose to command a quarter of the earth's territory and a fifth of its people … a task only made possible by the Royal Navy,' argues historian Daniel Owen Spence. In that navy, women were not the archetypal Jack Tars singing 'Hearts of Oak', nor their home-bound helpmeets. They were much different in attitude, in the marginal tasks they were allowed to do, and their social role, as ladies; mothers, daughters and desirable figures, rather than as hearty defenders of the nation.[39]

Fig. 10.5. Pilot Natalie Grainger in a Merlin, 2016.

These pages have shown the many different ways in which women have been involved in naval work. Without women as supporters – such as unwaged naval wives and mothers, as well as servicewomen – this immense and effective institution could not have had all the successes it has enjoyed. Women who did paid work – usually in uniform and sometimes with naval titles – enhanced the navy's strengths. This book has contextualised individual stories and highlighted some of the challenges the women, being accustomed to loyal positivity, were reticent about revealing. Naval services have become increasingly fair-minded about acknowledging women's contribution and giving them space to serve in even more satisfying ways. Women sometimes had to endure exceptional difficulties, on top of simply doing their jobs. But often they received exceptional rewards, especially pride, a sense of having done something worthwhile and all done with the intense joy of comradeship.

Women's changing position in wider society has meant that the exceptional ones who are in the services have to do several tasks simultaneously. Like men, they do what they are paid to do, which might include risking their lives for others and the greater good. They have also done the emotional labour among colleagues – such as encouraging civility and raising morale – that is expected of women. In addition women coped with relegation because they were not like the majority. Their values and traits – such as communicating in an egalitarian way, or being cautious about taking an action without full prior information – have not always fitted.

Over the twentieth and twenty-first centuries naval women have faced arguably greater challenges than women in any of the other UK armed forces. It is not just that the sea can kill, maim and cause distress, as well as bring metaphysical elation. Coping with unwarranted blocks to their acceptance as equals takes all the more stamina when people are away from home in a relatively small floating residential workplace with its own tight culture.

In addition, this period of history continues to pose problems. Gender and sexuality are still intensely knotty fundamental matters in the UK's hyper-sexualised society. Workplaces dominated by unenlightened male leaders are trying. These issues are even more challenging to tackle in traditional and conservative institutions such as the armed forces, which in part continue to be proud of their ruggedly hyper-masculine culture. It is even more difficult again in these live-in machines, ships, and in a social climate where people playing hard, fuelled by alcohol and freed from home constraints, sometimes act unwisely.[40]

Assessing the many centuries of women's exclusion from sectors of the navy means witnessing the squandering of talent, such as women with STEM ambitions; the wasting of public money paid in compensation for discrimination; and lost opportunities for positive change, especially for mothers, those who love other women, early would-be seafarers, high-flyers and the technically minded. In some cases women have endured anguish, frustration and career loss. Individuals have suffered when the tradition-bound, cash-strapped institutions behaved unfairly towards their less powerful members.

Despite the bigger, sometimes problematic, picture women have not only progressed to become esteemed contributors to the navy, they have also enjoyed themselves and basked in collective warmth. Being 'in the Andrew' has meant fulfilling ambitions and gaining an enormous sense of their abilities and power. Membership has brought opportunities to explore the world and their own potential. To be harnessed for the greater good is deeply rewarding. To be wisely harnessed is even better. Women's successes and pleasures have gone far beyond even Katharine Furse's dreams for them.

Historians rightly mistrust simple notions of cumulative progress, the idea that things get increasingly better. Real life is more stop-start-wiggle-and-detour than that. However, in the case of the Royal Navy, and indeed the services generally, progress for women has been achieved if it is gauged through widened opportunities and increased respect. Technological advancement has enabled women to move forward, using state-of-the-art equipment, not saturated sails. No longer the sometimes-annoying parasites on the military body, or the sometimes-welcome lady visitors to a moored ship, women in defence work are now almost full participants. In a few decades' time women will be so integrated that new naval personnel will find it unbelievable that they were ever treated as a separate category.

Fig. 10.6. Exhilarating camaraderie: World War II Wrens classically enjoying 'the time of their lives' in naval service, Plymouth, October 1945.

The UK naval services have been slower than those of other countries to move forward on diversity and inclusion. Women are 10 per cent of naval services but only one commodore is female; no woman is any higher than that. Of the Fleet Air Arm's 480 pilots, just ten are female. However, the navy is learning by example, particularly from the USA, the Netherlands and the Scandinavian and Australian armed forces. In the increasingly combined services women are willingly seen as not simply another source of labour, but real assets. Lieutenant Stephanie Buttery, the commanding officer of HMS *Smiter*, explained aboard on International Women's Day 2017 that at no point in her career had anyone said '"because you're a woman you can't be a Commanding Officer". I feel very empowered in the Navy and they are very supportive of everything to do with women in high places.' The navy's exemplary equal opportunities policies and practices have also provided an inadvertent model that has helped women in commercial shipping, too.

To this history-minded observer it looks as if today's diverse and integrated navy is extraordinarily willing, given all the practical constraints, to offer women scope that Nelson would never have dreamed of. Most women who try it say: 'I had the time of my life.'[41]

Appendices

1

Women and Naval Services: A Select Timeline

KEY
Grey = QARNNS, Nurses, Voluntary Aid Detachment (VADs), dentists and doctors and medical assistants
Bold = WRNS/naval women
Normal font = wider world

Earliest times
BC
480: Queen Artemisia of Halicarnassus, later called the 'world's first woman admiral'
31: Cleopatra is also called the 'first woman admiral'

AD
875: The first recorded 'English Navy' is controversially said to have begun
1160: Queen Eleanor of Aquitaine orders a record of the Oléron maritime court judgment
1588: Elizabeth I sends ships to repel Spanish armada
c1600: Keumalahayati from Indonesia also called the 'first woman admiral'

1600s
1660s First recorded women nurses on hospital ship

1690s: First three cross-dressed women sailors are recorded, including Anne Chamberlayne

1700s
1760s: Admiralty issues many orders forbidding wives to be aboard. In fact blind eyes were turned for the next 55 years

1800s
1854: Navy attempts to make naval hospital nursing males-only. This is largely achieved

1854–6: Six semi-professional British women nurses go to Crimean war at naval hospital Therapia

1876: Philanthropist Agnes Weston opens first Sailors' Rest, a key example of women concerned for naval welfare

1884: Naval Nursing Service (NNS) founded. Head sisters appear for first time in *Navy List*

1897–98: Isabella Smith and Eva Mary Keogh are first two NNS members to go to war at sea, in hospital ship, *Malacca*

1900s
1902: NNS renamed Queen Alexandra's Royal Naval Nursing Service (QARNNS)

1907: Hague Convention. Protects all servicewomen and gives immunity to marked hospital ships. It is amended by Geneva conference the following year

1909: Red Cross and Order of St John found the Voluntary Aid Detachment (VAD) system

1911: A reserve of QARNNS begins, August

World War I 1914–18
1914: Britain declares war on Germany, 4 August

1915: Munitions of War Act guarantees that women will only do such work until men return

1917: Germany announces it will no longer respect hospital ships. QARNNS afloat were supposed to be replaced by SBAs, February

Women's Army Auxiliary Corps, the first services' organisation of women, is set up, March
Women's Royal Naval Service (WRNS) begins, November, directed by Katharine Furse
Navy takes up VADs, December
1918: Women's Auxiliary Air Force begins April; Wrens at RNAS stations transferred into WAAF, May
War ends, 11 November

1920s

1920: Sea Guides founded, later become the Sea Rangers
1921: Association of Wrens formed, January
1922: The idea of re-organising of WRNS is dropped, August
1927: 'Head Sister in Chief, QARNNS' post introduced. The service now has first national head, August.
1928: All women may now vote. Representation of the People (Equal Franchise) Act, July
1929: Geneva Convention – affirms women, even if combatants, are protected by international law, July

1930s

1935: Navy considers a possible women's auxiliary for the coming war, but not yet

1938: Munich Agreement is signed 30 September, appeasing Germany
Medical Director General anticipates 400 nursing reserves will be needed and invites direct applicants, November
An Admiralty paper on a force to be known as the WRNS is circulated, November

**1939: Vera Laughton Mathews is offered WRNS directorship, March and appointed. Preparations begin
First Wrens are called up, July**
First QARNNS reserves sail to war zones, August. Large influx of VADs into naval hospitals

World War II

1939: Prime Minister declares Britain is at war after Germany invades Poland, 3 September
WRNS sent out across UK
QARNNS reserves and VADs are appointed to new and old naval hospitals

1940: Huge build-up of Wrens in spring
Germany attacks France and the Low Countries, 10 May
Dunkirk evacuation, from 26 May to 4 June. QARNNS and VADs nurse patients after evacuation.
Siege of Malta begins, 11 June. The eight-to-ten QARNNS stay
South coast bombed, in Battle of Britain 10 July–31 October. QARNNS nursing in hospitals under fire
Services Feminins de la Flotte is formed by Free French women

1941: WRNS expands hugely. First overseas draft of WRNS goes to Singapore, January
First Wrens go to Gibraltar, on *Aguila*; 21 Wrens and QARNNS Sister Kate Gribble lost in sinking, 22 August
Mobility of all Wrens over 21 is extended to wherever Admiralty wishes in UK. Wrens are trained in gun use for first time, September
Japanese bomb Pearl Harbor Hawaii base, which brings the USA into war, 7 December
Allies declare war on Japan, 8 December
Hong Kong falls, Christmas. Armed forces nurses and VADs are at risk of rape. Three QARNNS are later interned until 1945
Women's Royal Australian Naval Service WRANS formed (will continue until 1947)

1942: QARNNS increasingly work overseas and at sea
Singapore falls, 7–15 February. WRNS there had just been evacuated to Ceylon
National Service Act for women comes into force, March. All women aged 20–30 could be called up

Women's Royal New Zealand Naval Service starts, June (and continues until 1977)

Wrens and other British personnel evacuated from Egypt for safety, mid-year. QARNNS and VADs stay on

Allied Raid on Dieppe, 19 August. **Wrens involved in communications in UK**

Markham committee look into service women's rumoured sexual immorality, report 3 September

Women's Royal Canadian Naval Service (WRCNS) begins, with UK WRNS guidance, October

Eighth Army launches attack on Rommel's Forces in North Africa, 22 October. **WRNS at a distance are involved in communications work**

Operation Torch begins, the landing in North Africa, 8–16 November. QARNNS support invasion in hospital ships and nearby hospitals

Siege of Malta is lifted, 20 November. QARNNS continue to nurse there in consistent numbers. **Wrens can go out there from January**

QARNNS Matron-in-chief is now based at the Admiralty. Coincides with Rushcliffe committee moves improve civilian nurses' status and QARNNS' gaining equivalent ranks with the navy, November–December

Girls Naval/Nautical Training Corps begins

1943: Discussion in Commons, March, over whether WRNS should serve afloat. No, say Admiralty (QARNNS are not used as comparators, although they had served afloat since war's start)

Allies defeat of Axis Powers in North Africa, May

Eastern fleet headquarters moves from Kilindini (Kenya) to Ceylon, August. **Build-up of WRNS,** QARNNS and VADs in Ceylon

More women doctors and women dental surgeons begin to be accepted in view of shortages

VADs begin same training as sick berth staff

South African Women's Auxiliary Naval Service, is formed, October (ends in 1949)

40 WRNS are in first convoy to sail through the liberated Mediterranean, December

1944: Women's Royal Indian Naval Service is formed, February (continues until 1945)
RN College at Greenwich is bombed, April. WRNS officers instead trained at Stoke Poges, then Hampstead
Build up to D-Day. **All possible Wrens moved to Portsmouth.** Haslar staff train to be a major casualty reception centre
D-Day. Decisive allied landing in Normandy, from 6 June. **Some boats crew Wrens pilot ships across the Channel. WRNS fix damaged ships**
First party of Wrens crosses to France, August 15
Transfer of C-in-C British Pacific Fleet from Ceylon to Sydney, October. QARNNS and VADS and **WRNS drafted to Australia**
Women's service of the Royal Netherlands Navy founded, October 1944
Wrens serve in Germany, winter

1945: QARNNS begin bringing home Prisoners of War from Far East, January
Yalta Conference, 4–11 February. **WRNS involved in communications on ships**
Burma Landings, to capture Rangoon from Japanese, April–May. HMHS *Vasna* involved, probably with four reserve QARNNS aboard
RN medical air evacuation unit founded, April. Twelve QARNNS trained to fly with patients to Sydney
Victory in Europe (VE) Day: 8 May
WRNS officer training moves back to Greenwich, 9 June (where it continues until 1976). Wrens increasingly involved in navy's air-focused work
US bombs Hiroshima and Nagasaki on 6 and 9 August, effectively defeating Japanese

War ends, 15 August. **Unknown Wren rating at Kurunegala, Ceylon, types out terms of acceptance Japanese surrender**
Victory in Japan (VJ) Day celebrations, 2 September
QARNNS and VADs continue to nurse in Pacific theatres, until late 1946

1946–50
1946: Prolonged discussions about whether women's auxiliary corps should continue
Camp at Burghfield, near Reading, becomes the Central Training Depot for new Wrens, until 1981. It is commissioned HMS *Dauntless* in 1953
Danish women's navy corps, based on WRNS, is formed, June

1949: WRNS established as 'permanent and integral part of navy', February
Training for the Women's Royal Naval Reserves begins
VAD reserve for navy begins, summer
Sick berth category of WRNS ratings formed

1950s
1956: Select Committee decides that WRNS and QARNNS should continue to be outwith the Naval Discipline Act, February
1958: Grigg Report

1960s
1960: Recruiting begins for new Naval Nursing Auxiliaries section of QARNNS, February
1963: RN starts taking on women MOs again after ten year gap

1970s
1970: Equal Pay Act
1974: Pritchard Report on WRNS, November
 Women are allowed into the Japanese Maritime Self-Defense Force
1975: Sex Discrimination Act

1976: **WRNS officers' training switches from Greenwich to Dartmouth, Devon, and become mixed-gender**
1977: **Pivotally, WRNS and QARNNS are now under the Naval Discipline Act, 1 July**
Geneva convention (Protocol II) recognises any women in armed services is a combatant
The first WRNS to be deployed with Royal Marine Commandos go to Northern Ireland
In Belgium the Women's Naval Service is formed

1980s

1980: Servicewomen allowed into more roles, and will bear arms to a limited extent, April
WRNS ratings' training is integrated with males at HMS *Raleigh*, Tor Point, Devon
1981: Publication of study group report: *The size and shape of the WRNS in the 1980s*
1982: Falkland Conflict: 40 QARNNS serve for 113 days on hospital ship *Uganda,* April to August
1983: First male nursing officers join QARNNS
1985: Royal Norwegian Navy allows women to serve on submarines
1986: French Navy allows in women
1987: The first women Medical Assistant (Q)s (MA(Q))s begin training, September
1988: Twelve reservists (wrongly) acclaimed as 'first Wrens to serve at sea' in NATO Teamwork 88 exercise, Norway, September
1989: West Report, March
National Audit Office report, April

1990s

1990: Parliament announces women can serve on surface ships, February
First WRNS members to sail as ship's complement sail go to sea, October

First legal challenge to MoD compulsorily discharging servicewomen on pregnancy begins. In August the right to take maternity leave is introduced

1992: WRNS switch from blue lace to RN gold
Women are allowed to join the Royal Marine Band Service
1993: *The Integration of sea service, Final report*, **Lyn Bryant et al., September**
First women join RFA as officer cadets and the first RN Supply &Transport Service staff can go to sea.
WRNS and QARNNS members become fully integrated into RN and Royal Naval Reserve, November
WRNS who were dismissed for being pregnant (even if married) win compensation claims
1994: Women permitted to joining Irish Naval service
1995: QARNNS adopt RN ranks. Matron-in-chief post becomes Director Naval Nursing Service
1997: MA (Q)s become part of navy's medical service, no longer QARNNS, April

2000s

2000: QARNNS made fully part of navy
2002: House of Commons discusses why women cannot serve on submarines (January) and in Marines General Service (June)
Women allowed into Argentina's Navy

2010s

2011: Navy announces women will be submariners from 2013
2013: Naval Servicewomen's Network established
2014: First three female officers qualify for submarine service
2016: Bangladesh navy's first women complete training
Women in UK services to later be allowed in close combat, July

2

Finding Out More about Naval Services Women: Selected reading

For readers new to the subject of women connected with the Royal Navy, here is an annotated select list of books, easily available articles, and websites. They will enable you to go deep and wider. These are followed by information about what can be found in archives.

Real women

Nothing is better than asking *real* women in navy life about their experiences. Much of the information in this book – and certainly most of the insights – comes from the conversations I have had with women who have served. People who are not part of the naval world can meet them via published memoirs and websites.

To browse current news of naval women see:

- The Association of Wrens/ Women of the Royal Naval Service website: http://www.wrens.org.uk.
- WRNS Benevolent Trust Facebook pages
- Naval Servicewomen's Network facebook pages

For the latest information about women in naval health care see:

- https://www.qarnns.co.uk and its facebook pages
- Two Royal Naval hospitals have picture-rich sites: http://www.haslarheritagegroup.co.uk and http://rnhstonehouse.blogspot.co.uk

Women's activities in the reserves can be seen in the online magazine *The Maritime Reservist*, https://tinyurl.com/l485wyo.

WRNS and naval women

Published histories of the WRNS come in two sorts: factual accounts of the organisation; and lively personal stories of members' experiences. Of the first sort, the institutional histories include:

- Ursula S. Mason, *Britannia's Daughters: The story of the WRNS* (Leo Cooper, London, 1992) is by a former WRNS officer whose understanding was enriched by working at the National Maritime Museum.
- Marjorie H. Fletcher, *The WRNS* (Batsford, London, 1989) (This account by a former director of the service is awry on dates but full of pictures).

Of the women's own accounts, the very best is a compilation, *I Only Joined for the Hat*, edited by Christian Lamb (Bene Factum, London, 2007). Most of the memoirs are overwhelmingly about World War II, and are primarily jaunty anecdotes of social life, written with flair. 103 brief written stories by Wrens in World War II are online in various locations at WW2 People's War: https://tinyurl.com/k3xks7h. They have been poorly edited so there is some inaccuracy. By contrast Barbara Pym's autobiography *A Very Private Eye: An Autobiography in Letters and Diaries* (Panther, London, 1984) gives the story of a reserved person who did not feel easy with the jolly camaraderie. The very best full autobiographies are the lively and telling ones by the two ex-directors of the wartime WRNS:

- Katharine Furse, *Hearts and Pomegranates* (Peter Davies, London, 1940)
- Vera Laughton Mathews, *Blue Tapestry* (Hollis & Carter, London, 1948)

As yet there are no academic books on the WRNS as there are about other servicewomen. However there is an excellent thesis and a forthcoming book based on a thesis:

- Kathleen Sherit's PhD thesis, 'The integration of women into the Royal Navy and Royal Air Force, post-World War II, to the mid-1990s', (2013), https://tinyurl.com/ya3c83ya, is the best thought-through analysis of the WRNS and their struggle for official respect.
- Hannah Roberts, *Wrens in Wartime* (I.B.Tauris, London), will appear in late 2017.

Naval women in other countries

Up-to-date news of women in navies of both sorts in different countries appears on my blog: http://genderedseas.blogspot.com. Modern international comparison of women in defensive navies can be found in several academic books including Helena Carreiras and Gerhard Kümmel (eds), *Women in the Military and in Armed Conflict* (VS Verlag, Wiesbaden, 2008).

Australia: Shirley Fenton Huie, *Ships' Belles: The Story of the Women's Royal Australian Naval Service in War and Peace 1941–1985* (Watermark Press, Balmain, NSW, 2000).

Canada: Several histories of women in the Canadian military weave in the Women's Royal Canadian Naval Service, which only existed in World War II. Stand-alone works include:

- Rosamond 'Fiddy' Greer, *The Girls of the King's Navy* (Sono Nis Press, Victoria, 1983). This is part light memoir, part institutional history, and richly illustrated.
- Barbara Winters, 'The Wrens of the Second World War: their place in the history of Canadian Servicemen', in Michael L. Hadley et al. (eds), *A Nation's Navy: In Quest of Canadian Naval Identity* (McGill-Queen's University Press, Montreal, 1996), pp. 280–96.

China: *Roses on a Blue Sea: The Women of China's Navy* (2013), https://tinyurl.com/kenmahl.

Germany: Women's relationships with its navy are discussed briefly in *World War II German Women's Auxiliary Services* by Gordon Williamson (Osprey, Oxford, 2003).

India: D. J. E. Collins has written the fullest summary of Indian Wrens (WRINS) in World War II, in *The Royal Indian Navy, 1939–45*, https://tinyurl.com/knwz4o6.

Netherlands: The only easily available English language work on the Netherlands situation is Guns Nicolaas's 1988 thesis 'Women on board: a longitudinal study of attitudes towards and opinions about serving with women at sea in the Royal Netherlands Navy', https://tinyurl.com/m8z4x38.

USA:

- Jean Ebbert and Mary Beth Hall, *Crossed Currents: Navy Women in a Century of Change* (Brasseys, Washington DC, New York, 1999), is a comprehensive summary and a kind of parallel to this UK book.
- Joy Bright Hancock, *Lady in the Navy* (Naval Institute Press, Annapolis, 1972), summarises this veteran's push through two world wars for women's integration into the US navy. It is a US counterpart of Vera Laughton Mathews' UK story.
- Jean Zimmerman *Tailspin: Women at War in the Wake of Tailhook* (Doubleday, New York, 1995) summarises the 1991 scandal that exposed the sexism among the Navy Marine Corps aviation officers.

Nursing and medical staff and the navy

Naval health care workers appear in far fewer publications than Wrens. The books below are arranged in order of the amount of relevant information they offer.

- Kathleen Harland, *Queen Alexandra's Royal Naval Nursing Service* (The Journal of the Royal Naval Medical Service,

Portsmouth, 1989). This is the authoritative summary of QARNNS. Unfortunately it has no footnotes to enable further research, but many of the documents she used can be found in the National Archive, using my footnotes as signposts.
- Claire Taylor (ed.), *Nursing in the Senior Service, 1902–2002* (QARNNS Association, Gosport, 2001). This former matron-in-chief has included biographical fragments and added information about the twenty years after Harland's history ended.
- Jack Coulter, *History of the Royal Navy Medical Service* (HMSO, London, 1954). This is a thorough two-volume official history of World War II which includes nursing officers and VADs.
- Eric Taylor, *Combat Nurse* (Hale, London, 1999), is one of many popular histories of military nurses which includes QARNNS. Taylor has drawn more than most on the QARNNS archive. Often authors use the term 'QA' so it is not always clear when army nurses, rather than naval nurses, are the focus; it pays to be alert.
- Nora Lewis, *Nursing in The Navy*, 2016, available via http://www.carolinebrannigan.com/memoirs-by-caroline-brannigan.php. This is a brief story of a life, not just about being a QARNNS. It has a lively chapter on the 1970s, including overseas exchanges by naval sisters.
- Stories of post-1980s naval nurses (not officers) and medical assistants can be found on YouTube (see filmography). Heroic MA Kate Nesbitt's experiences are highly visible in newspapers' online archives such as http://www.webcitation.org/5lbgJIxS8.

VADs
Accounts of Voluntary Aid Detachment nurses working with the navy are hard to find in print. The main two are both focused on World War II:

- Joyce Drury, *We Were There* (Jupiter Press, Dudley, 1997)
- Doreen Boys (ed) *Once Upon a Ward* (Photobooks, Bristol, 1980)

The BBC *WW2 People's War* website has two accounts by VADs:

- Joan Holgate, who was at Haslar: https://tinyurl.com/ycsrjnlt
- Mildred Tulip, who did initial training at RNH Stonehouse: https://tinyurl.com/y9c5zhw2

Hospital ships

Nursing on hospital ships is not yet the subject of any complete work. However some details of their context – those floating 'palaces of pain' – appear in the following books, none of which has references you can follow up:

- Stephen McGreal, *The War on Hospital Ships, 1914–18* (Pen & Sword, Barnsley, 2008).
- John H. Plumridge, *Hospital Ships and Ambulance Trains* (Seeley Service, London, 1975). It covers the period to 1945.
- QARNNS Regular Sister Ruth Stone wrote the main available account of being on a hospital ship in the Korean War of the 1950s (which is included at length in Harland's history).
- Nicci Pugh, *White Ship, Red Crosses: A Nursing Memoir of the Falklands War* (Melrose Press, Ely, 2010). This is the only book which summarises nursing staff's roles on a hospital ship in any conflict.
- Lieutenant Audrey Johnston describes 'A Day in the Life of a Royal Navy Nurse' aboard an (unidentified) naval vessel in 2012, at *Nursing Times*, March 2012, https://tinyurl.com/y9ff7ntt.

Doctors

Women doctors in the navy are currently only visible in small items on a few websites, such as Dr Jo Laird's story of adventure, *Adventure Medic*, 8 July 2014, https://tinyurl.com/nxx8zr3. They are in no books. However, one book reveals the US situation, Judith Bellafaire and Mercedes Herrera Graf's *Women Doctors in War*, 2009.

Dentists

Katharine Cordner has created the only available record, 'My Life as a Young [naval] Dentist', *Young Dentist*, https://tinyurl.com/kqj99df.

Naval services

RN social media sites

The Royal Navy's official faces are at www.royalnavy.mod.uk, on Twitter at https://twitter.com/search/royal+navy and on Facebook at https://www.facebook.com/royalnavy. On the unofficial RN community's site http://www.navy-net.co.uk readers will find gossipy and blunt reminiscences flow unguardedly: use the search terms such as 'women', 'QARNNS', 'Wrens' and 'female'.

Navy List

An overview of women officers' place, and statistics, can be found in the *Navy List*. This internal directory can be partially searched (from 1766) online through www.navylistresearch.co.uk. That site is run by a very helpful webmaster Mike Coombes. Hard copies can be seen at the National Maritime Museum, and also at Portsmouth Central Library, where they (and an excellent collection of maritime books) are, very unusually these days, on open shelves.

Naval Review

Back copies of the *Naval Review*, the independent internal discussion journal contributed to by officers, can be found on line: www.naval-review.com. From the 1980s it reveals officers' attitudes towards naval communities and WRNS integration. Thirteen articles have had 'women' in the title since 1947, eight on Wrens and none on nurses or QARNNS, but other articles do deal with women.

Royal Marines

The Royal Marines' journal *Globe and Laurel* contains little about women, because their role has been relatively slight. Back copies can be seen at the National Museum of the Royal Navy in Portsmouth. The current editions can be read online via iTunes. Subscriptions can be organised via http://www.royalnavy.mod.uk/useful-resources-and-information/globe-and-laurel. By contrast the *Blue Band* magazine, the thrice-yearly journal of the RM Bands and RN Volunteer Bands, does carry stories and pictures by and about women 'bandies'.

The military

Books and articles on women in the military often refer to the army and air force more than navy, but they do enable comparisons with naval life.

- Mary A. Conley, *From Jack Tar to Union Jack: Representing naval manhood in the British Empire, 1870–1918* (Manchester University Press, Manchester, 2010). This explores the masculinity that was crucial in thinking about naval women's gendered situation.
- Christopher Dandeker and Mady Wechsler Segal, 'Gender Integration in Armed Forces: Recent Policy Developments in the United Kingdom', in the journal *Armed Forces & Society*, Fall 1996, vol. 23, no.1, pp. 29–47. Dandeker's work has been seminal; this is the most easily available text.
- Cynthia Enloe, *Does Khaki Become You? The Militarization of Women's Lives* (Pluto, London, 1988). Enloe is the leading light in discussing the military's impact on women's wide lives.
- Edmund Hall, *We Can't Even March Straight: Homosexuality in the British Armed Forces* (Verso, London, 1995). Many people have wondered where the navy's lesbian history can be found. It is largely absent from records, but pp. 34–49 of this book is a fine starting place.
- John Hockey, *Squaddies: Portrait of a Subculture* (Liverpool University Press, Liverpool, 2006). Military organisations have distinct lower and upper echelon cultures; naval women's subcultures can be interpreted through the lenses of this seminal work.
- Sue Jervis, *Relocation, Gender and Emotion: A Psycho-Social Perspective on the Experiences of Military Wives* (Karnac, London, 2011). A former naval wife she offers the best insights of

any book so far into the psychology of serving personnel, including women and their home-and-away lifestyle.
- Patricia Neville, '"In with the new, only more so…": The Politics of Change and Gender in the Irish Naval Service', *Journal of Gender Studies*, vol. 12, no.2, 2003, pp. 115–24. This offers a fascinating article about gender which can be used for comparison with the UK navy.
- Lucy Noakes, *War and the British: Gender and National Identity, 1939–1991* (I.B.Tauris, London, 1998), and *Women in the British Army: War and the Gentle Sex, 1907–1948* (I.B.Tauris, London, 2006). Noakes is acclaimed as the main modern historian of pre-1970 women's military history; the navy is a small part of her focus.
- Penny Summerfield, *Reconstructing Women's Wartime Lives: Discourse and Subjectivity in Oral Histories of the Second World War* (Manchester University Press, Manchester, 1998). This work in invaluable for usefully examining how veterans shape their stories, including proudly never grumbling.
- Janice D. Yoder and Loren Naidoo, 'Psychological Research with military women', in A. David Mangelsdorf, *Psychology in the Service of National Security* (American Psychological Association, Washington DC, 2006), pp. 211–23. Although US-focused, it usefully explores what motivates female armed forces workers.

Archives

I have written this essay with the assumption that readers of this book may not want to look at the substantial archives of original documents (which include, for example, correspondence between WRNS headquarters and the Admiralty, and MoD minutes about changes to QARNNS and female naval doctors' conditions). However, if you wish to explore such mines, the primary material is principally held here:

National Museum of the Royal Navy, Portsmouth. https://www.nmrn.org.uk/research/. The Museum's WRNS collection numbers over 6,000 items which has been acquired via the Director

WRNS office and private donations from former Wrens. Researchers wishing to view the collection should contact the library staff in the first instance to arrange an appointment.

National Maritime Museum, Greenwich. collections.rmg.co.uk/archive.html#!asearch. See especially the Dauntless collection, which contains several scrapbooks of WRNS' pre-1945 history. Catalogues can be digitally searched from your arm chair: use category 5: 'artificial catalogues previously assembled'. The only major QARNNS item is material from Sister Helen Fox Harvey, a World War I nurse.

National Archive, London. A quick way to do this is to go to a TNA summary of documents relating to women and war, then use the search term 'navy' to find a useful list: https://tinyurl.com/kphly83. For WRNS service records 1917–1919 see the research guide https://tinyurl.com/koot7cb. The TNA also has a guide to help people find records of naval nursing staff: https://tinyurl.com/mflmc4v. For a biography-based approach try this illustrated blog by an experienced browser: *The Women's Royal Naval Service and The First World War; The National Archive series ADM 318 and the WRNS Officers of World War One*: https://wrnsofficersofworldwarone.wordpress.com.

QARNNS archive, Gosport. It is currently run by a few volunteers but is in the process of being digitised. Email NAVYINM-QARNNS@mod.uk.

Imperial War Museum, London. The archive has 1,634 items on the WRNS and 73 relating to QARNNS, including photos and sound recordings. It is searchable on line at: http://www.iwm.org.uk/collections/documents.

Liddle Collection, University Of Leeds Special Collection. This includes 28 items about the WRNS but none on the QARNNS. https://library.leeds.ac.uk/special-collections/collection/723.

Online nursing archives

- Archive copies of the Royal College of Nursing's (in effect, their trade union) *Nursing Record* & *Hospital World*, can be searched digitally. The archive goes back to c1900 and has 941 items which refer to the navy, in which so many reserves served in wartime. Very little about QARNNS or VADs appears. https://tinyurl.com/lwxp6cv.
- The archives catalogue of the British Red Cross is digitally searchable. To find the personal records of naval VADs in World War I go to https://tinyurl.com/n5j9tkh. Insert the term 'naval' in the box marked 'location/hospitals'.

3

Filmography[1]

(Starred films are highly recommended)

WRNS and women in the modern navy

Feature films

1943   *Bell-Bottom George*. Cheeky chappie waiter rejected by navy befriends Wren Pat (Anne Firth). He foils a spy ring, is allowed into the navy and Pat accepts him. Comedy

1944   *Fiddlers Three*. Comedy about two sailors and Nora, a Wren (Elizabeth Welch). They are transported back to ancient Rome and treated as seers

*1945   *Perfect Strangers*. Poignant drama about married couple who join naval services. Cathy Wilson (Deborah Kerr) becomes a boats crew Wren despite his objections. Wartime separation and other relationships then broaden their horizons and reignite their marriage

1946   *Piccadilly Incident*. Weepie about a briefly married Wren (Anna Neagle) who is soon torpedoed off Singapore, and presumed dead. Returns from three years on South Sea island (with sailors) to find husband has new wife and child

*1953   *The Cruel Sea*. Classic drama battle of Atlantic action film, especially focusing on Hostilities Only sailors. WRNS Second Officer Julie Hallam (Virginia McKenna) was initially abjured by the *Compass Rose*'s second hero, who puts war first

1958   *The Silent Enemy* features naval frogmen in 1940s Gibraltar. Third Officer Jill Masters (Dawn Addams) is the minor love interest

1960   *Sink the Bismarck!* Naval war film in which WRNS Second Officer Anne Davis (Dana Wynter) is the calm and very competent assistant of the Admiralty's Chief of Operations.

	He turns their relationship towards romance the moment Germany's iconic battleship is sunk
1961	*Petticoat Pirates*. This is the only film to tackle female-male relationships within naval services at sea, excruciatingly. A comedy vehicle for Charlie Drake, it features many Wrens who, angered at being turned down for sea service, capture frigate HMS *Huntress*. They take it to sea in a NATO exercise, but then sunbathe and hang undies on the halyard. Finally the happy commander tells Admiralty that Wrens should be seagoing. Starring Anne Heywood as Chief Officer Anne Stevens
2010	Humorous 3D animations made with xtranormal technology, on YouTube. They need an adults-only warning but offer important insights into naval life and slang today. Titles include *Wrens Join Submarines!!!!!* Naval men discuss rumour of women submariners coming aboard, very hostile language. https://www.youtube.com/watch?v=Eo3OqJE3uZE

Documentaries

1918	*WAACS (1914–1918)*, British Pathé Gazette newsreel (mistitled) showing World War I Wrens drilling and in tug-of-war, https://www.youtube.com/watch?v=XBZ0HHKkYDs
1940	*How Time Flies!* Pathé Gazette of new WRNS officer arriving at Royal Naval College, Greenwich. https://www.youtube.com/watch?v=jQtPKzAQWEM
c1943	*WRNS Torpedoes*, British Movietone, showing WRNS ratings at HMS *Attack*, and their connection with male colleagues at sea. https://www.youtube.com/watch?v=gNtkH95pkVQ
1944	*WRNS at the Helm*, British Pathé, boats crew Wrens at work. https://www.youtube.com/watch?v=cyGWgHuI0C0
1949	WRNS recruiting trailer. Includes shots of dentistry, testing aircraft equipment. https://www.youtube.com/watch?v=oHku80SCUv8

*1950   *WRNS* British Pathé. Newsreel including RNAS Yeovilton with Wrens handling planes. https://wn.com/wrns

1960   *Look at Life – Girls Ahoy,* Rank recruitment film includes footage of Directors WRNS Jean Davies and Elizabeth Hoyer Millar, Imperial War Museum, http://www.colonialfilm.org.uk/node/3393

1977   *Gender Equality at RNAS Culdrose.* Amateur film focused on a several interviews with a new rating, WRNS officer, photographer and engineer, all un-named. http://player.bfi.org.uk/film/watch-gender-equality-at-rnas-culdrose-1977/

1988/9   *WRNS: A Girl Like You,* Promotional video giving information on a career beginnings including anonymised interviews, drilling, firefighting. https://www.youtube.com/watch?v=503GZ4iX548

*1988   *HMS Raleigh – A Day to Remember.* Home movie of gender-integrated training and passing-out parade, Class of Sirius 08 Division (WRNS). https://www.youtube.com/watch?v=hRMVvtDLeC0

*1994   *HMS Brilliant,* BBC TV series, episode 3, 'Rocking the Boat'. Very important footage of women's preparations for the Sod's Opera, where they critically sing about their reception on board. Unavailable, made by Uppercut Films, http://www.uppercutfilms.co.uk/

*2015   *Officers and Gentlemen (BRNC) – Part 1 Militarisation.* Official video of Britannia Royal Naval College officer training. Many interviews with women include a former reserve. https://www.youtube.com/watch?v=u91W442p2iU

2016   *Royal Navy School Season 1 Episode 7 In the Navy Passing Out.* Intercut home movie of HMS *Raleigh* training for ratings. Includes a woman in charge of drilling.https://www.youtube.com/watch?v=uG65feko-24

QARNNS, medical assistants, naval doctors and dentists

Feature films

There appear to be no UK feature films about QARNNS before 2000. The nearest are several about US navy nurses such as *Tell it to the Marines* (1926); *The Shores of Tripoli* (1942); *Navy Nurse* (1945); *South Pacific* (1958); *In Harm's Way* (1965); and *Pearl Harbor* (2001). The television series *Tenko*, about British women captured from Singapore is set in a Japanese internment camp in 1943–45. It offers a story that may illustrate the experience of Olga Franklin and her two accompanying nurses.

Documentaries

2013 *Surface Fleet Naval Nurse Student*. An official RN film interview with a practice nurse in a medical centre who explains routine at sea too. https://www.youtube.com/watch?v=bPcJzbbiDBE

2013 *Royal Navy Jobs: Meet Ashley (Qualified Naval Nurse)*, Official RN video re a QARNNS officer. https://www.youtube.com/watch?v=mfoKSfW09RM

*2013 *Surface Fleet Medical Assistant General Service*. Official RN video. Kate, a Medical Assistant, at sea describes her work. https://www.youtube.com/watch?v=F4N1bnec35g

2013 *Royal Navy Medical*. Official RN video: mini interviews with personnel including female doctor and nurses. https://www.youtube.com/watch?v=bXBeHQ4ODSo

2013 *Surface Fleet Dental Nurse*, Official RN video, interview with Daniele in HMS *Excellent*. https://www.youtube.com/watch?v=Kmz1yJoymas

2013 *Surface Fleet Dental Officer*, Official RN video, interview with Kirsty. https://www.youtube.com/watch?v=QJhEafmKT2Y

2014 *Royal Navy Jobs: Meet Sharon (Nursing Officer)* Official recruitment video. https://www.youtube.com/watch?v=QYKb2Q0kmx8

VADs

These films tend not to differentiate between naval and army VADs

Feature films

2014 *Testament of Youth*. Story based on World War I army VAD Vera Britain, who sailed to Limnos in the Gallipoli campaign and nursed in army hospital there

Documentaries

1918 *The V.A.D.'s Smart Ambulance Practice at Pevensey Bay*, 1914–18, British Pathé silent film. https://www.youtube.com/watch?v=vM9HFX_dr40

1930 *'Bravo ... 'Vads'!'*. British Pathé Compilation, includes nurses on parade. https://www.youtube.com/watch?v=BSY6lxqQdCA

1939 *Troops and Vad's For Warzone*. British Pathé footage includes nursing VADs embarking on troop ship. https://www.youtube.com/watch?v=nE3q4v62mgk

4

Women in Perspective: Other Organisations

Women in naval services are part of the wider world of women in naval and navy-related life. The bodies to which they belong include the following.

Charities

The Association of Wrens

Founded by ex-Wrens in 1920 for veterans, the Association of Wrens continues to be the lively focus of post-service networking but also serving female personnel including QARNNS members. The AOW has a parallel with the Royal Naval Association, the veterans' body to which some women also belong, especially if they have naval veteran husbands.[2]

The WRNS Benevolent Trust

A charity founded by Wrens in 1942 and made permanent in February 1949. Its aim is still to 'provide relief in cases of necessity or distress'. It also functions as a veterans' network.[3]

Reserves

The **Women's Royal Naval Volunteer Reserve** was founded in 1951, a century after its male counterpart. In 1958 the WRNVR became the WRNR, just as the two male reserves too became one: the Royal Naval Reserve. The WRNR was not only a 'try before you buy' opportunity for potential Wrens, but also a kind of practice area for trialling non-traditional jobs for naval women, such as the first two women divers in 1988. Naval integration led to the WRNR integrating with the Royal Naval Reserves in 1993. Muriel Hocking (born 1945), a former Wren, was the RNR's first woman commodore from 1997–1999 and the very first female commodore in the navy. As the navy decreases, reserves today are increasingly needed, including to work at sea. There have been a number of female commanding officers.[4]

Another naval civilian volunteer service allowed women in too. **The Royal Naval Auxiliary Service (RNXS)** ran from 1963 to March 1994 (until defence cuts led to closure). Women worked on small vessels. Denise St Aubyn Hubbard (1924–2017) became famous as its first women skipper in 1978. After the RNXS was disbanded the Maritime Volunteer Service began. Unfunded it now provides training and community support on waterways. There are approximately 97 women and 347 men.[5]

Girls' organisations

The Girls' Nautical Training Corps began in 1942 as the Girls' Naval Training Corps, part of the National Training Corps for Girls. Being in the GNTC was a way that a former Wren or would-be Wren, and her daughters, could connect with the navy in the evenings and at weekends.

Integration with males in the Sea Cadets came in several steps: 1963, 1972, 1981 and 1992. Today it exists as the Marine Society & Sea Cadets.

The GNTC was much more navy-minded then the **Sea Rangers**, which was begun in 1920 by ex-Wren Veronica Erskine. It grew out of the Girl Guide movement, offering wholesome recreation, rather than ever being a feeder organisation for the WRNS. It still exists as a females-only body.

Civilian organisations with navy connections

Merchant Navy

Commercial shipping became termed the 'Mercantile Marine' around the seventeenth century and the Merchant Navy in 1918. Such ships are not engaged in the nation's defence, but the transport of goods and people. Women sailed on MN vessels from at least 1821, as stewardesses. WRNS and QARNNS sometimes joined it. From the late 1960s women began doing non-traditional work such as engineering officers.

Royal Fleet Auxiliary

The RFA is a kind of cross-over of Royal and Merchant Navies. RFA personnel are civilian Merchant Navy personnel, although they look like Royal Navy and officers train at Britannia Royal Naval College. They work in the thirteen MoD-owned ships which are part of the Royal Navy's support network, replenishing far away warships with fuel, food and ammunition. The RFA began in 1905. Wives were sailing from the 1950s and women employees sailed from 1991. Dr Victoria McMaster was the RFA's very first seagoing woman in 1991.[6]

The Royal Naval Supply and Transport Service

Staffed by civilians, this service supported the navy and the Royal Fleet Auxiliary, for example in transporting food and fuel to RFA ships that would then take the material to ships and overseas bases. It existed from 1965 to 1994, and its women personnel were allowed to go to sea from 1993. Subsequently it became the Naval Bases and Supply Agency, the Warship Support Agency and is currently part of the Defence Logistics Organisation.[7]

5

Heads of WRNS and QARNNS[8]

WRNS Director/Chief Naval Officer for Women	QARNNS Head Sisters in Chief/Matrons-in-Chief/ Directors of Naval Nursing Services/ Head of Naval Nursing Service
1910s	
Katharine Furse, 1917–19	No such position, Instead there were head sisters at Haslar, Plymouth and Chatham naval hospitals from 1902–27
1920s	
WRNS did not exist	**Head Sister-in Chief** Margaret Keenan, 1927–9 Mildred Hughes, 1929–34
1930s	
WRNS did not exist	Catherine Renwick, 1934–7 **Title changed in 1935 to Matron-in-Chief** Bertha M. Martin, 1937–40
1940s	
Vera Laughton Mathews, 1939–46 Jocelyn Woollcombe, 1946–50	Annabella Ralph, 1940–41 Dame Doris Beale, 1941–4 Matilda Goodrich, 1944–7 Olga Franklin, 1947–50
1950s	
Mary Lloyd, 1950–4 Nancy Robertson, 1954–8 Elizabeth Hoyer-Millar, 1958–60	Jeannie Gillanders, 1950–3 Kathleen Chapman, 1953–6 Barbara Nockolds, 1956–9 Helen Moore, 1959–62
1960s	
Jean Davies, 1960–4 Margaret Drummond, 1964–6 Marion Kettlewell, 1966–70	Joan Woodgate, 1962–6 Mary Fetherston-Dilke, 1966–70
1970s	
Daphne Blundell, 1970–3 Mary Talbot, 1973–6 Vonla McBride, 1976–9	Christina Thompson, 1970–3 Cynthia Cooke, 1973–6 Patricia Gould, 1976–80
1980s	
Elizabeth Craig-McFeely, 1979–82 Patricia Swallow, 1982–5 Marjorie Fletcher, 1985–8 Anthea Larken, 1988–91	Margaret Collins, 1980–3 Jean Robertson, 1983–6 (*1985–6) Eileen Northway, 1986–90

WRNS Director/Chief Naval Officer for Women	QARNNS Head Sisters in Chief/Matrons-in-Chief/Directors of Naval Nursing Services/Head of Naval Nursing Service
1990s	
Anne Spencer, 1991–3 **Title changed in 1993 to Chief Naval Officer for Women** Julia Simpson, 1993–6 Pippa Duncan, 1996–9	Jane Titley, 1990–4 (*1992–5) **Title changed in 1995 to Director Naval Nursing Service** Claire Taylor, 1994–6 Patricia Hambling, 1996–2000
2000s	
Annette Picton, 2000–2005 **Post ended.**	J. Brown, 2000–1 (2001–2) Michael Bowen, 2001–2 Lynne Gibbon, 2003–8 Helen Allkins, 2008–11
2010s	
	Title changed in 2011 to Head of Naval Nursing Service Inga Kennedy, 2011–15 Steven J. Spencer, 2015–

NB. An asterisk means that this head of QARNNS was also Director of Defence Nursing Services. It is a role that existed until 2003, and was held in turn by the heads of nursing in the three armed services.

Patrons of the QARNNS and WRNS were and are members of the royal family, who had varying honorary ranks and titles while in that role. In the WRNS HRH Princess Marina, Duchess of Kent (1940–1960) was succeeded by HRH the Princess Royal from 1974. Since 2012 she was Admiral Chief Commandant for Women in the Royal Navy, as well as Commodore-in-Chief, Her Majesty's Naval Base Portsmouth since 2006. In QARNNS the patrons were HRH Queen Alexandra until 1925, HRH Queen Mary from 1926 and HRH Princess Alexandra from 1955. HRH the Duchess of Cornwall is currently Commodore-in-Chief Naval Medical Services.

Table A.1. Total Women and Men in Royal Naval Services, 1660–2016[9]

DATE	WOMEN (not QARNNS)	QARNNS) (Active reserves deployed in brackets, if data available)	Naval VAD	TOTAL WOMEN AND MEN IN RN SERVICES
1660				3,695
1750				9,797
1800				145,000 (in 1810, then 19,000 in 1817)
1850				39,000
1884		11		61,000
1900		28		113,000
1905		45		127,00
1910		47		131,000
1914		52 (pre-war figure)		250.000
1915		71 (+153)		350,000
1916		74 (+ 160)		n/a
1917		82 (+ 162)	n/a	400,000
1918	5,933	79 (+200)	534 (overall wartime total)	450,000
1919	2,630	79 (+ 14)	Category Naval VADs seemingly no longer exists	275,000
1920	WRNS not in existence	77		136,000
1925	WRNS not in existence	75		102,500
1930	WRNS not in existence	76		97,000
1935	WRNS not in existence	74		92,800
1939	1,601	90		98,200
1940	10,653	99 (+218)	265	102,800
1941	15,100	81 (+250)	500	405,000
1942	28,600	c90 (+ 318)	1,587	506,700
1943	53,300	c90 (+ 600)	2,800	671,000
1944	73,500	86 (+ 636)	2,800	790,000
1945	63,395	87 (+971)	3,893	788,800
1946	20,500	c90 (+825)	n/a	350,000
1950	5,400	106	361	132,500
1955	4,100	232	187	122,100

DATE	WOMEN (not QARNNS)	QARNNS) (Active reserves deployed in brackets, if data available)	Naval VAD	TOTAL WOMEN AND MEN IN RN SERVICES
1960	3,100	174	90	93,400
1965	3,100	182	1	94,600
1970	3,300	203	Category ended	86,000
1975	3,700	202		76,200
1980	3,800	157		72,000
1985	3,700	106		70,400
1990	3,600	n/a		63,200
1995	3,900	n/a		50,900
2000	3,436	227		38,500
2005	3,210	290		35,600
2010	3,623	270		35,000
2014	2,720	n/a		30,180
2015	n/a	n/a (+30)		33,450
2016	3,030	230(+30)		29,390
2017	c.3,000	n/a		29,480

NB: These totals are indicative and sources disagree. All these statistics should be treated with caution. In the case of RN totals they differ by several thousand, depending on sources. In some cases the original data has been calculated on different bases (e.g., in April or December, or has/not included QARNNS in 'Women's Services') and therefore is not quite comparable. Total naval numbers are rounded to the nearest hundred, as are naval women's numbers in some periods. QARNNS figures include men from 1983. Female naval nurses, doctors, dentists and MAs are excluded from this list; in other words this is only a rough guide to women giving health care.

Table A.2 **What Did Naval Women Do? 2004 and 2014**[10]

By branch of Naval Service	2004 Total women	2004 Women as percentage of total strength	2014 Total women	2014 Women as percentage of total strength
Warfare	1,170	9% of 11,800	850	9% of 8,650
Logistics	1,080	25% of 4,240	810	28% of 2,820
Engineer	380	3% of 12,170	420	3% of 10,150
Medical	310	32 % of 950	360	35% of 1010
QARNNS	200	71% of 280	150	68% of 220
Royal Marine Band Service	40	12% of 330	80	22% of 350
Careers Service	0	0% of 50	0	0
Dental Service	20	33% of 60	20	40% of 50
Royal Marine General Service	0	0 of 6,100	0	0% of 6,640
Royal Marine Fleet Air Arm	n/a	n/a	0	0% of 40
Chaplaincy Service	0	0% of 70	0	0% of 60
TOTAL	3,210	8% of 36,140	2,720	9% of 30,180

Notes

Introduction

1. Paul Higate, ed., *Military Masculinities: Identity and the State*, Praeger, Westport, CT, 2003; Suzanne J. Stark, *Female Tars: Women aboard Ship in the Age of Sail*, Naval Institute Press, Annapolis, MD, 1996.
2. Emotional labour is a term coined initially to describe the work airline cabin crew do, but now more widely understood to be a process largely done by women, managing their own and others' feelings, especially customers, superiors, and less emotionally able colleagues. In formerly male-only situations where there was still emotional illiteracy, such as the armed forces, this workload was significant. Arlie Russell Hoschild, *The Managed Heart; Commercialization of Human Feeling*, University of California Press, Berkeley, CA, 1983. Minghua Zhao, Emotional Labour in a Globalised Labour Market: Seafarers on Cruise Ships, SIRC Working Paper 27, 2002, http://orca.cf.ac.uk/78070/1/wrkgpaper27.pdf, accessed 20 September 2017. A key way of understanding women's helpful behaviour with naval colleagues is that it is thought that most women are hardwired to be allocentric in dealing with other people. This means they put others first and so enhance collectivity. Most straight men are thought to be neurologically ideocentric in human relating. This means one uses oneself, not others, as one's central reference point. The foundational work on this is H. C. Triandis, K. Leung, M. Villareal and F. L. Clack, 'Allocentric vs. Idiocentric Tendencies: Convergent and Discriminant Validation', *Journal of Research in Personality*, no. 19 (1985), pp. 395–415. doi:10.1016/0092-6566(85)90008-X. Cultural influences can change this. Living collectively with well-bonded colleagues on ship would tend to increase allocentricity, but no research has yet been done on this.
3. Penny Summerfield, *Reconstructing Women's Wartime Lives*, Manchester University Press, Manchester, 1998.
4. Greg Dening, *Mr Bligh's Bad Language: Passion, Power and Theatre on the Bounty*, Cambridge University Press, Cambridge, 1992, p. 5.
5. T. R. Harris, 'Missing Their Sea Mummies?', *Naval Review*, vol. 81, no. 2 (April 1993), pp. 141–2.
6. Royal Navy, *Diversity, Inclusion and You*, https://tinyurl.com/ltkt345, accessed 13 March 2016.

Notes

Chapter 1. 'Assisting Behind the Scenes' – and More: 875–1884

1 N. A. M. Rodger, *The Safeguard of the Sea: A Naval History of Britain 660–1649*, Penguin, London, 2004.
2 Travers Twiss, ed., *The Black Book of the Admiralty*, Cambridge University Press, Cambridge, 2012, p. lix; Thomas Asbridge, *The Crusades: The War for the Holy Land*, Simon & Schuster UK, London, 2012, p. 22; Natasha Hodgson, *Women, Crusading and the Holy Land in Historical Narrative*, Boydell, Woodbridge, 2007; Helen Nicholson, 'Women on the Third Crusade', *Journal of Medieval History*, vol. 23, no. 4 (1997), pp. 335–49, discusses the problems of the colourful sources and the extent to which women were really warriors and cross-dressed on the battlefields.
3 George and Anne Forty, *They Also Served*, Midas Books, Tunbridge Wells, 1979; Margaret Vining and Barton C. Hacker, 'From Camp Follower to Lady in Uniform: Women, Social Class and Military Institutions before 1920', *Contemporary European History*, no. 10 (2001), pp. 353–73.
4 Wool merchants including Rose de Burford travelled overland, but are not recorded as sailing. Eileen Power, *Medieval Women*, Cambridge University Press, Cambridge, 2012, p. 48. Women at sea tend not be recorded in maritime histories nor medieval women's histories.
5 Stark, *Female Tars*. Julie Wheelwright, *Amazons and Military Maids: Women Who Dressed as Men in Pursuit of Life, Liberty and Happiness*, Pandora, London, 1990.
6 A fireship was a vessel deliberately packed with combustibles and sent to destroy the enemy's fleet. It later became the word for someone with a sexually-transmitted disease who infected others. Anne married but died giving birth to her daughter. Thomas Faulkner, *An Historical and Topographic Description of Chelsea and Its Environs*, vol. 1, London, 1829, pp. 246–7.
7 Rudolf M. Dekker and Lotte C. van de Pol, *The Tradition of Female Transvestism in Early Modern Europe*, Macmillan, London, 1989; Diane Dugaw, *Warrior Women and Popular Balladry, 1650–1850*, Cambridge University Press, Cambridge, 1989; Jo Stanley, *From Cabin 'Boys' to Captains: 250 Years of Women at Sea*, History Press, Stroud, 2016, p. 245; Frank Felsenstein, 'Unravelling Ann Mills: Some Notes on Gender Construction and Naval Heroism', *Eighteenth-Century Fiction*, vol. 19, nos. 1–2 (2006–2007), pp. 206–16. Re Bundy: see Rictor Norton, ed., 'A Female Husband Exposed, 1721', *Homosexuality in Eighteenth-Century England: A Sourcebook*, 27 November 2000, http://rictornorton.co.uk/eighteen/1760fema.htm, accessed 25 May 2017.
8 Hannah Snell, http://www.hannahsnell.com/, accessed 8 March 2017.
9 *William Brown, 'A female African'*, tinyurl.com/llfl8eb, accessed 7 March 2017.
10 Stark, *Female Tars*.
11 No records support her claims, which may mean she embroidered the truth, or that naval records overlooked her.
12 Stark, *Female Tars*, pp. 47–81. The *Minotaur* story appears in the *Naval Chronicle*, vol. 14 (July–December 1805), p. 478. Re births at sea: *Nelson and His World*, tinyurl.com/k7szxx6, accessed 14 July 2016.
13 Charles Napier Robinson, *The British Tar in Fact and Fiction*, Harper & Brothers, London, 1911, p. 235.
14 A possible minimum rough total for the year 1700 is 716 wives, calculated on the basis of three standing officers per ship multiplied by 272 vessels. British naval ship displacement grew from 196,000 to 459,000 displacement tons. 131,818 men were in the Navy by 1801 so the nominal 2,850 wives would have been the equivalent of 2 per cent of the navy. Fleet statistics: Jan Glete, *Navies and Nations: Warships,*

Navies and State Building in Europe and America, 1500–1860, vol. 1, Almqvist & Wiksell International, Stockholm, 1993; B. R. Mitchell and Phyllis Deane, *Abstract of Historical Statistics*, Cambridge University Press, Cambridge, 1962. Note the figures on wives are ballpark figures and can never be confirmed. However, they can and should be disputed as they drastically understate the more likely story. I thought it politic to err on the side of underestimates. The Marines were formed in 1664 and termed Royal Marines from 1802. In the French Revolutionary and Napoleonic Wars there was usually one marine per ship gun. Marines' wives were more likely than navy wives to become battle widows as their men worked on the open main deck; *Per Mare Per Terram – the Royal Marines 1793–1815*, https://www.napoleon-series.org/military/organization/Britain/Marines/c_marines.html, accessed 16 July 2016.

15 See John B. Hattendorf, 'The Struggle with France, 1689–1815', in J. R. Hill, ed., *The Oxford Illustrated History of the Royal Navy*, BCA, London, 1995, pp. 116–7.

16 Mennes' letter to Pepys, 16 April 1666, discussed in N. A. M. Rodger, *The Command of the Ocean, 1649–1815*, WW Norton, New York and London, 2005, p. 134; G. J. Mark, *Hearts of Oak: A Survey of British Sea Power in the Georgian Era*, Oxford University Press, London 1975, p. 224; Jedediah Stephens Tucker, ed., *Memoirs of Adml the Right Honourable, the Earl of St Vincent*, vol. 1, Richard Bentley, London, p. 193; Stark, *Female Tars*, pp. 55–7.

17 John Wells, *The Royal Navy: An Illustrated Social History 1870–1982*, Sutton, Stroud, 1994, p. 271.

18 Matthew Neufeld, 'Portsmouth Landladies and Care for Naval Casualties in Late Stuart England', *Port Towns*, 17 June 2015, http://porttowns.port.ac.uk/care/, accessed 25 June 2016. The main works are on naval health are John J. Keevil, Christopher Lloyd, and Jack Leonard Sagar Coulter, *Medicine and the Navy, 1200–1900*, E & S Livingstone, Edinburgh, 1957; and David McLean, *Surgeons of the Fleet: The Royal Navy and Its Medics from Trafalgar to Jutland*, I.B.Tauris, London (a book which is unusually aware of women).

19 Account was written by unnamed aunt of Richard Higham, who seems to be related to Bellamy. Nelly Giles' obituary appears in the *Gentlemen's Magazine*, July–Dec 1860, p. 210; Henry Giles, *Nelson and His world*, tinyurl.com/n8obl3l, accessed 23 March 2014.

20 Kathleen Harland, *Queen Alexandra's Royal Naval Nursing Service* (Journal of the Royal Naval Medical Service, Portsmouth, 1989), pp. 1–2; John H. Plumridge, *Hospital Ships and Ambulance Trains*, Seeley, Service & Co, London, 1975, pp. 13–16; Stark, *Female Tars*, pp. 68–71.

21 In date order, the British RN hospitals were Haslar, Gosport, 1753; Stonehouse, Plymouth, 1760; Great Yarmouth, 1793; Deal, Kent, 1800; Paignton, 1800; Melville Hospital, Chatham, 1828. Overseas hospitals were built from 1701 (Jamaica). Usually their nurses were locals. Staffing information is in Harland, *QARNNS*, p. 3; Christopher Lloyd and Jack L. S. Coulter, *Medicine and the Navy 1200–1900*, vol. 4:1815–1900, E. & S. Livingstone, Edinburgh, 1958, pp. 63–4; McLean, *Surgeons*, especially pp. 97–8; *Parliamentary Register*, vol. 15, Stockdale, London, 1802, p. 274. Mary Shoveller shared the same surname as the agent's clerk, indicating family networks helped people gain employment.

22 From 1884 the earlier category of untrained rating acting as sick berth attendant, a kind of steward or loblolly boy, was replaced by trained sick berth staff. In the usual absence of applicants civilians were allowed to take the jobs. *RNMB Ratings and Sick Berth Staff Association*, http://www.docrn.org/index.php/history, accessed 11 December 2016.

23 Gamp appears in *Martin Chuzzlewit*, first serialised in 1843. R. G. Huntsman et al., 'Twixt Candle and Lamp: The Contribution of Elizabeth Fry and the Institution of Nursing Sisters to Nursing Reform', *Medical History*, vol. 46 (2002), pp. 351–80; Harland, *QARNNS*, pp. 5–12.
24 John A. Shepherd, *The Crimean Doctors. A History of the British Medical Services in the Crimean War*, vol. 1, Liverpool University Press, Liverpool, 1991, p. 550.
25 Mary Erskine's letter to Aunt Mary, 21 September 1855, kindly loaned to author by David Luard. Park Village nurses were those in the very first Anglican community for females. Genteel ladies were educated to assist the poor in St. Pancras. They were barely trained, even less so than Elizabeth Fry's early nurses.
26 'Pioneering Nurses', http://www.kingscollections.org/nurses/s-u/stewart-henrietta, accessed 6 May 2016; 'Another sad case', *The Nursing Record and Hospital World*, 7 March 1896, p. 202; Harland, *QARNNS*, p. 19; Juliet Piggott, *Queen Alexandra's Royal Army Nursing Corps*, Leo Cooper, London, 1990, p. 15.
27 Report cited in 'The Naval Nursing Service', tinyurl.com/kmghjyg, tinyurl.com/lmel4l8, accessed 6 May 2016; Harland, *QARNNS*, p. 21.
28 From 1883 the sick berth staffs were expected to be 396-strong, including 223 afloat. McLean, *Surgeons*, p. 221.

Chapter 2. The War Needs Veiled Warriors – in Navy Blue: 1884–1919

1 Anne Marie Rafferty, *The Politics of Nursing Knowledge*, Routledge, London, 1996, p. 13; Harland, *QARNNS*, p. 1418.
2 Re Henrietta: Harland, *QARNNS*, pp. 22–3; *The Nursing Record & Hospital World*, 7 March 1896, p. 202; Anne Summers, *Angels and Citizens, British Women as Military Nurses 1854–1914*, Routledge, London, 1988, pp. 72–90.
3 Harland, *QARNNS*, especially pp. 16–8. Much of this chapter derives from her detailed work on the QARNNS' primary sources (which she does not list). Small stories of individual nurses appear in Claire Taylor's *Nursing in the Senior Service*, QARNNS Association, Alverstoke, 2002, pp. 9–13. The QARNNS' working relationships with SBAs are referred to in Gregory Clark's *'Doc' 100 Year History of the Sick Berth Branch*, HMSO, London, 1984.
4 *The Nursing Record and Hospital World*, 9 November 1895, 2 December 1911; Harland, *QARNNS*, p. 22; Lynn McDonald, *Collected Works of Florence Nightingale, Wars and the War Office*, vol. 15, Wilfrid Laurier University Press, Waterloo, Canada, 2011, p. 234; Summary of BNA, tinyurl.com/kgory5z, accessed 28 March 2016.
5 Comments on Eva by Sue Light, 26 September 2011, *Great War Forum*, http://tinyurl.com/lnhrkhz, accessed 7 March 2017.
6 Harland, *QARNNS*, pp. 149–50. For the broad naval context see Duncan Redford and Philip D. Grove, *The Royal Navy: A History Since 1900*, NMRN/I.B.Tauris, London, 2014; *Naval Women Make Music*, https://tinyurl.com/ksaj3fx, accessed 29 April 2017.
7 Harland, *QARNNS*, p. 32.
8 Harland, *QARNNS*, pp. 24–6.
9 *British Journal of Nursing* (hereafter *BJN*), 21 June 1902, p. 494.
10 Professor Christine Hallett, *Angels of No Man's Land*, 2014, tinyurl.com/lhujq7n, accessed 2 August 2016.

11 *BJN*, 11 December 1909, p. 479; Summers, *Angels*, p. 237–70; Thekla Bowser, *The Story of British V.A.D. Work in the Great War*, IWM, London, 1917, p. 85; William Macpherson, ed., *Medical Services: General History*, vol. 1, HMSO, London, 1921, p. 56.

12 *BJN*, vol. 47, 9 September 1911, p. 208. See also Admiralty discussions of a possible scheme for a reserve for QARNNS: London, The National Archive, (hereafter TNA), TNA T 1/11194/5589/10 and T 1/11356/22630/11. Re matrons/army MOs selection tensions in the Boer War and then with VADs: Summers, *Angels*, pp. 237–70; Harland, *QARNNS*, p. 29 and onwards.

13 Summers, *Angels*, p. 290; *Scottish Women's Hospitals*, tinyurl.com/mwxcnzf, accessed 8 March 2017.

14 Mike Farquharson-Roberts, *A History of the Royal Navy – World War I*, I.B.Tauris/NMRN, London, 2014, p. 19. Totals statistics: Wells, *The Royal Navy*, p. 274; Thomas John Mitchell and G. M. Smith, *Medical Services: Casualties and Medical Statistics of the Great War*, HMSO, London, 1931.

15 Harland, *QARNNS*, p. 151. Re 'charming': *BJN*, 24 March 1917, p. 312; Table VII, *Statement of the First Lord of the Admiralty*, Naval Estimates 1919–1920, https://tinyurl.com/ljtonxr, accessed 1 July 2016.

16 Harland, *QARNNS*, p. 151; Plumridge, *Hospital Ships*; Stephen McGreal, *The War on Hospital Ships 1914–1918*, Pen & Sword, Barnsley, 2008; Campbell McCutcheon, *Hospital Ships & Troop Transport of the First World War*, Amberley, Stroud, 2015.

17 Harland, *QARNNS*, pp. 29, 151.

18 When war ended 10,404 had enrolled in QAIMNS. There were also 9,000 Army VADs. Many Australian sisters were involved in nursing casualties from Gallipoli. Piggott, *Army*, pp. 46–61; Harland, *QARNNS*, p. 151.

19 McGreal, *Hospital Ships*, pp. 34–9, 172–5, 214; Harland, *QARNNS*, pp. 33–4.

20 Harland, *QARNNS*, pp. 34–8; *Gallipoli Casualties by Country*, tinyurl.com/m6zmqvz, accessed 11 March 2017.

21 Harland, *QARNNS*, p. 30.

22 Harland, *QARNNS*, pp. 30, 151.

23 British Red Cross, VAD Members' Records (digital archive), www.redcross.org.uk/ww1, accessed 31 August 2016; Kingston upon Hull War Memorial 1914–1918, http://www.ww1hull.org.uk/index.php/home/hull-in-ww1/hospitals, accessed 23 May 2016; Katharine Furse, *Hearts and Pomegranates*, Peter Davies, London, 1940, p. 371.

24 Furse, *Pomegranates*, p. 300.

25 Bristol, University of Bristol Special Collections (hereafter JAS Bristol), John Addington Symonds Archive, Folder VII 'The VAD', Katharine Furse's draft autobiography, p. 648. Re substitution rates: Macpherson, *Services*, p. 142.

26 Harland, *QARNNS*, pp. 38, 151.

27 Harland, *QARNNS*, p. 151.

28 Table VII, Naval Estimates; *BJN*, 26 August 1922, p. 133, lists the women's names; Table V, Naval Estimates.

29 *BJN*, 20 April 1918, p. 272; 'Military Medals', http://www.scarletfinders.co.uk/121.html, accessed 9 July 2016; 'Awards of the Royal Red Cross', http://www.naval-history.net/WW1NavyBritishLGDecorationszzRRC.htm, accessed 13 August 2016; RN Nursing Service, Roll of Naval War Medals, TNA ADM 171/1333.

30 Tables IV and VII, Naval Estimates. This percentage is calculated mainly on the basis of 15 November 1918 figures: i.e. 5,652 women, of whom 297 QARNNS,

534 VADs and 4,821 WRNS. They are part of the total 407, 316 personnel (which may exclude WRNS). All these statistics are problematic, so this figure must be used with caution.

Chapter 3. Wrens in World War I

1. Katharine Furse's letter to her sister Madge Symonds Vaughan, 3 July 1918, cited in Furse, *Pomegranates*, p. 377.
2. Letter from Furse's mother to Annie Ritchie, c. 1890, Furse's Folder vol. II, 'Adolescence', p. 155, 111–17, 221/9; Katharine Furse, *Pomegranates*, pp. 286, 298; Furse's Folder VII 'VAD', pp. 535d/66y, 535f, 551. Furse's Folder 'After Death CWF', vol. VI, pp. 489–90. All documents are at JAS Bristol.
3. Beatty letter, 10 December 1914, cited in Stephen Roskill, *Admiral of the Fleet Earl Beatty*, Collins, London, 1980, p. 95.
4. The Submarine Service increased from 1,418 to 6,058. The WRNS grew from 0 to 5,550, in half the time. Farquharson-Roberts, *Navy*, p. 158.
5. Gail Braybon, *Women Workers in the First World War*, Routledge, London, 2012; Introduction of women clerks and other posts for women, TNA ADM 1/8425/181. Re femininity in military: Lucy Noakes, *Women in the British Army: War and the Gentle Sex, 1907–1948*, Routledge, London, 2006, pp. 72, 84; Keith Grieves, *Sir Eric Geddes: Business and Government in War and Peace*, Manchester University Press, Manchester, 1989, p. 67. Re Lady Rocksavage: Ursula Stuart Mason, *Britannia's Daughters: The Story of the WRNS*, Leo Cooper, London, 1992, p. 2.
6. Furse, *Pomegranates*, pp. 561–2; Mason, *Britannia's*, p. 3.
7. Edith Bass photo, IWM WWW D8-5-925, https://tinyurl.com/lnb6hxy; Lady Drury photo, IWM, 205380258, http://tinyurl.com/lnltrf7, both accessed 10 March 2017.
8. Furse, *Pomegranates*, pp. 351, 358.
9. Furse, *Pomegranates*, p. 360. The Geddes were cousins of pioneering women doctor Elizabeth Garrett Anderson, through their mother, powerful Edinburgh radical reformer Christina Geddes, nee Anderson.
10. Furse, *Pomegranates*, p. 361.
11. Furse, *Pomegranates*, p. 363.
12. Furse, *Pomegranates*, pp. 361–2, 370; Noakes, *Army*, pp. 72, 84; Janet Watson, *Fighting Different Wars: Experience, Memory, and the First World War in Britain*, Cambridge University Press, Cambridge, 2004, pp. 29, 53; Doron Lamm, 'Emily Goes to War: Explaining the Recruitment to the Women's Army Auxiliary Corps in World War One', in Billie Melman, ed., *Borderlines; Genders and Identities in War and Peace 1870–1930*, Routledge, London, 2013, p. 389. Re pay: Furse, *Pomegranates*, p. 362; Watson, *Fighting*, pp. 30, 170.
13. Similarly the army underestimated the size of women's contribution: 12,000 WAACs (later called Queen Mary's Army Auxiliary Corps) were anticipated but 56,000 served. 17,000 of the 56,000 served overseas. Samantha Philo-Gill, *The Women's Army Auxiliary Corps in France, 1917–1921: Women Urgently Wanted*, Pen and Sword, Barnsley, 2017; Elisabeth Shipton, *Female Tommies: The Frontline Women of the First World War*, The History Press, Stroud, 2014; Furse, *Pomegranates*, p. 377.
14. Alexandra Chalmers Watson, www.oxforddnb.com/index/67/101067666, accessed 13 March 2017; Furse, *Pomegranates*, p. 365.
15. Furse, *Pomegranates*, p. 363.

16 The key foundational document Dame Katharine's team produced was *Advance Instructions Pending the Issue of Complete Instruction, WRNS*, undated but around mid-December 1917, NMRN 206/92 (47). Re femininity: Lucy Noakes, *War and the British: Gender, Memory and National Identity*, I.B.Tauris, London, 1998, pp. 16, 68B; Furse, *Pomegranates*, p. 377.
17 Furse, *Pomegranates*, pp. 364–5; *WRNS: Organisation and Uniform Allowance Regulations*, TNA ADM 116/3455. Their badges and details of their braid can be seen at Godfrey Dykes, 'The Wrens', tinyurl.com/mqufcsa, accessed 10 August 2016.
18 Furse, *Pomegranates*, pp. 365, 368. On pay: *Navy List*, 1918. Re family wage: Braybon, *Workers*, p. 16.
19 Furse, *Pomegranates*, pp. 367–74; Mason, *Britannia's*, pp. 10–11.
20 Mason, *Britannia's*, pp. 15–18.
21 Furse, *Pomegranates*, p. 369.
22 Form WS4, Application and Enrolment for Admission as Officer to the Women's Royal Naval Service (included in every folder, in TNA ADM 318), Guidelines 'instructions to officers in general', p. 10, DM1227, JAS, Bristol. Re bluffing: Furse, *Pomegranates*, p. 370.
23 Re humane: Hester Lethbridge's record (TNA ADM/318/32). Officers' service records (TNA ADM 318) include notes by interviewers, which are sometimes astonishingly offensive. In one case interviewers recorded they 'could not think why they had passed her previously, as she obviously had Negro blood in her' (ADM/318/335). Re Craster: ADM 318/128.
24 *Instructions for Principals and Divisional Directors*, 1918, NMRN, 206/92 (46), Appendix C, pp. 85–6.
25 Furse, *Pomegranates*, p. 367.
26 *Kings Regulations and WRNS Ideals*, Abbey Press, February 1918; Bristol JAS, DM 190, papers of Katharine Furse, section 2; Quote from Charles Hankey, *The Beloved Captain*, 1917, https://archive.org/details/belovedcaptainh00hankgoog, accessed 20 September 2017; Letter from Furse to Jermyn, TNA ADM 31/ 819 11; Letter of appreciation from Beale to Furse, NMRN 206/92 (137*2).
27 Furse, *Pomegranates*, p. 371. Bristol JAS, DM 190, papers of Katharine Furse, section 2, KF letter to W. Ernest Martin, Harwich, 4 January 1919.
28 Furse, *Pomegranates*, p. 371. Testosterone was only in the late twentieth century recognised as a significant hormone in collective male behaviour. Stephen Peter Rosen, *War and Human Nature*, Princeton University Press, Princeton, NJ, 2009. Picture postcards from 1900 to the 1960s reflected the idea of the sailor figure as jolly roué (in author's Eve Tar Archive).
29 Re Heath: Mason, *Britannia's*, p. 13. Re toast: Furse, *Pomegranates*, p. 369. The usual Saturday toast was 'To our wives and sweethearts!', to which the unofficial response was a saucy 'And may they never meet!' In 2013 it was amended to the neutral 'To our families'.
30 Furse, *Pomegranates*, pp. 368–9; WRNS Divisional office log, SW division, 1918, NMRN, 206/92 (72) (mislabelled 1919).
31 Bristol JAS DM1227/ Wrens VAD etc., in elderly buff folder called 'KF WRNS', Temporary Instruction to Principal WRNS, 18 March 1918.
32 Furse, *Pomegranates*, p. 369; TNA ADM 336, *WRNS Ratings Registers of Service*, showing their first job. Data extracted and kindly shared by M. A. Fish. For his discussion of totals see *Wrens Project*, 22 June 2016, tinyurl.com/lo7xboo, accessed 5 August 2016.
33 *Ratings Registers*.

34 Furse, *Pomegranates*, p. 369.
35 Furse, *Pomegranates*, pp. 373–4. Finally, 32,000 WRAF women served. Dame Katharine was involved in sorting out major tensions over the management of the WRAF by Violet Douglas-Pennant. There was a sex scandal and formal enquiry. Katharine was in effect managing two forces, and was indeed invited to formally take over. Matters straightened out somewhat from September when Helen Gwynne-Vaughan, the former WAAC Chief Controller in France, replaced Violet.
36 Jermyn Record of Service, letter dated 17 July 1918, TNA ADM 318 819/06; *Thwarted Expansion?*, http://tinyurl.com/mdmrrr5, accessed 20 September 2017; Mason, *Britannia*'s, p. 15.
37 WRNS hostels, NMRN 206/92 (1732). Re pride: Furse, *Pomegranates*, p. 376.
38 Furse, *Pomegranates*, p. 380.
39 JAS Bristol, DM 1584/14, Journal of Isobel Crowdy, 1918–19; Furse, *Pomegranates*, p. 380.
40 Furse, *Pomegranates*, p. 381.
41 Furse, *Pomegranates*, p. 380.
42 Beale letter to her mother dated 21 January 1919, cited in Walker, *Fighting*, p. 170; Divisional office log, SW division, 6 September 1919, NMRN; KF's letter to Women's Section of Comrades of the Great War, Devonport, 6 October 1919, NMRN 206/92 (121).
43 Furse *Pomegranates*, p. 388.
44 Re awards: *Supplement to the London Gazette*, pp. 5775–6, 9 May 1919; Mason, *Wrens*, p. 39. Re establishments closing: National Maritime Museum (hereafter NMM) DAU 216; Bristol JAS DN 190; papers of Katharine Furse, section 2.
45 The Naval Estimates say there were 4,821 on 15 November 1918.
46 Re mobiles: I am indebted to M. A. Fish for this data, extracted from NMM DAU/179 and TNA ADM/318. In mismatching data he found 3,040 mobiles and 3,840 immobile ratings. Only 22 had switched to being mobiles. Raw figures on marital status from *WRNS Officers of WW1*, 4 August 2014, https://tinyurl.com/kb73tzn, based on at least 80 per cent of officers findable at TNA ADM 318.
47 Cutting, Liddle Archive, University of Leeds, WW1/WO/040, 'Personalities and Powers, Dame Katharine Furse, GBE, RRC', no author or date but early 1919.

Chapter 4. Nursing in the Peacetime Navy: 1919–38

1 Olga Franklin's WRNS record: TNA ADM 318/111; QARNNS records: TNA ADM 104–161/3; see also *The Times* obituary, 23 April 1987. Her uncatalogued material is at the NMM, MSS/77/165.
2 Harland, *QARNNS*, pp. 39–53. Redford and Groves, *History*, pp. 101–32. Keyes Papers, British Library Manuscript Collections.
3 The first quote is from 'Nancy Astor the Viscountess Astor Quotes', tinyurl.com/mnxytco, accessed 13 November 2016. The second is from Navy Estimates, House of Commons debate (hereafter HC Deb), 11 March 1937, pp. 144–3.
4 A little can be grasped from documents on pay for reserves and the VAD nursing members: TNA T161/35, ADM 1/8609/133; ADM 1/8715/186.
5 Minutes from 1920. Compensation for injuries, etc. to members of … nursing services attached to HM Forces: TNA T 1/12560 (10600/20; 9584/20; 8356/20; 5521/20; 50406/19). *BJN*, 15 March 1919, p. 165; 6 September 1919, p. 146; 13 September 1919, p. 162.

6   Harland, *QARNNS*, p. 39; Franklin, QARNNS Service record.
7   *Lives of the Fellows*, tinyurl.com/mneow8k, accessed 22 March 2017.
8   Harland, *QARNNS*, p. 40; TNA ADM 104/161; Matrons and Senior Nurses, https://tinyurl.com/ycm2le9v, accessed 30 August 2017.
9   Adapted from Harland, *QARNNS*, p. 152.
10 *BJN*, November 1927, p. 263; Discussions in 1928 about QARNNS conditions, and the rank of head sister-in-chief are at TNA, ADM 1/8727/149; Piggott, *Army*, pp. 64–5; QARNNS service records, TNA ADM 104–43; 104/ 161/1, p. 9; *BJN*, 19 December 1914, p. 484.
11 Medical director's quote is cited in Harland, *QARNNS*, p. 43, pp. 46–8, 51; Report of Warren-Fisher Committee, TNA ADM T162/738/6 and ADM 116/4550.
12 JLS Coulter, *The Royal Naval Medical Service, vol. 1: Administration*, HMSO, London, 1953, p. 57.

Chapter 5. Naval Women Win World War II

1   Vera Laughton Mathews, *Blue Tapestry*, Hollis & Carter, London, 1948, p. 277.
2   Mathews, *Blue*, pp. 51–2. The now-untraceable Mrs Beatrice Wyatt could have been the Beatrice Wyatt who was the Secretary of the International African Institute, whom Barbara Pym knew, and/or related to Harold F. Wyatt, co-founder of the Imperial Maritime League in 1907.
3   HMS Victory Girl Cadet Corps, TNA DM 1/21197; Mason, *Wrens*, p. 50.
4   Mathews, *Blue*, pp. 50, 51.
5   Mason, *Wrens*, p. 52; Mathews, *Blue*, pp. 53–4, 60.
6   Mathews, *Blue*, pp. 59, 201.
7   Mathews, *Blue*, p. 60.
8   Mathews, *Blue*, pp. 62, 68.
9   Mathews, *Blue*, p. 69–70. 'Tugboat Annie Brennan' was a (usually male) reference to her burly size and to a tugboat operator in a 1933 film *Tugboat Annie*. The picaresque anomalous Mrs Annie (Madge Dressler) was based on Thea Foss, the Norwegian-born founder of the largest tugboat company in the western USA.
10 Mathews, *Blue*, pp. 70, 71.
11 Mathews, *Blue*, pp. 61–4.
12 Duncan Redford, *A History of the Royal Navy: World War II*, NMRN/I.B.Tauris, London, 2014, p. 165; Christian Lamb, Ed, *I Only Joined for the Hat*, Bene Factum, London, 2007.
13 Sylvia Jensen case, 1941–2, Entry into the WRNS, nationality, 1942, TNA ADM1/ 11747. Of the 226 senior officers, 78 were wives/widows and 34 were daughters of naval men: HC Deb, 13 December 1939, vol. 355, 1222.
14 Mason, *Wrens*, p. 59.
15 Powell is cited in Mathews, *Blue*, pp. 104–5.
16 Drummond, *Blue*, pp. 117, 133, 153.
17 Mathews, *Blue*, p. 108.
18 Paul Lund and Harry Ludlam, *Nightmare Convoy: The Story of the Lost Wrens*, W. Foulsham, London, 1987, p. 36; Re Cunningham: Mathews, *Blue*, pp. 147–8.
19 Paddy Gregson, *Ten Degrees Below Seaweed: A True Story of World War II Boat's Crew Wrens*, Merlin, Braunton, 1993; Rozelle Raynes, *Maid Matelot: Adventures of a Wren Stoker in World War Two*, Castweasel, Newark, 2004; Mathews, *Blue*, pp. 201–6,

211; Hayes, *One Wren's War*, typescript, Leeds University Special Collection, LIDDLE/WW2/HFIU/025.
20   Mathews, *Blue*, pp. 115–17; Mason, *Wrens*, p. 60.
21   Script of WRNS Pageant, *c*. 1945, in ex-WRNS Jane Eldridge's collection, shown privately to author.
22   Mathews, *Blue*, p. 114. This crucial distinction is discussed very fully in Hannah Roberts, 'The Women's Royal Naval Service 1917–1945: A History of Female Military Inclusion and Exclusion', PhD thesis, 2016, Department of War Studies, King's College London.
23   Mathews, *Blue*, p. 149.
24   No breakdown of the services exists. My sample investigation of people with surnames beginning with 'A' found 31 WRNS, 76 other women, 33 men, and 32 whose gender not stated. Bletchley Park Roll of Honour, http://rollofhonour.bletchleypark.org.uk/search/, accessed 1 December 2016.
25   The WRINS story is at https://www.ibiblio.org/hyperwar/UN/India/RIN/RIN-9.html, accessed 20 September 2017, and *1945 Report of the Royal Indian Navy 1943–1944. Formation of the Women's Royal Indian Nursing Service*, TNA, ADM 1/17377. Mathews' views about Women Accepted for Volunteer Emergency Service (WAVES), the wartime women's branch of the United States Naval Reserve, can be found in Mathews, *Blue*, p. 153.
26   Win Cluny, later Hayhurst, *Airwaves*, http://tinyurl.com/n3kv3kb, accessed 1 December 2016.
27   Mathews, *Blue*, p. 178.
28   Mrs Cazalet-Keir (whose name is often written Kerr) was a firm supporter of the women's services and member of the 1942 Markham Committee enquiring into their morals, HC Deb, 10 March 1943, vol. 387, cc. 758–830.
29   Ibid.
30   Mathews, *Blue*, pp. 219, 222. Barbara Pym recycled her time in Italy as fiction, found Anne M. Wyatt-Brown, *Barbara Pym: A Critical Biography*, University of Missouri Press, Columbia, 1992, p. 64; Chris Howard Bailey, '"Ambassadors of England": Work and Leisure for the Wrens in Malta, 1944–1950', *Oral History*, vol. 21, no. 2 (1993), pp. 55–64.
31   Mathews, *Blue*, pp. 183, 235–6.
32   *Ginger Thomas's D-Day: Working for Cossac*', https://tinyurl.com/khszmkz, accessed 17 March 2016.
33   Drummond, *Blue*, pp. 122, 135–48.
34   *D-Day Experience: A Wren at Portsmouth*, https://tinyurl.com/kop22mg, accessed 14 December 2016.
35   *In the WRNS with Laura Ashley*, https://tinyurl.com/lamnghl, accessed 14 December 2016.
36   Drummond, *Blue*, p. 149; Peggy Carmichael, formerly Morris, briefing to author, 27 March 2016. Re Patricia: *My War in the WRNS; Dartmouth after D-Day*, https://tinyurl.com/l89s78u, accessed 14 December 2016.
37   Drummond, *Blue*, p. 152; Thornycroft, *My War in the WRNS*.
38   A list complete until 1985 can be found in Fletcher, *WRNS*, pp. 145–9; Morris, briefing to author, 27 March 2016.
39   Eileen Trubody: *London Gazette*, 2 July 1946, p. 3391. Re Beth Booth: Tina Rowe, 'The Woman Whose Bravery Inspired a Generation of Girls', *Western Morning News*, 9 March 2013. Accounts of other earlier awards include P. B. McGeorge, TNA ADM 1/11385, and M. W. Lunnon, TNA ADM 1/11483.

40 HC Deb 3 August 1943, vol. 391, cc. 2091–3; Public Administration Select Committee, *A Matter of Honour: Reforming the Honours System*, HMSO, London, 2004, pp. 19, 45; 'New Year Honours List: How Men Edge Out Women for Top Honours', *Telegraph*, 4 January 2016.
41 See Mason, *Britannia's*, p.136, for details of awards; Mathews, *Blue*, p. 196.
42 Cartland story told to author by Anne Dickerson, 14 November 2015. 'Leading Steward (O) Lois Lade, (née Price) WRNS', https://tinyurl.com/kylvl89, accessed 19 September 2017. Obituary of Molly Rimington [Shakespear], *Telegraph*, 3 April 2010.
43 In *Tomboys and Bachelor Girls: A Lesbian History of Post-War Britain 1945–71,* Manchester University Press, Manchester, 2007, Rebecca Jennings included only two references to the WRNS. Re Nancy Spain: see *Nancy Spain: Wrens and Same-Sex Love*, https://tinyurl.com/y9y4su7w. Cynthia Gilbert's material is at NMRN 119/110.
44 Ursula P. Foulis, 'In Retrospect', *Ditty Box*, no. 29 (November 1946), p. 48; Peggy Carmichael, formerly Morris, briefing to author, 27 March 2016.
45 Freda Bonner, private papers, IWM 19649; Dorothy Runnicles, phone briefing to author 2 August 2016, and 'D-Day Anniversary Veterans', *Guardian*, 8 June 1915.

Chapter 6. Women Care for Wartime Patients: 1939–45

1 A fuller history can be found in Kathleen Harland's history of QARNNS and J. L. S. Coulter's *The Royal Navy Medical Service,* vol. 1 and vol. 2, HMSO, London, 1954 and 1956. Army and naval nurses are included together in the works by Eric Taylor, including *Combat Nurse,* Robert Hale, London, 1999, and Brenda McBryde, *Quiet Heroines: Nurses of the Second World War,* Chatto & Windus, London, 1985.
2 Harland, QARNNS, p. 86.
3 Coulter, *Service,* vol. 1, p. 72.
4 Coulter, *Service,* vol. 1, p. 9. Rewcastle details: National Maritime Museum blog, 15 March 2016, https://tinyurl.com/hpabtgy, accessed 3 July 2016. The MWF pushed for the women's rights, as the British Medical Association was not strong on this. Re Summerskill: HC Deb 3 August 1943, vol. 391 cc. 2111–2011.
5 Coulter, *Service,* vol. 1, pp. 3, 50.
6 Derived from Coulter, *Service,* vol. 1, pp. 8–15, and for dentists pp. 642–4. The dental and total strength figures were calculated on a different time basis so are for a month later. Coulter notes that this list is not complete. Also, the numbers given for 1944 are largely the same as for the previous year and are probably an early administrative error.
7 Coulter, *Services*, vol. 1, pp. 462, 466.
8 Re Waistell: Unnamed writer *of Nights in the Cellars,* within papers of Mrs D. Boys, IWM, 6467, pp. 259, 261. (This is the rather confusing early typescript of what finally became the definitive history of VADs, mainly naval: Doreen Boys, ed., *Once Upon a Ward: V.A.D.s' Own Stories and Pictures of Service at Home and Overseas, 1939–1946,* Lion Books, Kidderminster, 1980.) For a photograph of Miss Waistell see https://tinyurl.com/m3uuw4m, accessed 19 September 2017. Author's interview and correspondence with Norma Hanson, June 2016. Re uniforms: *Caring on the Home Front*, https://tinyurl.com/l69ytfu, accessed 11 March 2017.
9 Coulter, *Service,* vol. 1, p. 72.
10 In all 600,767 naval ratings plus 64,276 Royal Marines ratings had joined up as hostilities-only personnel, as well 32,8000 entering on normal engagement basis: Coulter, *Service,* vol. 2, p. 34.

Notes

11 *A VAD Arrives at Haslar*, https://tinyurl.com/l5uth45, accessed 14 August 2016; Coulter, *Service*, vol. 1, p. 83.
12 Harland, *QARNNS*, pp. 153–60; Coulter, *Service*, vol. 1, pp. 50, 56, 120.
13 Coulter, *Service*, vol. 1, p. 19.
14 See Table 6.1. Hospital details are in Harland, *QARNNS*, pp. 57–62. Unfortunately, Rajendresen Perusram's name is often misspelt, including as Rajendraseh Purusram. Rajendresen Perusram is the correct spelling as it appears in the *Navy List* of 1984.
15 Harland, *QARNNS*, pp. 79, 74.
16 Coulter, *Service*, vol. 1, pp. 99, 103. Robinson cited in McBryde, *Quiet Heroines*, pp. 194–5. Statistics calculated from Harland, QARNNS, p. 155.
17 Coulter, *Service*, vol. 1, p. 61.
18 Coulter, *Service*, vol. 1, p. 48; Harland, *QARNNS*, pp. 54–5. The figures vary slightly.
19 Women's involvement in the evacuation is barely mentioned in Coulter, *Service*, vol. 2, pp. 308–27. Re Greenwood: Barbara Mortimer, *Sisters: Heroic True-Life Stories from the Nurses of World War Two*, Random House, London, 2013, p. 98.
20 Brian James Crabb, *Beyond the Call of Duty*, Shaun Tyas, Donington, 2006, pp. 59–60. Kate Gribble is pictured at https://tinyurl.com/leg7849, accessed 3 March 2017.
21 Coulter, *Service*, vol. 2, pp. 273, 282.
22 The story of Sister Anne Griffiths in the *Oxfordshire* appears in Eric Taylor, *Combat*, pp. 113–17. A British Pathé film of nurses in the *Oxfordshire*, 1943, can be seen at https://tinyurl.com/leuqml9, accessed 2 March 2017. A nurse in HMHS *Vita* is cited in Claire Taylor, *Nursing*, p. 24; Coulter, *Service*, vol. 2, pp. 468–91; Nicola Tyrer, *Sisters in Arms: British Army Nurses Tell Their Story*, Phoenix, London, 2009, pp. 172–80.
23 Harland, *QARNNS*, pp. 55–6.
24 Coulter, *Service*, vol. 2, p. 531.
25 Author's interview and correspondence with Norma Hanson, June 2016; Coulter, *Service*, vol. 1, p. 53; Harland, *QARNNS*, pp. 79–84.
26 A. V. Alexander, Oral Answers to Questions, Royal Navy, HC 28 November 1945.
27 Coulter, *Service*, vol. 1, p. 71; *Marriage on HMHS Amarapoora*, TNA ADM 178/347; Norma Hanson, June 2016.
28 Coulter, *Service*, vol. 1, pp. 70, 71.
29 Coulter, *Service*, vol. 2, p. 509. The QAIMNS was ten times the size of QARNNS: 12,000.
30 Total navy casualties were 63,787 out of 860,000. Don Kindell, *Casualty Lists of the Royal Navy and Dominion Navies*, 2008, http://www.naval-history.net/xDKCas1003-Intro.htm, accessed 24 June 2016. ARRC, RRC, RRC and bar awards were given out less generously in World War II. In the previous war 6,741 women had received the wartime RRC by 1922. Sue Light, *The Royal Red Cross and the Great War*, http://www.scarletfinders.co.uk/174.html, accessed 19 September 2017; *Supplement to the London Gazette*, 1 January 1946, pp. 83–6. Re Ann: 'GA Ramsden, obituary', *Independent*, 15 November 2004.
31 Coulter, *Service*, vol. 1, p. 63.
32 Cited in Claire Taylor, *Nursing*, p. 28.

Chapter 7. Struggling Seawards: The WRNS 1946–90

1. Cited in Mason, *WRNS*, p. 131. This chapter is highly indebted to the many insights of Kathleen Sherit's PhD thesis on the integration of the WRNS. Her study gives a fuller picture of what can only be summarised here: 'The Integration of Women into the Royal Navy and the Royal Air Force, Post-World War II to the Mid-1990s', King's College, London, 2013, https://tinyurl.com/maa8ecj, accessed 4 March 2017.
2. Mathews, *Blue*, pp. 129, 271. Woollcombe's father Maurice became Admiral in 1928. She was remembered in the Woollcombe block of WRNS Quarters, 1973.
3. Statement for Royal Commission, 3 October 1945, TNA ADM 1/18884.
4. Mathews, *Blue*, p. 276. Report of the Committee on the Women's Services, 24 June 1943, TNA CAB 66/38.
5. Minutes of Senior Wrens Officers Conference, 24 January 1947, NMRN 198.350.
6. Mathews, *Blue*, pp. 276–7.
7. Tables 136 and 137, *Annual Abstract of Statistics*, No 93, HMSO, London, 1956.
8. Mason, *WRNS*, p. 127.
9. Conference of Senior WRNS Officers, March 1952, NMRN, 1988.350.28.1–4.
10. Mason, *WRNS*, p. 128.
11. HC Deb 17 April 1957, vol. 568, cc. 1981–2059.
12. HC Deb 16 December 1958, vol. 597, cc.1051–64; HL Deb 15 December 1958, vol. 213, cc. 253–317.
13. Nine years later, of the 1959 intake 66 per cent of 251 cadets were from 56 independent schools. HC Deb, 14 December 1959, vol. 61, cc.1204–16. Author's emailed discussions with Penny Melville-Brown, 14 March 2017.
14. Mason, *WRNS*, p. 131.
15. 'You can count on the women!', *Evening News*, 30 August 1939.
16. Jacqueline Warwick, *Girl Groups, Girl Culture: Popular Music and Identity in the 1960s*, Routledge, London, 2007.
17. 'Angela Green' (pseudonym) briefing to author, 13 July 2016; Minutes of Senior WRNS officers' conference, 1963, NMRN, 1988.350; Note to minister from Mary Talbot, undated but just before the post-Pritchard cuts, TNA DEFE 13/1342.
18. Sherit, *'Integration'*, p. 133; Family Planning, TNA DEFE 49/18.
19. Mason, *WRNS*, p. 131.
20. Phone briefing by Lord Judd to author, 8 February 2017.
21. *Annual Abstracts of Statistics* for example show that 1,093 women entered in 1966, and 825 in 1979. The peak year for intake was 1972; 1,179 entered. In 1978/9, to take a snapshot year, 975 left and 813 entered. Career duration figures were given in HC Deb 19 May 1977, vol. 932, cc. 727–836.
22. *WRNS Study Group Report*, November 1974, TNA ADM 105/99; Sherit, *'Integration'*, p. 157.
23. *Study Group Report*.
24. Jean Ebbert and Mary Beth Hall, *Crossed Currents: Navy Women in a Century of Change*, Brasseys, Washington DC, New York, 1999, pp. 242–5. Re tights: see Godfrey Dykes, https://tinyurl.com/lnzo4j2, accessed 14 June 2016.
25. HC Deb 19 May 1977, vol. 932, cc. 727–836; Townsend letter to *Naval Review*, vol. 80, no. 2 (April 1992), p. 163. The Mason Review identified priorities for cuts. Talbot biographical details were given anonymously to the author; others appear in William Stewart, *Admirals of the World: A Biographical Dictionary, 1500 to the Present*, McFarland, Jefferson, NC, 2009, p. 272.

26 Re armbands: 'Snapdragon', a WRNS officer, in letter to *Naval Review*, vol. 76 (75th anniversary issue, 1988), p. 38; Carolyn Stait, briefing to author, 3 March 2017; Mason, *WRNS*, p. 132; Anonymous, email to author, 30 April 2017.
27 Rosie Ball, https://tinyurl.com/lnzo4j2, accessed 1 February 2017; Mason, *WRNS*, p. 135. Re Northern Ireland: Memo of 21 July 1976 from Head of DS5, TNA DEFE 3/1342.
28 Sherit, *'Integration'*, p. 165.
29 Principal Personnel Officers Committee minutes, 13 December 1979, TNA, DEFE 71/31; Sherit, *'Integration'*, p. 139; Penny Hockley, email to author 3 January 2017.
30 Wilson, interview with Katy Elliott, 14 October 2006, NMRN 2006, CD2; Stait, 6 March 2017.
31 HC Deb 22 April 1970, vol. 800, cc. 505–12; HC Deb 29 April 1980, vol. 983, cc. 1174–300.
32 *The Size and Shape of the WRNS in the 1980s* (1981); Mason, *Britannia's*, p. 114.
33 It appears that the first woman to join Dartmouth as a senior observer (the person who sits behind the pilot) was in 1991. By 2002 there were three WRNS helicopter pilots and 15 observers, at least one of whom was a trainer. Tlam999, Professional Pilots Rumour Network, 18 March 2011, https://tinyurl.com/lw3nmwa, accessed 2 February 2017; HC Deb 22 July 1981, vol. 9, cc. 326–409; Dennis Barker, *Ruling the Waves: An Unofficial Portrait of the Royal Navy*, Penguin Viking, Harmondsworth, 1986, p. 267.
34 The four who were awarded BEMs are listed in Max Hastings and Simon Jenkins, *The Battle for the Falklands*, Pan, London, 1983, pp. 452–68; Mason, *Britannia's*, pp. 116–17.
35 Anthea Larken, interview by Katy Elliott, 24 July 2006, NMRN 20006.65; Stewart, *Admirals*, p. 198.
36 Re education: *Report of a Study into the Employment of Women's Royal Naval Service Personnel in the Royal Navy*, March 1989, p. 13.
37 Franklin letter, *Naval Review*, vol. 78, no. 2 (April 1990), p. 158; 'Just Call Her Sir, Female Sailor Says', Associated Press, 1 May 1990, https://tinyurl.com/y7t92vfz, accessed 20 September 2017.
38 West Report, Annex A, cited in Sherit, *'Integration'*, p.186. From 1988 moves were afoot to try to alter *Re-entry after Pregnancy Regulations*, DCI (RN) (1/C 1/88. As early as 1964 the US had begun refusing women the right to leave after marriage (which meant in effect breaking their contract).
39 No copy of the report is available in any public archive. Kathleen Sherit has seen a private copy and she is the main person who discusses it: *'Integration'*, pp. 184–92.
40 Rosie Wilson, interview; Caroline Coates briefing by phone to author, 10 February 2017.
41 National Audit Office, *Ministry of Defence: Control and Use of Manpower*, HMSO, London, 1989, pp. 24–5; Sherit, *'Integration'*, p. 185; Carolyn Stait, correspondence with author, 6 March 2017.
42 Aeneas, 'To Sea, WRNS, or Not to Sea', *Naval Review*, vol. 77, no. 3 (July 1989), pp. 230–2. His article was in response to the seminal one by Cassandra, 'The Future Employment of the WRNS', vol. 77, no. 1 (January 1989).
43 Alan West, interview, 5 June 2007, cited in Sherit, *'Integration'*, p. 194.
44 Sherit, *'Integration'*, p. 202. Brian Brown interview by Chris Howard Bailey, 6 December 1983, NMRN 456/1993.
45 HC Deb 5 February 1990, vol. 166, c. 648.

Chapter 8. Women become Doctors and Men become Nurses: 1946–90

1. Poem from *COHSE Journal*, November/December 1963, cited in Penny Starns, 'Military Influence on the British Civilian Nursing Profession, 1939–69', PhD thesis, University of Bristol, 1997, p. 240, https://core.ac.uk/download/pdf/33133758.pdf, accessed 19 September 2017.
2. Re numbers: Of the 971 civilian women active in the reserve in 1945 only 16 per cent went back to civilian life. Reserves' numbers dropped only slightly to 825 in 1946 and to 174 in 1960: Harland, *QARNNS*, pp. 100–2, 150–69; *Annual Abstracts of Statistics*.
3. HC Deb 19 October 1949, vol. 468, cc. 36–7W.
4. Re Ruth: Harland, *QARNNS*, pp. 103–10; IWM interview 16421, http://www.iwm.org.uk/collections/item/object/80015900, accessed 19 September 2017. Re Barbara: Claire Taylor, *Nursing*, pp. 40–1; portrait at https://tinyurl.com/kncgzu8, accessed 3 April 2017. Re Alfreda: Drury, *We Were There*, p. 177.
5. HC Deb 10 March 1960, vol. 619, cc. 703–11.
6. Briefing to author by Ann, now Dickerson, 2 January 2016. Re Alfreda: Harland, *QARNNS*, p. 111.
7. The State Registered Nurse (requiring a three-year training period) was a forerunner of today's registered general nurses (RGNs). The SENs similarly preceded the enrolled nurse (general). They were trained for two years. Harland, *QARNNS*, p. 114.
8. Nora Lewis, née Miller, *Nursing in the Navy*, 2016, and briefings to author, February 2016; Carole Ralph, telephone briefing to author, 27 February 2016; 'Cynthia Cooke, Naval Nurse', *Telegraph*, 14 June 2016.
9. Harland, *QARNNS*, p. 118; Lewis, *Nursing in the Navy*. The Royal College of Nursing Defence Forum apparently began only thirty years later: *Defence Nurses' Experiences from Iraq and Afghanistan: The RCN Defence Nursing Forum's Oral Histories Project*: https://www.rcn.org.uk/professional-development/publications/pub-005367, accessed 20 September 2017.
10. Nicci Pugh, *White Ship, Red Crosses: A Nursing Memoir of the Falklands War*, Melrose, Ely, 2010.
11. 'Tough Initiation for Newly-Qualified Nurse', *Navy News*, October 2007, https://tinyurl.com/y8al2o77, accessed 24 August 2017.
12. Liz Ormerod, telephone briefing to author, 16 June 2016. 'Recalling Casualties of Conflict 30 Years On', *Craven Herald*, 20 April 2012.
13. Men trained as SRNs had served before, but were called medical technicians. After qualifying many served as medical secretaries in hospitals, rather than being in charge of wards. Harland, *QARNNS*, p. 126; Nora Lewis, telephone briefing to author, 22 March 2017.
14. S. Pragnell cited in Claire Taylor, *Nursing*, pp. 42, 48. Re Maggie Freer: Pugh, *White Ship*, p. 148. Re pregnancies: 'No "excessive" award for sacked pregnant officer', *Guardian*, 24 December 1994.
15. Claire Taylor, *Nursing*, pp. 62, 69. Email and telephone briefing to author from Carol Murray-Jones, March 2017.
16. Letter from Platt to Padmore, Treasury, 20 July 1949, TNA T213/305, cited in Sherit, '*Integration*', p. 88. Re Patricia: *The Journal of The Radiology History and Heritage Charitable Trust*, vol. 19, 2003; *Navy List*, 1955, 1956.
17. *Royal Naval Reserve (RNR): Scheme for Recruitment of Medical and Dental Students*, TNA ADM 1/28183; Judith Bellafaire and Mercedes Herrera Graf, *Women Doctors in War*, Texas A & M University Press, College Station, TX, 2009, p. 120; Joy Bright

Hancock, *Lady in the Navy: A Personal Reminiscence*, Naval Institute Press, Annapolis, MD, 2013, p. 85; 'Wanted to Do Something Different', *Navy News*, August 1963, p. 13.

18 Sources include *Navy Lists* and the *Annual Abstracts of Statistics*. The former may be a little inaccurate as they are a compilation involved counting individual names. In some cases it was not clear whether the first name – such as Beverley – was female or male, so these statistics are almost certainly an under-representation. I am indebted to Mike Coombes of Navy List Research for his efforts here.

19 Rick Jolly, *The Red & Green Life Machine*, Red & Green Books, Saltash, 2007, pp. 8, 16.

20 Women Dental Officers, 1951, TNA ADM 1/22457; Cadetships, TNA N1/54/5/63A; *Navy Lists* 1951–73. Thanks to Mike Coombes and Rachel Bairsto for help here.

21 Mary Milton, telephone briefings and emails to author, December 2016–January 2017.

22 *(U) 499 – WRNS – Ratings – Introduction of Dental Hygienist Specialisation*, https://tinyurl.com/m3zswtr, accessed 13 January 2017.

23 Interview with Lesley Thomas by Carol Hanson, 30 March 1992, NMRN 450/92 (1); E. J. Grant, *The Toothwrights' Tale: A History of Dentistry in the Royal Navy 1964 to 1995*, Chaplin Books, Gosport, 2012, p. 67.

24 Carol Murray-Jones phone briefing to author 28 March 2017. Re Kay: Jean Morton's correspondence with author, Match 2017. Re Sally: *Navy News,* October 2007.

Chapter 9. All in the Defence Medical Services Team: 1991 to Today

1 Inga J. Kennedy, on https://uk.linkedin.com; Royal Hospital School, 19 October 2013, tinyurl.com/lp6n8o4, both accessed 1 June 2016.

2 Re DSAs: Mason, *Britannia's*, p. 127. The number of naval women health care staff among the 1,500 UK reserves who were called up to all three services, is not recorded; the majority were NHS medics, *Guardian*, 27 October 2002. Re the USA: 'Women's Role in Combat: The War Resumes', *New York Times*, 26 May 26, 1991, and 'Female Medic Initially Told She Couldn't Deploy for Gulf War', *The Leaf-Chronicle*, 24 February 2016. The pride story was given to the author in 2017 by the jubilant male medical officer, who wishes to be nameless here.

3 The Taylor story reached the author in March 2017 through two who choose anonymity.

4 'Ship's Doctor: One Woman out of a Crew of 292', *Daily Press*, 23 July 1996.

5 'Military Cross for Plymouth Woman Medic', *The Herald*, Plymouth, 11 September 2009.

6 Lara Herbert, 'Going Commando', *Anaesthesia News*, 8 February 2011, pp. 6–8.

7 Kate Prior, 'Obituary, Surgeon Commander Jane Risdall', *Journal of the RN Medical Service*, vol. 103, no. 2 (summer 2017), p. 148. Her roots were in both early women's higher education and the navy. She qualified at Girton and was related to a Boer War and World War I naval surgeon, Ernest Lomas.

8 FOI request 2016/05166, Defence Statistics (Navy), 30 June 2016, https://tinyurl.com/ny6ohfp, accessed 19 September 2017; *QARNNS Reserves*, http://tinyurl.com/m5xe5gh, accessed 28 June 2016; *The Maritime Reservist*, Spring 1916, p. 14.

9   *Navy News*, February 2002.
10 In addition in the reserve less than five of the 30 MOs were women, and under 15 of the 30 QARNNS members were female: FOI 2016/06075,30 June 2016. Women in the UK were 51 per cent of GPs but only 32 per cent of specialists. General Medical Council, http://tinyurl.com/p3hm2qd, accessed 3 July 2016.
11 MoD email to author, 8 June 2016; FOI 2016/06075.
12 The clearest explanation of the current DMS structure appears at *Defence Medical Services*, tinyurl.com/n8vywfy, accessed 28 December 2016. Re RCN DNF: tinyurl.com/zqytcpe. Re BMA AFC: tinyurl.com/lht624x, both accessed 11 March 2017.
13 House of Commons Defence Committee, 15 November 2016, *Navy Medics on Patrol in Helmand*, *https://tinyurl.com/ybsemopj*. Re Ship numbers: House of Commons Defence Committee, 15 November 2016, https://tinyurl.com/mecsqtc (both accessed 4 March 2017).
14 Re Debbie: *RCN Defence Nursing Forum Newsletter*, Spring 2007; *Ark Royal Medical Department*, https://tinyurl.com/lf4ubn7, accessed 24 February 2017.
15 *The Young Dentist*, http://tinyurl.com/kqj99df, accessed 11 June 2016. In 2003 Rear Admiral Carol I. Turner became the first female Chief of the US Navy Dental Corps. No UK naval woman has risen so high.
16 Statistics supplied to author by MoD, 23 August 2016.
17 Re Laird: *The Adventure Medic*, http://tinyurl.com/nxx8zr3, accessed 16 January 2017. Lieutenant Angela Lewis was, in 2015, the Royal Navy's only female search and rescue officer, 'Hogmanay will see the last Royal Navy shift for Prestwick Search and Rescue', *Daily Record*, 21 December 2015; MA-SM information from Laird.
18 Telephone briefing to author by Carole Ralph, 27 February 2017.

Chapter 10. On towards Diversity and Inclusion: 1991 to Today

1   Wilson interview by Katy Elliott, 29 August 2006, CD 2, NMRN.
2   Wilson, interview.
3   Mason, *Britannia*'s, pp. 126–7. Ships' complements: J. J. Colledge and Ben Warlow, *Ships of the Royal Navy: The Complete Record of all Fighting Ships of the Royal Navy*, Chatham Publishing, London, 2006.
4   'Wrens' sea role call: Jennies Now Able – How Many Willing?' *Navy News,* March 1990.
5   WEO Stef Dowson, serving in *Hecla*, drew the cartoon 'Girls Go Green', *Navy News*, September 1990, https://issuu.com/navynews/docs/199009, accessed 19 September 2017; Re Smiles cartoon: *Navy News*, February 1991, https://issuu.com/navynews/docs/199102, accessed 3 April 2017.
6   'Film of HMS *Brilliant* Wren's Interview', November 1990, IWM ADM 90139. Unfortunately, current technology does not allow it to be viewed. Cobbold email to author, 13 April 2015; Elliott cited in Mason, *Britannia*'s, pp. 127–8.
7   Re bridegroom cartoon: *Navy News*, March 1991. Re unloading cartoon: *Navy News*, April 1994.
8   Mason, *Britannia*'s, p. 127. Re Babbington: 'Royal Honour for Top Cadet'*, Navy News*, July 1998. Re commanders: 'Women Taking the Helm', *Maritime Heritage*, vol. 24 (November–December 1998), pp. 34–7.
9   UK Defence Forum, *The Future Role of Women in the Armed Forces*, 1996, http://www.ukdf.org.uk/assets/downloads/m6.htm, accessed 1 March 2017; Julia

Simpson cited in Dick Abram and Patrick Binks, eds, *Not Just Chalk and Talk: Stories of Schoolies in the Royal Navy*, 2012, and briefing to author, April 2016.
10 Re Maggie: 'All the Nice Girls Love a Sailor', *The Times*, 2 November 1993. Re Knuckles: 'Sex and the Services; Legislating for Love', *Daily Mail*, 2 April 1992. NAAFI story emailed to author by anonymous petty officer, 25 June 2016.
11 Re media: Letter from Commander P. G. Hore to *Naval Review*, vol. 78, no. 2 (April 1990), pp. 58–9. Opponents of the 'No Touching' rule argued that it would never work, was against nature and spoilt the camaraderie expressed in innocent pats on the back. Wilson and Larken comments are in NMRN interviews, Re Claire: 'Wren Loses Case against Navy', *The Herald*, 25 October 1996. This summary of cases is based on author's own study of the limited online newspaper reports.
12 Scapegoat discussion: Midshipman E. R. Hayman, 'Women at Sea', *Naval Review*, vol. 82, no. 3 (July 1994), p. 216.
13 Christopher Chris, *HMS Brilliant: In a Ship's Company*, BBC, London, 1995, pp. 157–8; Terrill briefings to author, April 2015.
14 Lyn Bryant, Joan Chandler and Tracey Bunyard, *The Integration of Sea Service: Final Report*, Royal Navy/University of Plymouth, 1993.
15 Re arms: 'Private View: A Wren with the Will to Shoot and Kill', *Financial Times*, 23 October 1993. Re typical conversions: Carolyn Stait, email to author, 6 March 2017.
16 Sherit, '*Integration*', p. 248; Mason, *Britannia's*, pp. 124–8.
17 Re class action: *The Independent*, 9 October 1992 and 12 July 1994; Rupert Hollins, 'A Review of Compensation for the Unlawful Dismissal of Pregnant Servicewomen', *Naval Review*, vol. 84, no. 2 (April 1996), pp. 147–51; 'Wren Sacked for Being Pregnant Resumes Career', *The Times*, 31 March 1995.
18 *Equality, Diversity and Inclusion*, http://www.royalnavy.mod.uk/equality-and-diversity, accessed 18 February 2017.
19 Muriel Hocking, briefings to author, August 2014. A studio portrait of Annette can be seen at Jane Brettle, http://www.janebrettle.com/a13.htm, accessed 15 February 2017. The 'ships aren't she' controversy is discussed in Stanley, *From Cabin 'Boys'*, pp. 251–2.
20 *Committee on Women in the NATO Forces UK Armed Services Report 2003*, Annex A, p. 8. 'Royal Navy Vessels Travel to London to Mark International Women's Day', *Forces Network*, 8 March 2017, https://tinyurl.com/lrp2c35, accessed 19 September 2017.
21 'It's a Woman's Life at Sea for the Royal Navy's Captain Charlotte', *Herald Scotland*, 27 January 2004. Re Vanessa: Interview with Katy Elliot, 2006, NMRN.
22 'Military's "Brass Ceiling" to Melt as Women Take Command', *Independent*, 7 March 2015; Carolyn's email to author.
23 'Women on Subs – Not all that New', *The Old Salt Blog*, 7 June 2010, https://tinyurl.com/khcoasg, accessed 10 March 2016.
24 'The Liberation of the Sexes…', *Guardian*, 6 April 2007, https://www.theguardian.com/commentisfree/2007/apr/06/comment.gender, accessed 19 September 2017.
25 Examples include 'Wild Night for "HMS Lusty" Crew after Visit by Queen', *Telegraph*, 28 May 2008. Re removing the W: *The Wren*, no. 357 (September 2006), p. 28.
26 Re Becky: 'Former Teacher to Become First Female "Black Cats" Pilot', *Telegraph*, 22 March 2010. Re Kay: MoD, 18 January 2011, https://tinyurl.com/kg3ofrm. Re Sarah:

'First female Navy Commander Removed after Affair Claim', *BBC News*, 8 August 2014, http://www.bbc.co.uk/news/uk-28700446, all accessed 19 April 2017.

27   This draws on the author's off-the-record conversations with former and serving personnel, 2015–17.

28   Information sent to author under Navy FOI 2016/06560, 11 July 2016. Couples also cohabit, but the armed forces reward those who formally tie the knot, including same-sex civil partners. 'Army chiefs trial flexitime to stop women soldiers leaving service', *Express*, 3 September 2015.

29   'Meet the Commander Giving the Royal Navy a Female Touch', *Telegraph,* 8 March 2013. 'Moving from Fitting in to Adding Value', *Nautilus Telegraph,* January 2017, https://issuu.com/redactive/docs/tel_january2017. NSN is at https://www.facebook.com/RoyalNavyWomen1/. Harmony Guidelines, Table 7, MoD, https://tinyurl.com/kayqjxj, all accessed 4 March 2017.

30   Normal conception rates for women aged between 15 and 44 are 77 per thousand. By that token, 231 navy women (7 per cent of 3,000) would be pregnant at any one time. In fact, 6 per cent is currently typical. FOI 2016/06560: UK Armed Forces Biannual Diversity statistics, October 2016, https://tinyurl.com/kceszro; Office for National Statistics, *Conceptions in England and Wales: 2014*, https://tinyurl.com/z9wv982, all accessed 3 March 2017.

31   Policy appears in Chapter 35, BR 3 (1), *Naval Personnel Management*, 2016, https://tinyurl.com/mmrgauw, accessed 23 March 2017. The returns after maternity leave figures are found in MoD diversity statistics, 2016, https://tinyurl.com/kceszro, accessed 3 March 2017.

32   'Sex Discrimination Payout for Former Wren Who Wasn't Promoted Because She Refused to Go to Sea', *Daily Mail*, 23 July 2012.

33   *The Findings of the Tri-Service 2014 Review of the Exclusion of Women from Ground Close Combat (GCC) Roles*, 2014, https://tinyurl.com/mof38h6. 'Women to Serve in Close Combat Roles in the British military', *BBC News*, 8 July 2016, http://www.bbc.co.uk/news/uk-36746917, both accessed 1 March 2017.

34   Statistics are from FOI2017/02306, 17 February 2017, and *Biannual Diversity Statistics, 2016*. Cultural evidence was gathered informally by author as part of NMRN's *Sea Your History* project, 2008, and remains unpublished; Mandy's email and phone correspondence with author, July 2016.

35   Liz's email to author, 13 June 2016; author's off-the-record discussions with former and serving personnel, 2008–17; 'RAF Women Banned from Wearing Skirts on Parade', *The Times,* 28 February 2017.

36   Tennis story from Tamsin Benton, interview by author, 6 July 2008, NMRN sound archive. 'Fourth Member of the Same Family Joins the Royal Navy', *The News* (Portsmouth), 11 February 2016.

37   MoD responses to author's Freedom of Information requests: FOI 2016/05652, 21 June 2016; 2016/06114, 4 July 2016; 2016/06560, 11 July 2016.

38   HMS *Raleigh*, https://tinyurl.com/y75ynz3m; '846 Pilot Wins Award', https://tinyurl.com/ybw8wrp8, both accessed 1 March 2017.

39   For summary see Daniel Owen Spence, *A History of the Royal Navy: Empire and Imperialism: The British Empire*, I.B.Tauris/NMRN, London, 2015.

40   See for example, 'Top General Admits Gay Soldiers Still Face Bullying', *Mail on Sunday*, 5 March 2017.

41   MOD Annual Diversity Statistics, October 2016, https://tinyurl.com/kceszro. Author's FOI requests, 2016/05652, 21 June 2016; 2016/06560, 11 July 2016; 'International Women's Day', https://tinyurl.com/lrp2c35, all accessed 3 April 2017.

Appendices

1. For discussion of the subject see Ralph Donald and Karen MacDonald, *Women in War Films: From Helpless Heroine to G.I. Jane*, Rowman & Littlefield, Lanham, MD, 2016; Victoria Carolan, 'British Maritime History, National Identity and Film, 1900–1960', PhD thesis, Queen Mary, University of London, 2012, especially pp. 225, 243–4, 262, https://core.ac.uk/download/pdf/77038573.pdf, accessed 8 April 2017.
2. Association of Wrens, http://www.wrens.org.uk/, accessed 4 April 2017.
3. WRNS BT, http://wrnsbt.org.uk/history, accessed 4 April 2017; *Seventy Years of Trust: An Illustrated History of the Women's Royal Naval Service Benevolent Trust, 1942–2012*, Portsmouth, 2012.
4. Author's correspondence with Muriel, August 2014–17.
5. Denise St Aubyn Hubbard, *In at the Deep End*, Janus, London, 1993, and phone conversations with the author, February 2014. Correspondence re MVS with Lynn Peppitt, April 2017; approximate MVS statistics from Chris Todd, email to author, 1 May 2017.
6. Author's correspondence with Victoria McMaster, 2014.
7. *Defence Equipment & Support Annual Report and Accounts 2015–16*, pp. 54–5, https://tinyurl.com/y6woleux, accessed 19 September 2017.
8. Images of QARNNS leaders can be found at http://www.qarnns.co.uk/about/former-matrons-chief.
9. Sources: Chris Howard Bailey and Lesley Thomas, *The WRNS in Camera: The Work of the Women's Royal Naval Service in the Second World War*, Sutton Publishing, Stroud, 2000, p. 101; Harland, QARNNS; Fletcher, *WRNS; Annual Abstract of Statistics 1935–2015*, using Ministry of Defence data; MOD Freedom of Information data sent to author, 2014–17; calculations on WRNS kindly made by M. A. Fish from raw data at TNA and NMM; John Wells, *The Royal Navy*, Alan Sutton, Stroud, 1994, pp. 209–74; MoD Royal Navy and Royal Marines Monthly Personnel Situation; MoD Biannual Diversity Statistics.
10. Source: compiled by author from 'Trained Regular Strength… Split by Branch', July 2004 and July 2014, FOI 2014/04346, 11 September 2014.

Index

Italic page numbers refer to an illustration.
Bold indicates 'main focus' pages.

Ablett, Ellie *xiv*, 193–4, 198
accommodation, naval women's 17, 27, 51, 57, **62**, 64, *95*, 92, 103, *208*
    wrenneries, hostels and nurses' homes 40, 92, *95*, 118, 134, 138
admirals, women as 203
Admiralty 17, 92, 220, 223, 224
adultery 12, 156, 181, 191
adventure 13, 23, 87, 93, 98, 138, 217
Aguila, SS 96, 123, 206
alcohol use 17, 51, 35, 36, 66, 102, 106, 107, 145, 186, 201, *colour plate 4*
Alexandra, Queen/Princess *42*, 43, 58, 60, 172, 232
'amazons' 23, 13, *15*
Archdale, Betty 60, 95, 110
arms bearing 17, 23, 129, *135*, 140, 146, 147, 148, 174, 186
'associate members', idea of women as navy's **2**, **21**, 29, 201
Association of Wrens xxii, xxiv, xxv, 87, 107, *192*, 205, 212, 228
attitudes towards women's services 35, 43–4, 50, 55, 59, 61, 74–5, 80, 81, 83, 84, 87, 88, 89, 98, 103, 106, 111, 125, 131, 205
    Civil Establishment of 88, 90, 98
    civilian women employees in 55, 56, 78, 89
    orders from 45, 50, 61, 64–5, 68, 75, 92, 94, 99, 132, 204, 206, 207
    women's attitudes towards 44, 58, 62, 79, 85, 87, 89, 90, 98
    women's presence in Admiralty buildings 4, 43, 58, 62, 79, 85, 89, 90, 93, 124, 207
Australia 101, 105, 120, 124, 126, 154, 202, 206, 208, 214

auxiliary/marginal status of women's services 3, 31, 55, 56, 61, 84, 88, 209, 215
awards/honours 52, 75, 108–9, 126. 159, 173

bad luck, women aboard as **10**
BAME (black and minority ethnic) personnel 26, 33, 189, 196, 109
Beale, Doris 118, 124, 231
Beale, Helen 66, 73, 76
Bletchley Park 13, 100
'blue Wrens' 191, *192*, 195, 196, 197
boarding officers (WRNS) 103, *103*
boats crew wrens (WRNS) 96, 97, 105, 208, 223, 224
bombings of naval women's locations 95, 124, 206, 208
Bowen, Mick 174, 232
boyfriends, sailors as *5*, 23, 52, 60, 65–6, 105, 139, 140, 186, *colour plate 6*
Britannia figure 3, 7, 19, *20*
Britannia Royal Naval College, aka Dartmouth 11, 63, 136, 145, 148, 151, 152, 183, 193, 210, 225, 230
brotherliness/brothers 23, 55, *60*, 99, 105, 106, 136, 196

camaraderie 8, *9*, 14, 72, 107, 110, 187, *202*, 213
Canada 101, 214
career, *see under* QARNNS and WRNS, and retention, sea service
casualties 33–4, 48–9, 51, 67, 84, 107, 122, 123–4, 126, 164, 172, 174
Ceylon (now Sri Lanka) 104, 105, 106, 120, 123, 124, *125*, 206, 207, 208, 209

256

Index

Chalmers Watson, Mona 56, 57, 58, 61
Chamberlayne, Anne 23, 24, 204
Chatham 32, *44*, 47, 79, 82, 120, 231
civilian status of naval services women 11, 38, 40, 41, 45, 54, 46, 130, 131, 134, 138, 146, 160, 161, 162, 163, 166, 207, 229
civilianisation of navy 134, 155, 175, 176
class, social 3, *15*, 21, 33, 34, 35, 57, 59, 91–2, 136, 164
clerical work 45, 55, 56, 59, 68, 75, 87, 93, 98, 104, 110, *114*, 118, 155
clothes, civilian 24, 61, 73, 92, 94, 110
Coates, Caroline 153–6, *153*
Cobbold, Richard 180, 181, 182
coders, cypherers (WRNS) 68, 77, 93, 96, 98, 103
Cold War 129, 133, 140, 160, 161, 169
conscription 55, 58, 131
contraception 138–9, 154, 170
combat 32, 51, 72, 119, 131, 187
 females' exclusion from 6, 12, 16, 20, 45, 56, 99, 129, 130, 131, *135*, 142, 146–7, 148, 152, 153–4, 154, 155, 157, 165, 168, 172, 173
 grey areas 99, 157
 ground close (GCC) 190, 191, 195
 increasing involvement in 173, 177, 178, 182, 187, 189–90, 191, 195, 205, 210, 211
combined services/tri-service 12, 55, 87, 124, 175, 176, 195, 202, *colour plate 24*
communications work (WRNS) 68, 93, 102, 105, 113, *146*, 148, 207, 208
Cooke, Cynthia 124, 165, 169, 231
cooks 55, *58*, 92, 93, 105, 113, 120
Crimea War 11, **33–4**, 204
cross-dressed women sailors **23–6**, *25*, *colour plate 1*
cutbacks and policy reviews, impact on naval women 35, 130, 134–5, 142–3, 148–9, 151, 153–4, 162, 166, 172–3, 174, 185, 190, 229

danger
 sexual/moral danger 8, 17, 65, *99*, 103, 123, 139, 149, 206
 war/sea danger 16, 18, 25, 41, 48–9, 50, 67, 72, 76, 78–9, 80, 94–5, *95*, 96, 97, 99, 101, 103, 104, 109, 111, 122, 123, 137, 156, 157, 160, 164, 165, 200, 204, 205, 207, 223
 women as dangerous 56, 60, 66, 104
Davies, Jean 129, 140, 225, 231
'daughters of Senior Service' *15*, *58*, 92
D-Day 104–5, 124, 150, 160, 208
demobilisation 71–5, *74*, 106, 107, 110–11
dental staff 113, 115, 116–7, 155, 166, 167, 168–9, 172, 175, 176–7, 207, 218, 224, 226, 235, *colour plate 18*
Devonport *1*, 1–2, 66,73, 77, 134
discipline 17, 38, 40, 43, *44*, 63, 65, 83, 145, 195
discrimination **66**, 80, 109, 147, 148, 195, 196, 201, 209
Diversity and Inclusion 2, 18, 189, 196, 201
domestic work 21, 23, 59, 68, 73, 87, 93
drivers, motor 71, 93, 108, 110, 113, 188
Dunkirk 93–4, 123, 204, 206
duty, women's sense of 14, 71, 45, 46–7, 99, 104, 107, 135, 151

electricians 67, 143
engineers 67, 140, 149, 180, 184, 197, 225, 229, 235, *colour plate 20*
essentialism, female 79, 137,119, 154

Falklands Conflict 1 49, 150, 153, *164–5*, 168, 170, 210, 217
families 23, 76, 189
 family support for service personnel 78, 109
 navy as 'family' 14, 56, 59, 107, 132, 136, 138, 164, 132
 women from maritime family of origin 33, 56, 62, 67, 77, 80, 81, 85, 88–9, **92**, 129, 197
 women as responsible for 28, 62, 172
Faslane 140, 177, 190
fathers/daughters 10, 63, 65, 91, 92, 173
father figures, fatherlessness, patriarchy 6, 59, 181
femininity 2, 7, 8, *47*, 55, **67**, 104, **135–7**, 141, 146–7, 154, 181–2, 186, 196, 197
feminism 12, 87 198
film, representation of naval women in 7, 38, 138, **223–5**

Fleet Air Arm 14, 108, 110, 140, 144, 147, 149, 177, 192, *192*,197, 202, 235
Fletcher, Marjorie 213, 231
France 48, 54, 59, 93, 94, 101, 104–6, 123, 124, 210, 206, 208
Franklin, Olga 77, 81, 89, 123, 126, 226, 231
Furse, Katharine 50, 51, 53, *54*, 56–7, 58, 60, 61, 62, 63, 64, 65–6, 69, 70, 71, 72, 74, 76, 87, 88, 89, 91, 98, 132, 137, 201, 205, 213, 231

Geddes, Eric 55, 58,
gender 66, 109, 136, 173, 174, 177, 178, 178, 180, 183, 185, 189
gender-free terms and testing 162, 183
Geneva Convention 16, **147**, 205, 210
Germany 44, 45, 55, 71, 79, 93, 95, 107, 147, 163, 204, 205, 206, 208, **215**, 224
Gibraltar 41, 48, 70, 83, 96, 120, 123, *146*, 163, 169, 206, 223
Giles, Nelly 31–2, 178
Girls' Nautical Training Corps (GNTC) 111, 207, 229
glass ceiling 151, 189, 190
Goodenough, Angela 88–9, 90
Gould, Patricia 163, 169, 231
Green, Collette 166–7, *167*
Greenwich 90, 100, 107, 148, 152, 208, 210, 221, 224
Grigg Report 134–5, 155
Guides (Girl/Sea) 75, 87, 90, 205

Hague Convention 48, 204
Hamilton, Archie 157, 179
Hare, Dorothy 81, 115
Haslar 11, 32, 33, 37, 38, 39, *39*, 41, 47, 49, 80, 82, 113, 117, 119, 120, 124, 127, 160, *161*, 175, 208, 212, 217, 231
Heath, Herbert 58, 62, 66, 71, 75
'heroism', women's 6, 7, 13, 23, 52, 108, 109, 123, 165, 166, 173, 178, 216
HMS *Dauntless* 143, 148, 165, 209
HMS *Dryad* colour plate 14
HMS *Illustrious* 174, colour plate 24
HMS *Raleigh* 148, 165, 198, 210, 225
HMS *Sheffield* 165, colour plate 26
HMS *Somerset* 177, colour plate 21
HMS *Sultan* colour plate 20

HMS *Victory* 31, 87, *colour plate 2*
Hocking, Muriel 189, 228
Hogg, Louisa *39*, 41, 43
home
  home-and-away life 18, 131, 165, **178**, 181, 189, 193–4, 200, 219
  naval life/premises as homelike 14, 18, 16, 40, 92, 120, *121*, 200
  proper place for females 6, 8, 18, 22, 55, 60, 65, 75, 181, 198
  service women and responsibilities for 76, 111, 189, 219
  site of constraint 8, 12, 14, 72, 110–11, 132, 138, 201
Hong Kong 78, 82, 120, *121*, 123, 160, 206
hospitals 3, 31, 32, 37, 159, 164, 204, 206, **212**, 222
  civilian 33, 35, 37, 41, 45, 51, 81, 84, 118, 119, 126, 163
  combined services facilities **175–6**
  decisions about female staff being used in 2, 35, 37, 50, 204, 205
  Royal Naval Auxiliary Hospitals 3, *46*, **47**, 51, 83,113, *114*, 118–19, **120–1**, *121*, 123, **124**, 160
  Royal Naval Hospitals 3, 11, 33–4, 35, 37, 39, *39*, **41**, *44*, **47**, 48, 49, 50–1, 80, **82**, **83**, 84, 113, 118–19, **120–1**, 124, 160, 163, 231
hospital ships *42*, 82, 204, **217**
  pre-World War I 31, **32**, 35, 203, 204
  World War I **48**, 50, 51, 84, 204
  World War II 84, 119, *121*, **122**, 123, 124, 125, 207
  post-World War II 82, *160*, 161, 164, *164*, 169, 172, **177**, 210
  women not/allowed in some at times 48, 50, 82, 83, 84, 122, 204

India *100*, 101, 104, 208, 215
Institute of Naval Medicine 177
institutions, services as 7, 12, 13, 18, 55–6, 71, 85, 90, 107, 139, 148, 180, 190, 200, 201, 213
internment of naval women 123, 206
Ireland 47
Italy, Sicily 54, 79, 101, 104

Jack Tar 2, 4, 3, *5*, 31, 39, 59, 65, 198, 196, 219

Index

Japan 79, 99, 106, 107, 123, 125, 161, 206, 208, 209

Keenan, Margaret 83, 231
Kennedy, Inga 171, 198, 232
Korean War 133, *160*, 161, 163, 169, 217

labour, unpaid emotional 7, 200
ladettes 24, 66, 97, 139, 143, 152, 154, 155, 156, 186, 196
'ladies'/ladylike behaviour 17, 22, 34, 35, 36, 37, 38, 40, 42, 56, 65, 98, 111, 129, 136, 139, 154, 198
lady superintendents 34, 56, 78
language 41, 46, 92, 97, 136, 186, 187, 224
Larken, Anthea *151*, 152, 155, 231
laundry, laundresses 21, 28, 30, 32
law 20, 21, 24, 34, 40, 63, 98, 131, 139, 143, 147, 165, **184–5**, 196, 203, 205
Law, Liz, *164*
lesbian 24, 110, 196, 219
Lloyd, Mary 133, 231
Lloyd's List 189
loblolly boys 31, 38
logistics work (WRNS) 235
  see also communications work, cooks, secretarial work, stewards, supply

Mackenzie, Eliza 34
McBain, Mandy 196, *colour plate 23*
McBride, Vonla 146, 231
McFeely, Elizabeth Craig 151, 231
McHugh, Annette 189
McMaster, Victoria 230
makeup 141, 182, 186, 196
Malta 49, *69*, 70, 78, 82, 99, 104, 120, 163, 206, 207
marriage 1, 24, 100, 113, 118, 107, 131, 138–9, 154, 164, 165, 195, 193, 196, 211
  compatibility with service life 17, 54, 76, 81, 119, 132, 13
  marriage/partnerships with serving personnel 125, 126, 131, 189, 193, 223
  weddings 110, 125, *126*, 186, 196, *colour plate 23*
Martin, Bertha 84, 113, 118, 123, 231
masculinity, military/naval 2, **4–6**, 8, 25, 44, 54, 201, 169, 186, 191, 197

'masculinity', women's 137, 143, 186, 191, 197, 219
maternity leave 154, 188, 194, 195, 211
Mathews, Vera Laughton 85, *86*, 87, 88, 89, 90, 91, 92, 95, 97, 98, 101, 106, 112, 129, 131, 132, 205, 213, 231
mechanics 59, *101*, 102, 105, 106, 149, 181, 184, 111, 131
media attention 89, 108, 180, 184, 190, 191
medical assistants, MA (Q)s 3, 162, **165–6**, 172, 175, 177, 216, 226, 235
medical officers (MOs) 116, 120, 167, 169, 171, 175
  female 115–16, **116–17, 166–9**, *167*, 207, 217, 230
  male 34, 35, 40, 43, 51, *colour plate 24*
menstruation 64, 154, 184
merchant shipping 10, 22, 24, 54, 91, 150, 230
Middleton, Sally 164–5, 170
Millar, Elizabeth Hoyer 134, 225, 231
military, women as part of 11, 21, 23, 41, 51, 59,79, 98, 117, 140, 155, 190, 191, 201,214, 216, **219–20**
militarisation 4, 45, 225
Ministry of Defence (MoD) 107, 142, 143, 155, 165, 177, 183, 185, 188, 189, 195, 211, 218–19, 220, 230
mobile/immobile serving women 59, 62, 67, 70, 76, 80, 82, 84, 88, 89–90, 93, 100, 101, 118, 132, 206
mobility, naval service as enabling 94, 107, 131, 136
Moore, Suzanne 11, 183
moral anxieties 65–6, 139, 181, 200–1, 207
morale, women's impact on naval men's 7, 21, 40, 84, 144, 200
mother
  figure 28, 137, 198;
  motherhood and service, compatibility of 28, 50, 85, 87, 113, 132, 154, 165, 178, 188–9, 191, 193–5, 201
  mothers of serving personnel 23, 25, 43, 62, 92, 107, 197
motives for joining naval life **12**, 14, 23, 53, 65, 91, 92, 137, 164, 176, 182, 213

National Audit Office report 155, 210
Naval Discipline Act (NDA) 38, 63, 81, 97–8, 130–1, 137, 142–3, 144, 145, 163–4, 169, 188, 209, 210
Naval Nursing Auxiliary Service, later NNS **162–3**, 165, 170, 172, 173, 177, 178, 216, 226, 234
Naval Nursing Service (pre-QARNNS) 3, 33, 35, **37–43**
Naval Servicewomen's Network 193–4, 211, 212
naval tradition 44, 85, 90, 91, 104, 106, 113
Navy Board 143, 144, 152, **157**
Navy League 42, 56
Navy List, women significantly in 40, 71, 78, 204, 218
Nelson, Horatio 4, 7, 8, 26–7, 28, 29, 30, 31, 91, 202; *colour plates 2 and 6*
Netherlands 101, 143, 202, 208, 215
Networks 39, 41, 43, 56, 57, 80, 83, 87, 90
nicknames 1, 6, 38, 50, 59–60, 90, 92, 116, 118, 124, 160, 168
Nightingale, Florence 3, 33, 34, 35, 37, 38, 39
North Africa 3 5, 37, 49, 97, 98, 99, 101, 104, 110, *114*, 120, 123, 207
Northern Ireland 146, 189, 99, 210
Norway 108, *170*, 174, 210
nuclear warfare 129, 133, 140, 161, 190

operational effectiveness 17, 18, 41, 133, 139, 154
overseas service 41, 82
  World War I 45, 48, 49, 52, 59, 60, *69*, 70
  World War II 84, 94, 96, 98, 99, 100, 104,105, 119, 120, 124, 127, 206, 207
  1946–90 *114*, *125*, 133, *146*, 161, 163, 166, 216
  1990 onwards 199

pacifism, women's 14, 42, 79, 111
patriotism 4, 12, 14, 19, 42, 43, 198, *colour plate 5*
pay rates 33, 43, 59, 60, 83, 95, 117, 124, 131, 155
  compared with men's 33, **62**, **88**, 116, 131, 132, 147, 166, 178
pensions 21, 26, 29, 83, 87, 132
Perriam, Ann 26–7
pilots
  in air 127, 149, 192, 197, 198, *199*, 202
  on water 6, 105, 208
Plymouth 32, 37, 47, 79, 80, 82, 94, 95, 120, 134, 176, 177, 185, 202, 231
political correctness 155, 157, 182
popular culture 10, 23–4, 46–7, 93, 97, 136, 138, 191, **223–7**
Portsmouth 12, 37, *73*, 79, 82, 89, 93, 94, 95, 104, *167*, 176, 177, 178, 197, 208, 218, 220, 232, *colour plates 3*, *8*, *22*, *25*
pregnancy 66, 138, 139, 154, 165, 188–9, **194–5**
press gangs 7, 26, 44
Pritchard Report 142–3

Queen Alexandra's Imperial Military Nursing Service (QAIMNS) 43, 60, 82, 83
Queen Alexandra's Royal Naval Nursing Service (QARNNS) 12
  early origins 3, **42–4**, *44*
  World War I **44–52**
  interwar **77–84**
  World War II **113–27**
  1946–90 **159–70**
  1990–2017 **171–8**
  army/RAF nursing connections 43, 47, 48, 118, 122, 126, 175
  as authority figures 52, 117, 119
  career progression 49, 77, 82, 83, 118, 119, 122, 125, 126, 159, 163, 165, 170, 171, 172–3
  changes in role, status, titles 43, 50, 81, 124, 165, 177, 216
  civilian connections 43, 44, 45–6, 52, 80, 160, 170
  Naval Nursing (Auxiliary) Service, relations with **162–3**, 164
  navy medical service including SBAs and MAs, relations with 14, 43, 45, 46, 50, 51, 81, 115, 119, 120, 127, 160–1, 163–4, 165, 172, 174
  numbers 81, 116, 118, 119, 123, 126, 171, 174, 176, 177

Index

organisation 44, 45, 46, 47–8, 50, 51, 78, 80, 83, 84, 114–15, **118–19**, 119–20, 122, **124**, 126, 159, 161–4, 165, 172–4, 178

overseas service 48, 49, 78, 82–3, 84, *114*, 119, 120, 123, 124, 161, 163, 164, 169

reserves 45, 46, 47, 51 84, 118, 120, 123, 124, 160, 162

sea service 48, 49, *49*, 50, 51, 82, 84, **122**, 123, 124, 125, *160*, 161, 166,172, 173, 174, 176, 177, 178

training 162–3, 165, 170, 175

uniforms 40, 46, *49*, 124, 163, 165, 176, 178

VAD, relations with 46, 50–1, 52, 77, 80, 113, 117–18, 119, 120, 160, 161, 162, 170

WRNS connections 50, 52, 77, 84, 160, 161, 162

racism 196

recruitment 45, 64, 65, 75 116, 134, 135, 137, 138, 146, 151, 160, 161, 166, 169, 186, 224, 225, 226, *colour plates 7*, *11*, *12*

remembering **13–14**, **76**, 111, *130*

rescue
  of women 17, 44, 93, 94, 96, 166
  women as rescuers 53, 123, 177

reserves 3, 4, 212, 225, **228–9**
  concept of 133, 161
  health care personnel 4, 44–5, 46, 47, 51 120, 159–60, 161, 162, 168, 170, 172, 204, 205, 206, 208, 209, 211, 222, 233–4
  WRNS 152, 161, 209, 211
  see also Women's Royal Naval Reserve, Royal Naval Reserve

retention 29, 40, 51, 83, 106, 125, 132, 133, 135, 137, 140, 151, 152, 154, 159, 165, 178, 194, 196; *see under* QARNNS and WRNS

Rewcastle, Genevieve 113, 115, 126, 178

riders, despatch (WRNS) 67, 93,

role models 53, *108*, *181*, 193, 197

Royal Air Force (RAF) 6, 16, 18, 71, 158, 163, 169, 171, 195, 197, 205, 214, 219

royal family *42*, 58, 71, 135, *139*, 147, 157, 178, 172, 193, 232

Royal Fleet Auxiliary (RFA) 149, 172, 211, **230**, *colour plate 27*
  RFA *Argus* 169, 172, **177**
  RFA *Engadine* 149
  RFA *Maine* 161, 82

Royal Marines 14, 25, 29, 34, 168, 169, 174, 211, 218–19, 235, *colour plates 1*, *17*
  bands 177, **197**, 198, 211, 235
  commandos 173, 174, 189, 190–1, 195, 198, 210

Royal Naval Air Service 69

Royal Naval Air Stations 69, 102, 111, 119, 140, 205, 225, *colour plate 15*

Royal Naval Auxiliary Service (RNAX), now Maritime Volunteer Service 4, 229

Royal Naval Friendly Union of Sailors' Wives 56

Royal Naval Reserve 4, 211, 228

Royal Naval Supply and Transport Service 211, 230

Royal Navy
  early times–1884 **19–36**, 203–4
  1884–1918 **37–76**, 204–5
  Post-World War I–1990 **129–70**, 209–10
  interwar **77–87**, 20
  World War II **88–127**, 205–9
  1990–2017 1–2, **171–202**, 210–11
  essential things to understand about women's naval context **3–9**, 11–13, **14–18**, 21–3, 107, 111–12, 137, 155, *colour plates 5*, *6*, *12*
  navy's attitudes towards WRNS, as civilian lady incomers/'daughters'/ visitors 7, 9, 46, 52, *58*, 60, 64, 71, 87–8, 89, 90, 91, 95, 97, 98, 99, *103*, 104, 106, 106, 131, 132, 152, 153, 201; to having combatant status/becoming 'like men' 131, **147**, 152, 191; to becoming seagoing 97, 153, 155, 157, 168, 180–2,186, 187, 224
  women's equivalent ranks, rates, titles, 165, 172, 183, 188
  women in RN, not in WRNS now, 1–2, **179–202**, *colour plates 17*, *19*, *21*, *22*, *26*

WRNS attitudes to navy, as 'hosts'/parent organisation 70, 72, 75, 76, 85, 88, 104, 111, 146
  see also Admiralty, combat, Diversity and Inclusion, families (naval), gender, sea service

Scotland 37, 45, *46*, 46–7, 62, 94, *96*, *100*, 102, 104, 106, 111, 120, 140, 169, 171, 177, 190, 199
sea, keenness about 2, 65, 87, 93, 111, 186
Sea Rangers 4, 85, 87, 90, 91, 111, 205, 229, *colour plate 10*
sea service, women's integration into 2, 18, 103, 142, 141–58, 170, 179–88, 189–91, 195
  combat's link with 131, 142, 147, **148**, **152**, **153–4**, **157–8**, **180–2**, **191**, **195**
  early as nurses and laundresses **30–2**
  early unofficial, disguised as males **23–5**, *25*
  early unofficial as wives **26–30**, *27*
  economic/demographic pressures impelling 2, 11, 130, 140, 144, **151–2**, 153, 155, 181, 185
  mixed feelings about desirability of in 1950s–1960s, 130, 131, 136
  naval wives, attitudes to 12, 181
  nursing staff 30–2, 34–5, 41, 48, 49, 51, 82, 84, 122, 123, 125, 142, 144, 153, 157, *160*, 166, 162, 172, 173, 174, 176, 177, 178, 179, 186, 188
  opposition to 12, 17, 154, **155–7**, **180—1**; 183–5, 190, 191
  women freeing men for 3, 32–3, 50, 55, 67, 95, 103, 104, 107, 118
  women in post-1990 navy serving at sea 1, **1–2**, 5, 17, 18, 157–8, **179–91**, *181*, **195**, **197**, 200, 202, 211
  working towards in 1970s and 80s **141–3**, **146–8**, **150–8**
  Wrens who did not serve at sea 62, 155, 180, 188, 195
  colour plates 1, 2, 21, 26, 27
Senior Service image 3, 14, *15*, 58, 137
sex/sexual activity 12, **17**, 23, **65**, 110, 139, 180–1, 191, 200, 207

sex industry 4, *colour plates 3, 4*
sexual attacks on women 7, 123, 185, 186
sexual objectification of women by men 5, 65–6, 144, 184, 186
sexually transmitted diseases 35, 65, 81
Sherit, Kath 142, 157, 214
ships 2, 17–18, 19, 22–3, 24, *25*, 28, *49*, 79, *96*, 97, *121*, 122, 141, *160*, 173, 176, 180, 182, 185, 190, 194, 230
  'combatant'/'non-combatant' 147, 154, 155, **157**
  as 'she' 189
  'suitable for women' 1, *1*, 35, 50, 155, 156, 179–80
  visits to ships by women (brief) 5, 9, 28, 30, 96, *100*, *103*, 149–50, *150*, 152, 163, 201
  see also entries prefixed *HMS* and *RFA*, hospital ships, sea service, submarines
sick berths/bays 3, *114*, 119, 166, 169
sick berth staff (SBAs) 120, 169
  connections with medical assistant role 162, 166
  male 33, 35, 38, 44, *45*, 46, 40, 53, 81, 115, 117, 118, 119, 160–1, 162
  nursing sisters' interchanges with male SBAs 50, 204
  VADs as akin to 118, 161, 162, 207
  WRNS SBAs *114*, **160–1**, *161*, 162, 209
Simpson, Julia *184*, 232
Singapore 78, 96, 99, 106, 140, 206, 223, 226
sisterhood 84, 90, 107, 126, 178
Snell, Hannah 25, *colour plate 1*
social life 5, 5–6, 8, *9*, *28*, 30, *80*, 106, 140, 149, 201, 213
South Africa 101, 120, 207
spiritual/noble ideals, chivalry 6, 16, 44, 47, 60, 61, 64, 66, 99, 137
sports 140, 193, 196
Stait, Carolyn 145, 148, 152, 187, 190
stereotypes of women 7, 8, *20*, 21, *22*, 33, 131, 137, 186
stewards (WRNS) 1, 22, 24, 30, 31, 68, 74, 92, 93, 110, *114*, *134*, 189, *colour plates 15, 16, 21*

Index

Stewart, Henrietta 34–5, 37, 38, 39
Stonehouse 37, 212, 217
strength, women's physical 16, 17, 40, 68–9, 131, 143, 156, 149, 195
submarines 42, 55, 140, 163, 177, **190–1**, 210, 211, 224
suffrage (women's) movement 12, 42, 45, 90
supply, stores work 32, 33, 68, 93, 94, **104**, 140, 196, 211, 230
Swallow, Patricia 107, 145, 149, 231

technical workers (WRNS) 67, 93, 101, 101–2, 140, 154, 201, *colour plate 13I see also* electricians, engineers, mechanics
   pre-World War I 3, 30, 45
   World War I 59, 60, 64, 65, 68
   interwar 81, 83, 87
   World War II 90, 92, 93, 95, *101*, 102, 111, 118, 119, 120, 124, 125, 126, 206, 207, 208
   post-World War II 140, 143, 145, 147, 148, 149, 150, 151, 152, 159, 162–3, 164, *167*, 168
   1980s onwards *170*, 174, 175, 176, 177, 178, 179, 186, 187, 188, 190, 198, 209, 210, 225, 229, 230
   naval *16*, 44, 85, 90, 91, 104, 106, 113, 155, 182, 183, 191, 196, 200, 201, *colour plate 23*
   women's services 137, 141, 149, 154, 174, *181*, 228
   training 4, 8, 33, 34, 35, 41, 68
   see also under QARNNS, WRNS
travel, service life as enabling 'cost-free' 8, 14, 45, 59, 132

Uganda, HMHS 164–5, 169, 210
uniforms 155, 176, 196, 197, 200
   braid colour 61, 89, *151*, 163, 188
   brassieres 61
   compared with other services 50, 61, 91, 197
   corsets 61
   design changes over time, 89, 99, 163
   head wear 40, 46, *49*, *54*, 71, 91, 102, 165, 178, 213
   MAs' 165
   medical and dental officers' 117
   men's interest in women's 61, 92, 154, 176
   QARNNS' 40, 46, 124, 163, 178
   sailor-like 40, *60*, 102, 163
   stockings/tights 144, 154
   supplying 3, 61, 92, 197
   trousers as new step 178, 197
   VADs 61, 117
   women's attitudes towards 2, 59, *60*, 64, 197
   WRNS' **61–2**, *54*, 64, 73, 88, 89, 92, 94, 102, 102, 144, *151*, 188, 196–7, 211
USA 100, 101, 106, 125, 133, 143, 185, 192, 202, 206, 215
USSR 133, 142

veterans 11, *27*, 34, 35, 37, 71, 83, 84, 108, 111, 117, 155, 162, 165, 170, 188, 191, 197, 215, 220 228
Voluntary Aid Detachments (VADs) 3, 12, 14, 117, 118, **216–17**, 222, 226–7, 233–4
   early foundations **44–5**, 204; in World War I 46, 47, **50–1**, 52, 53, 54, 57, 59, 61, 62, 63, 65, 75, 76, 77, 80, 205
   as partial model for World War I WRNS 59, 61, 62, 65, 75
   in World War II 84, 90, 113, *114*, 115, 116, **117–18**, 119, 120, **121**, 122, 123, 124, *125*, 206, 207, 208
   post-war 126, 160–1, 162, 165, 169, 170, 209

war 2, 7, *15*, 21, 23, 31–2, *96*, 104, 137, 146, 147, 157, 181, 190, 214, 220, *colour plate 2*
warfare 50, 157, 235
warrior concept 6, 21, 44, 60, 75, 95, 96, 99, 130, 137, 149, 155, 190
   women as assistants to male warriors 21, *22*, 23, 26, 76, *109*
   women's acceptance of warrior role 186–7, 190
wars (excluding World War I and World War II) 22, 26, 31, 32, 33, 34, 37, 41–2, 133, 150, 160–1, 168, 170, 172, 173, 176, 182, 190, 191, 204

see also World War I, World War II, and wars by name (e.g. Cold)
weaponry, women working with 26–7, 147, 150, 180, 186–7, *187*, 190, 206
welfare/pastoral support 4, 30–1, 35–6, *42*, 56, 60, 78, 87, 94, *109*, 150
West Report/Alan West **153–6**, 210
Weston, Agnes 94, 204
Whitehouse, Ailsa *114*, 116, 166
widows, naval 7, 32, 50, 62, 76, 110, 132
Wilson, Norma *114*, 117, 124, 126, 160
Wilson, Rosie 148, 152, 155, 179, 184
wives of naval personnel 4, 12, 17, 19, 21, 24, **26–30**, *27*, *28*, 29, 31, 54, 56, 58, 66, 83, 105, *109*, 110, *129*, 156, 166, 219, 228
Women's Army Auxiliary Corps (WAAC), later Auxiliary Territorial Service (ATS) 55, 57, 58, 59, 60, 61, 63, 66, 92, 224
Women's Royal Air Force (WRAF/WAAF) 6, 49, 61, 63, 69, 71, 135, 137, 142, 205
Women's Royal Naval Reserve (WRNR) 4, 209, 228
Women's Royal Naval Service **213–15, 223–6**
    World War I **53–76**
    interwar **74–5, 85–8**
    World War II **85–112**
    post-war–1990 **129–58**
    1990–2017 **179–202**
    army and air force connections with 55–6, 57, 58, 69, 87, 129, 131, 135, 137, 147, 142, 158, **200**, 202
    awards 75, **108–9**, 150
    career progression 60, 134, *134*, 145, 148, 151–2, 188–9, 190, 192–4, **195**, 201, 202
    civilian status 58–9, 62, 63, 66, 87, 88, **89**, 97, **98–9**, 99–100, 130–1, 137, 142–5
    intake, outflow and retention 59, 63, 71,73, **74**, 75, 91, 92, 94, 106, 107, 110–11, 132, 133, 134–5, 136–8, 140, 154
    naval shortages necessitate women's inclusion 54–5, 87, 101, 104, 149, 151–3, 196
    numbers 53, 87, 103, 107, 132, 141, 142, 156, 180, 182–3, 189–90, 192, 193, 197, 199, 233–5
    organisation 53, 57–8, 62–3, 65, 66, 69, 70–1, 74, 75, 87–8, 89, 96, **98–9**, 102–3, 107, 129–30, 133–4, 140, 142–3, 145–6, 148, 151–8, 179–80, 183, 185–6, 188, 191,194–6, 209, 210
    overseas service 70, 71, 96–7, 98, 99, 100–1, 104, 105–6, 107, 140, 142, 183, 191, 206, 208
    QARNNS, connections with 50, 52, 56, 57, 76, 77, 84, 160, 161, 162
    roles 56, 67–9, 85, 93, 94,97, 102, 103, 105–6, 131, **132**, 133–5, 140, 141–2, 145–6, 148, 150, 154, 152, 180, 183, 185, 202, 231–2; *see also under* specific job title (e.g. engineer)
    sea service 141–3, 146–8, 150–8, 179–88
    sexuality 65–6, 138–9, 144, 184, 186
    training 59, 60, 64, 68, 90, 92, 93, 95, 140, 143, 148, 149–50, 208, 210
    uniform 61–2, 89, 91,92, 94, 102, 144, *151*, 188, 211
    VAD, connections with 59, 61, 62, 65, 75, 76, **160–2**, *161*, 165
'women's work'
    as assistants supplementing 26, 28, 31, 57, 88, 112, 223
    traditional ideas about 21, 24, 54, 55, 56, 67, 95, 131, 145–6, 148, 149, 150, 151, 155, 168, *colour plate 9*
Woollcombe, Jocelyn 129, 132, 231
World War I
    female health care staff in **37–52**
    WRNS in **53–76**
World War II
    female health care staff in **113–27**, 217
    WRNS in *16*, **88–112**, 213, 214–16
WRNS Benevolent Trust xix, 108, 187, 212, **228**

youth 4, 12, 14, 17, 18, 106, 138, 139, 140, 193, 197, 227